READING AND ITS DIFFICULTIES

A PSYCHOLOGICAL STUDY

READING AND ITS DIFFICULTIES

A PSYCHOLOGICAL STUDY

BY

M. D. VERNON, M.A., Sc.D.

Emeritus Professor of Psychology,
University of Reading

CAMBRIDGE

AT THE UNIVERSITY PRESS

1971

Published by the Syndics of the Cambridge University Press
Bentley House, 200 Euston Road, London NW1 2DB
American Branch: 32 East 57th Street, New York, N.Y.10022

© Cambridge University Press 1971

Library of Congress Catalogue Card Number: 73–153013

ISBN: 0 521 08217 X

First published 1971
Reprinted 1973

First printed in Great Britain
at the University Printing House, Cambridge
(Brooke Crutchley, University Printer)
Reprinted in Great Britain by
Redwood Press Limited, Trowbridge, Wiltshire

CONTENTS

Foreword   *page* vii

I   INTRODUCTION   I

II   THE ASSESSMENT OF READING ACHIEVEMENT   6

III VISUAL PERCEPTION AND READING   10
     (1) Development in the perception of form, pattern
         and sequence   10
     (2) Visual perception of printed material   23
     (3) Relation of reading to perceptual deficiencies   30

IV   AUDITORY AND LINGUISTIC FACTORS IN
     READING   38
     (1) Auditory and linguistic development in children   38
     (2) Phonic analysis and synthesis of words   47
     (3) Reading of continuous prose   58
     (4) Relation of reading to auditory deficiencies   63
     (5) Auditory and visual sequences   67
     (6) Relation of reading to deficiencies in speech and
         language   70

V   THE RELATION OF READING TO REASONING,
     AND TO INTELLIGENCE AND OTHER ABILITIES   77
     (1) Conceptual reasoning   77
     (2) Intelligence and other abilities   83

VI   THE EFFECT TO MOTIVATIONAL AND
     EMOTIONAL FACTORS ON LEARNING TO READ   95
     (1) Conditions in the social environment   95
     (2) Effects on children's motivation of the home
         environment   103
     (3) Motivation and the school environment   109
     (4) Emotional maladjustment   115

CONTENTS

VII   SPECIFIC DEVELOPMENTAL DYSLEXIA   *page* 123

(1) General consideration of backwardness in reading   123

(2) The nature of specific developmental dyslexia   128

(3) Visual deficiencies in dyslexia   131

(4) Linguistic deficiencies in dyslexia   145

(5) The causes of dyslexia   149

   (A) *Neurological impairment*   149

   (B) *Maturational lag*   159

   (C) *Hereditary factors*   164

(6) The effects of remedial treatment on dyslexia   168

VIII   CONCLUSIONS   173

References   181

Index of Authors   203

Index of Subjects   209

FOREWORD

Since the publication of the author's book, *Backwardness in Reading*, in 1957, a great many books and articles have been written not only on reading in general, but also on reading backwardness specifically. Many of these are discussions of these topics in which are expressed opinions based mainly on the writers' experiences in teaching. Although they suggest a number of interesting lines of thought, they lack verification by means of controlled observation and investigation, and they exhibit considerable disagreement on almost every aspect of the reading process. But in addition there has been a number of experimental investigations and clinical studies. Some of these have shown great expertise in experimental design and performance; others have been inadequate in these respects. Thus it is not surprising to find disagreement here also in the results obtained and the conclusions drawn from these.

It did not appear to the author that it would be possible to discuss and evaluate all the new publications in a revised edition of *Backwardness in Reading*. Therefore a new book has been prepared which contains or refers to some of the material included in *Backwardness in Reading*, and, more important, is in the main a critical exposition of work published more recently. Moreover, since there still appeared to be considerable doubt as to the basic psychological processes involved in learning to read and in experiencing difficulties in reading, the present volume is intended as a contribution to the elucidation of these psychological processes. Thus it does not claim to include discussion of all recently published work on reading; and there may indeed be important studies which have been treated too briefly or even overlooked. However, in addition to consideration of the visual perceptual and reasoning processes, an outline is given of recent work on psycholinguistics in so far as this appears to be relevant to reading. Some consideration is also given to the motivational factors which may be involved. The perennial problem of specific developmental dyslexia is discussed at length. It is clear that the problem persists, and that the author's conclusions as to its nature and origin are speculative and extremely tentative. But it is hoped that this book may stimulate further experimental and clinical investigation along the lines suggested.

Since this book was written, an excellent short book has appeared, *Children and Learning to Read* by E. J. Goodacre (London, Routledge & Kegan Paul, 1971), which includes a discussion of the developmental psychological processes involved in reading. The present author is pleased to find a considerable amount of agreement between Dr. Goodacre and herself as to the fundamental nature of these processes.

ACKNOWLEDGMENTS for permission to reproduce figures are made to the following: *American Academy of Pediatrics*: Fig. 6, from *Pediatrics*, vol. 37, p. 352, by L. Eisenberg. *American Psychological Association*: Fig. 1, from the *Journal of Comparative Physiology and Psychology*, vol. 55, p. 898, by E. J. Gibson *et al.*: Fig. 4, from the *Journal of Abnormal and Social Psychology*, vol. 41, p. 305, by F. K. Graham and B. Kendall. *Cassell & Co. Ltd*: Fig. 7, from *Standards and Progress in Reading*, by J. M. Morris, 1966, p. 246: Fig. 8, from *The Second International Reading Symposium*, 1967, p. 247, article by T. R. Miles. *W. R. Henderson's Trust*: Fig. 10, from *Cerebral Dominance and its Relation to Psychological Function*, by O. L. Zangwill, 1960, pp. 18 and 20. *Professor J. Piaget*: Fig. 3, from *Archives de Psychologie*, vol. 34, pp. 211 and 224, by J. Piaget and B. Stettler-von Albertini. *Professor P. E. Vernon*: Fig. 5, from unpublished test material. *Souvenir Press*: Fig. 9, from *Reading and the Dyslexic Child*, by R. M. N. Crosby and R. A. Liston, 1968, p. 160. *University of Illinois Press*: Fig. 2, from the *American Journal of Psychology*, vol. 69, p. 580, by L. Ghent.

CHAPTER I

INTRODUCTION

The ability to read is generally regarded not only as the basis of education, but also as an essential possession of the citizens of civilized countries. Whereas in earlier centuries literacy was the prerogative of the aristocracy and bourgeoisie, in the nineteenth and twentieth centuries it was gradually recognized, especially in democratic countries, to be the right of all. Thus the decrease in illiteracy between 1850 and 1950 was from 45–50 per cent to 8 per cent in the adult population of Western Europe; and from 90–95 per cent to 10 per cent in Russia (Cipolla, 1969). Indeed, in Russia the increase in literacy was a direct result of the revolution. Whereas before the revolution about 80 per cent of the population was illiterate, by 1959 98.5 per cent were claimed to be literate (Jeffries, 1967). It is generally recognized that the efficient conduct of a modern civilized country depends on the possession by its members of a certain degree of literacy, if only to read the mass of printed notices, forms and instructions with which they are daily confronted. What use they make of the higher ranges of literacy is another matter, as Hoggart has pointed out in *The Uses of Literacy* (Hoggart, 1957).

It is not surprising, therefore, that with the advance of egalitarianism in this country over the last thirty years, the pressure on all children to learn to read has increased. The discovery that there was a considerable number of illiterate recruits to the British Army during the 1939–45 war caused much dismay. A survey carried out in 1948 in Britain under the auspices of the Ministry of Education showed that 5.7 per cent of 15-year-old children were illiterate or semi-literate, and a further 24 per cent were backward in reading (Ministry of Education, 1950). This high incidence of poor reading, which was said to compare unfavourably with pre-war standards, appeared to be due mainly to the disruption of education by war conditions. Nevertheless, alarm over illiteracy persisted. It was discussed by Lewis (1953), in his book *The Importance of Illiteracy*, which demonstrated that any increase in illiteracy other than that due to war conditions was probably illusory. Subsequent surveys by the Ministry of Education (1957) and other similar surveys seemed to indicate that illiteracy had sunk to the low figure of about 1 per cent, especially if only children of normal intelligence were considered. Indeed, Barker, Fee & Sturrock (1967) obtained a figure of 1 per cent for marked reading backwardness in children of 8–9 years in Dundee schools. However, Reid (1968) pointed out that the average improvement shown in the Ministry of Education surveys was more towards the upper end of the scale of reading achievement than the lower. The lowest 10 per cent of 11-year-old children scored so badly as to make it likely that a similar proportion of school leavers would be almost illiterate.

Kellmer Pringle, Butler & Davie reported in 1966 that 18 per cent of 11,000 children entering the junior school were poor readers and 9.8 per cent were non-readers. Morris in 1954 had found there to be 19.2 per cent of such children who could scarcely read at all (Morris, 1959). Moreover, she concluded that about half of those who were severely backward at 7–8 years would still be backward on leaving school at 15 years. In her view, these children would be unable to employ reading as a useful tool. A figure of 15 per cent at 7 years of children with R.Q.s* of 85 or less was obtained by Clark (1970) in a recent study of over 1500 children forming a whole age group in Dunbartonshire. These children had been taught to read for two years.

It is right that everything should be done to teach reading to all children who are capable of learning. Any pressure exerted by society to make available an adequate supply of facilities, and particularly of teachers suitably trained to teach reading, can do nothing but good. The enquiry of Morris (1966) indicated that this supply was not sufficient and that training of teachers in the

* The Reading Quotient, R.Q., is similar to the I.Q.; it is a percentage of the 'Reading Age' in years on the chronological age. Reading Ages are calculated from the average chronological ages of children making given scores on a reading rest; they are analogous to mental ages.

teaching of reading was often inadequate. Recent complaints have been made as to the continuing lack of suitable teacher training in many Colleges of Education.*

Nevertheless, the importance attached by society to the capacity to read has had certain unfortunate consequences. In the first place, teaching of reading in many schools begins at an age when, as we shall discuss in a later chapter, many children are not ready for it, and might indeed profit more from devoting their time and energies to other pursuits. Moreover, teaching may be carried out with undue pressure. It should be noted that in Scandinavia children do not go to school and begin formal reading teaching until the age of 7–8 years. It may well be that it is easier to learn to read their languages than it is to learn to read English. But the delay does not appear to produce a high incidence of illiteracy.

An even more unfortunate consequence is the plight of those children who fall behind their peers in reading achievement. True, many of these come from homes in which no great value is attached to the more advanced type of literacy. Yet even in these it may be felt that a child or young adult who cannot, for instance, read the newspaper is handicapped. Illiteracy is regarded particularly in middle-class families as a social stigma as well as a bar to entry to a profession. In recent years appreciable numbers of parents have been shocked to realize that their otherwise normal children cannot read at all, or read so slowly and inefficiently as to threaten their future careers. Moreover, educationists may have been slow to recognize the existence of their condition, and to provide suitable remedial treatment.

There is continuing argument and disagreement as to the best methods of teaching children to read competently, and as to the difficulties they encounter in learning. It may be that the failure to solve these problems is due at least in part to the lack of careful consideration of the nature and development of the relevant basic

* Goodacre (1970b) has cited the results of surveys carried out recently with young infant and junior school teachers, 20–40 per cent of whom reported that they had had no instruction or no adequate instruction in the teaching of reading at their Colleges of Education.

1-2

psychological processes occurring naturally in children; that is to say, the processes of perception, language acquisition and thought. It is true that explanations in terms of these processes are often advanced in support of certain methods* or for the abandonment of others. But too often these explanations are purely speculative, and their validity has not been adequately investigated.

There is a tendency to regard reading as a single unitary capacity which all normal children should be able to acquire automatically, as they learn to speak. However, careful study of reading, objectively and without bias, demonstrates that: (1) reading is an activity which varies considerably in nature according to the degree of proficiency with which it is performed; (2) the psychological processes involved are numerous and complex, and vary at different stages in learning to read; (3) the various processes must be adequately integrated together if reading is to become efficient and fluent.

Given this degree of complexity in the reading processes, it is not surprising to find that when a child fails to learn to read normally, the process or processes which are not operating satisfactorily may vary in different cases. Unfortunately there has been inadequate investigation of the stage of breakdown, and far too little is known as to where it has occurred in any particular individual case. This is due in part to the difficulty of locating the failure; but also to the aforementioned tendency to regard reading as a single unitary entity. It is inferred that there is a continuum of proficiency in reading from very high to very low; and that backward readers differ only quantitatively from normal, and normal from good readers. But it is not apparent whether the lower mean scores of the backward group is caused by equal decrements in every backward reader, or by varying decrements in different cases. Nor is it clear that severely backward readers do not differ qualitatively from others.

It appeared to the author that a thorough understanding of the course of learning to read, the effects on it of various teaching

* See, for instance, the discussion by Diack (1960) of the relation to Gestalt psychology of the 'whole word' method of teaching reading.

methods and the breakdowns which occur, might be gained only through a detailed investigation of the psychological processes involved. Whether or not children learn to read competently must depend on the manner in which their cognitive processes develop and function. Thus the intention of this book is to study and when possible assess the experimental and clinical observations which have been made of the psychological processes involved in the reading of normal and backward readers; and to draw some conclusions from their results as to the nature and development of these processes, and the difficulties they may engender. Attempts are made to trace the development of visual and auditory perception and linguistic and other cognitive processes, and to demonstrate the part played by these in reading. Furthermore, it would seem that in some children there may be a specific constitutional incapacity to perform these processes effectively. Investigations relating to the existence, nature and possible causes of this disability, sometimes termed 'specific developmental dyslexia', will be considered in some detail.

It would seem that actual reading achievement depends not only on the possession of the necessary cognitive abilities but also on the child's motivation, his will to acquire and operate these abilities. There is a variety of factors in the child's environment which may impair either ability or motivation, or both. It is important to consider these effects.

It cannot be claimed that this book will provide any complete exposition of the nature of all the psychological processes involved in reading, nor of the causes of their variations and defects. Nevertheless, it attempts to cover the principal data, to weigh the validity of these and to arrive at certain hypotheses as to the nature of reading and of difficulties in learning to read. Throughout it is obvious that further enquiry is essential to provide answers to many of the questions asked.

CHAPTER II

THE ASSESSMENT OF READING ACHIEVEMENT

It has already been noted, and will appear frequently in the course of this book, that there is considerable disagreement as to the nature of the processes involved in reading; and as to the frequency, nature and causes of difficulties in learning to read. In the first place, we saw that different surveys provided different estimates as to the frequency and severity of backwardness in reading.* These variations were no doubt due in part to differences in sampling of the population. The amount of backwardness certainly varies in different schools and in different parts of the country. But also discrepancies are produced by the use of different tests of reading achievement. In some studies 'word recognition' is tested – the ability to read aloud lists of isolated words without much regard to their meaning. Thus these tests relate only to a limited range of reading. Different authors select different sets of words, and the difficulty of reading these may vary according to the method by which the children have been taught and the vocabulary they have acquired. The norms for the tests have of course been standardized; but these variations have not always been eliminated.

Tests of oral reading must be administered individually, and are thus too time consuming for large-scale surveys. It is customary in these to employ tests which depend on the comprehension of sentences, as demonstrated by the capacity to fill in missing words or answer questions on content, and these are more representative of all-round reading capacity. The addition of a missing word was employed in the Watts–Vernon test used in the British Ministry of Education surveys (1950, 1957) and by Morris (1959). Clearly efficient comprehension necessitates correct word recognition. But it may also depend on intelligence (Kolers, 1968), though it is

* For a valuable discussion of the inadequacies of survey data, see Appendix E by B. S. Cane in Morris (1966).

stated in the report on the first Ministry of Education survey (1950) that sentences were devised which were sufficiently straightforward not to involve much reasoning capacity or 'g' factor. But in assessing any data derived from such tests, it is advisable to control for variations in intelligence, as was done by Morris. Otherwise the incidence of low scores on the test may reflect the effects of low intelligence and not of reading disability.

We shall be more concerned in this book with more circumscribed studies relating to the processes involved in reading and reading difficulties than with large-scale surveys, and no detailed discussion of reading tests is intended. It is not always clear in investigations of the perceptual and other cognitive processes which may function in reading whether these have been related to tests of ability for word recognition or for comprehension of continuous prose. The two abilities are of course interdependent. But as the child becomes adept in word recognition, his reading is to a less extent a function of this ability, and depends more on the ability to perform certain cognitive processes which may not operate at the earlier stages.

Many inconsistencies between the findings of different investigators may have resulted from inadequacies in experimental design method. Thus studies have been carried out by comparing the characteristics of groups of 'backward readers' with groups of 'average' or 'superior' readers. But the criteria of backwardness and superiority are not always clearly stated; and when they are, 'backwardness' may be seen to range from a few months to several years. Traxler (1960) has shown that reading achievement may fluctuate greatly from year to year; hence the deviation from the mean for any one child may be marked in one year and slight in the next. Thus children should not be designated as backward readers unless they diverge from the mean by an appreciable amount, of the order of $1\frac{1}{2}$ years, or more in older children.

Again, it may appear that the degree of backwardness in the backward reader group is uniform. Or even if it varies in amount, it is implied, as we noted on p. 4, that there is no variation in kind, and that the characteristics and deficiencies are similar in all backward readers. As we shall see in Ch. VII, this is certainly untrue in cases of specific dyslexia; and there may well be similar variations in other backward readers. Still more unsatisfactory is the practice of many American writers in particular of quoting school grades rather than ages. These grades have been converted into ages wherever possible; but the age range in any one grade may be wide.

By contrast with experimental investigations of groups of backward readers, those carried out by clinicians, medical and psychological, mainly with severely backward readers, are generally devoted to the intensive study of individual children and their difficulties. Yet their methods of investigation are not always satisfactory. Sometimes only general observations are made, without quantitative assessment. When testing techniques are employed, their application is not always sufficiently skilful, thorough or carefully controlled. Often no control group of normal readers is employed for comparison. It is true that standardized tests possess age norms obtained from normal readers. But they seldom explore adequately the qualitative differences which may be involved in the poor performances of backward readers. Thus specific experimental probes are preferable, comparing the performances of backward readers and matched control groups of normal readers. Again, because the number of children available may be small, the age range is often wide, and insufficient attention may be paid to variation with age in the processes and abilities investigated. Furthermore, when numbers are very small, the problem of the generality of conclusions drawn from them is raised.

Conclusions as to the nature of the reading processes have frequently been related to the postulated success of particular teaching methods. Yet judgments as to the success of these methods have been based on *a priori* beliefs as to their efficacy, without any systematic assessment of this. It is true that there are formidable difficulties in evaluating reliably the efficacy of teaching methods. It is essential that the performance of the experimental group, taught by the method to be assessed, should be compared with that of a control group of children matched in various important respects to those of the experimental group, who are taught by some other method. This is usually the traditional method. Certain

8

of the matched variables can be assessed fairly readily; namely, age, sex, intelligence and socio-economic status. However, other conditions which should be controlled because they are frequently important causes of variation are the general efficiency of the school, the skill of the teachers, the amount of time spent in teaching and the prominence it is given in the curriculum. These conditions are much harder to equate in the experimental and control groups. There are further difficulties. When the teaching method to be assessed is a new one, in which its originators are personally involved, whereas in the control group an old and familiar method is employed, the new method almost always produces better results initially than does the old one. The novelty of the former and the enthusiasm of its originators stimulates the teachers to make more effort; and the children are in turn motivated by their teachers' increased interest. Thus it sometimes appears that the introduction of any new method is a change for the better. But this of course tells us nothing about the intrinsic merits of the new method, or about the significance of the processes it stresses. The most satisfactory investigations are those which are prolonged over a considerable period of time. These considerations have been discussed at length by Warburton & Southgate (1969) in relation to experiments on Pitman's 'initial teaching alphabet' (i.t.a.). Many of them are relevant to investigations of other teaching methods.

However, no attempt is made in this book to provide any final assessment of the value and efficacy of different teaching methods. Certain of these methods are described in order to illustrate the varying emphasis which they have placed on different processes essential to learning to read.* Only a brief survey is given in this chapter of the many imperfections which unfortunately often impair the validity of the findings obtained in studies of reading and reading difficulties. These imperfections were more noticeable in earlier studies of reading, and they have decreased as experimental method in psychology has improved.

* An excellent description, together with some evaluation, of the principal methods employed in this country for teaching reading is given in *Reading – Which Approach?* by Southgate & Roberts (1970).

9

CHAPTER III

VISUAL PERCEPTION AND READING

(1) DEVELOPMENT IN THE PERCEPTION OF FORM, PATTERN AND SEQUENCE

Although reading may be classified as a linguistic process, since it is a form of apprehension of language, it differs from the main linguistic processes of speech in that it involves also the visual perception of printed symbols which the child must be taught to use. We shall discuss later the various complexities and difficulties related to symbolism. We must first consider the developing perceptual abilities in children in relation to the all-important processes of perceiving, differentiating, remembering and identifying printed letters and words.

Until comparatively recently, little was known of the ability of young children to perceive other than quite simple outlined geometrical shapes and objects. Piaget's studies of the early development of his children showed that they learnt to identify familiar objects during the first year of life. But it could not be assumed that their percepts were anything but global and crude. Any object provides a redundancy of perceptual information, and a small amount of this would be adequate to enable identification. Moreover, Piaget also demonstrated that there might be difficulty in differentiating objects from their settings; thus an object might be recognized only when it appeared in its customary surroundings. Gibson (1969) pointed out that infants, at a surprisingly early age, might search for and distinguish the '*invariant*' features of objects, that is to say, those which remain substantially the same despite minor variations in the whole configuration in which they are contained. This is particularly noticeable in the case of human faces. Differentiation of characteristic features such as the eyes begins as early as one month; and by five months a number of different features is differentiated, such that the child seems to recognize a human face and distinguish it from a dummy. As we shall see, this extraction of the invariant characteristic features from amongst irrelevant minor variations continues to be of the utmost importance in perceiving our perpetually varying environment. It is highly significant in reading, in which the invariant features of letters must be differentiated from unimportant variations in type face, etc. Indeed, this is a task of such complexity that it may require conceptual reasoning, as we shall consider in Ch. iv.

However, it would appear that the *perception of form* develops so early in life as to substantiate the claim made by the Gestalt psychologists that it is primary and innate. In recent years, a remarkable series of experiments, initiated by Fantz (1958), indicated that young infants were aware of certain features of meaningless forms and patterns. In these studies, pairs of forms or patterns, or a patterned and an unpatterned surface, were presented above the head of an infant lying prone. It was then observed that his gaze was not directed at these at random, but that in many cases he looked longer or more frequently at one than at the other. From the first weeks of life infants looked more at patterned surfaces, such as checkered patterns, than at unpatterned surfaces; though they did not discriminate between different outlined shapes such as a cross and a circle. When pairs of patterns were presented, the infants, as they became older, gazed increasingly at more complex patterns, that is to say, checkered patterns with larger numbers of squares (Brennan, Ames & Moore, 1966). It may be concluded therefore that the infants could discriminate between patterns from an early age; and that as age increased, they spent longer in exploring the more complex patterns in order to examine them and discover their nature.*

But it must be emphasized that ability to discriminate between two patterns exposed simultaneously does not lead automatically to *identification* of these, although it constitutes the first step. Identification – knowing a pattern – necessitates remembering it. During the early months of life impressions are fragmentary, and the infant soon forgets what he has seen. Thus Bower (cited by

* This evidence is described more fully by Hershenson (1967) and by M. D. Vernon (1970).

Bruner, 1966) presented to infants a stimulus which passed behind a screen and emerged in altered form. The change and novelty of the new form produced a cardiac acceleration in 2-month-old infants, but only if it re-emerged within about a minute. With a longer interval, the infant had forgotten the initial shape. However, at 2–3 months infants presented with pairs of patterns at intervals of one minute, one of which varied while the other remained the same, ceased to look at the repeated pattern and preferred the novel one (Fantz, 1964). Therefore their memories for repeated patterns were expanding. And thereafter the memory span increased fairly rapidly. A series of boxes, each with a picture or geometrical shape on the lid, was shown to children of ages from $1\frac{1}{2}$ to 5 years (Babska, 1965). Immediately after each of these the child was presented with four boxes, and required to pick out the box with the same picture or shape on the lid as the one previously shown. Up to an age of two years choice was mainly by chance; but accuracy improved rapidly in the next year, and thereafter more slowly until an age of five years.

However, in such tests the child is recognizing pictures and forms from their general appearance, and need not remember all their *details*. There is evidence to show that perception of general form, and especially of contour, develops fairly early. Children under five years old could remember the differences between pairs of shapes more easily when they handled them, which suggests that visual perception of contour may be reinforced and improved by tactile perception (Luria, 1961). Awareness and accurate perception of detail, especially of interior detail, develops later, a fact of some significance in learning to read. Thus Ames *et al.* (1953) presented the Rorschach ink-blots to children of 2–10 years, asking them to say what they saw in the blots. The responses of the younger children were to the general form of the blots, perceived vaguely and inexactly.

The lack of exact perception is demonstrated when children are required to *reproduce* pictures and shapes. Thus Maccoby & Bee (1965) found that children of 3–5 years, who could discriminate correctly between a circle and a triangle, could not copy them with even approximate accuracy. They hypothesized that this was due to the necessity of utilizing more aspects of the model in copying than in mere discrimination. Again, copying from models of shapes such as a square, circle and triangle was found by Piaget & Inhelder (1956) not to be completely accurate before 5–6 years. However, other experimenters obtained somewhat different results. Graham, Berman & Ernhart (1960) presented eighteen shapes varying in complexity from simple straight lines to a diamond to children aged between $2\frac{1}{2}$ and 5 years, and required them to copy these. Copying of over-all form was reasonably accurate by $4\frac{1}{2}$ years. But certain features such as orientation and size of angles were not grasped until considerably later. Reproduction from memory is naturally more difficult. Boguslavskaya (cited by Zaporozhets, 1965) found that children of 3–5 years, after making a brief visual examination of pictures of objects, could recognize these subsequently, but could not reproduce them by drawing them. Even 5–7-year-old children were not always able to do this. This inability may be of some importance in learning to write.

The shapes of letters of the alphabet are far more complex and intricate than are those of simple outlined geometrical forms, and the letters are therefore in all probability harder to perceive and remember. Even discrimination of such shapes may present some difficulty. Gibson *et al.* (1962) investigated the discrimination of '*letter-like*' forms, such as those shown in Fig. 1, in children of 4–8 years. Twelve letter-like forms were presented, each with twelve 'transformations' which differed from the original standards by changes of form, including straight to curved lines (and *vice versa*); broken to closed lines (and *vice versa*); and tilting, rotation and reversal. Each child had to select a copy of the standard from among the transformations. Confusions were frequent at 4 years but much fewer at 5 years, and infrequent at 8 years. But the frequency of different types of error varied considerably. Errors of break and close were few throughout. Errors of straight line and curve, and of rotation and reversal were high in the youngest children, but decreased almost to zero by 7–8 years. Errors of tilt were high throughout, indicating that the children thought that shapes retained their identity when tilted backwards or forwards.

Now it must again be noted that *remembering* the essential characteristics of shapes such as these is harder than discriminating between them when they can be directly compared. Trieschmann (1968) carried out a study in which the same material was used. But the transformations of each standard were exposed after the standard had been shown; thus the children had to remember the special characteristics of each standard in turn. The children, aged 7–9 years, made more errors than did those in the Gibson study

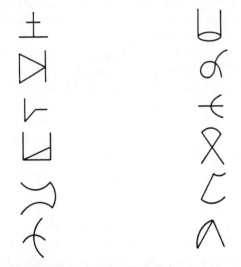

Fig. 1. 'Letter-like' forms. (After E. J. Gibson *et al.* 1962, p. 898.)

who employed direct comparison; but the same types of error were most frequent – rotations, reversals and backward tilt. Long-term memory for such forms, as in reading, would probably be even harder than this short-term memory.*

* Some doubt as to the validity of these 'matching to sample' techniques as measures of form discrimination is aroused by a recent experiment of Taylor & Wales (1970). They found that, in children tested at about $3\frac{1}{2}$ years and 5 years, judgments of 'same' depended to a considerable extent on the degree of similarity between the standard and comparison figures. Whereas in some of the younger children matching was at random, others realized that certain of the comparison figures possessed several attributes in common with the standard figure though were not

The difficulty of perceiving and copying *complex meaningless figures* has frequently been demonstrated in the performance of the *Bender* test, in which nine figures of varying complexity must be reproduced.* The nine figures constitute a distinctly heterogeneous collection of complex forms originally designed by Wertheimer (1923) to demonstrate various Gestalt effects such as the tendencies to perceive continuity and closure. But Bender (1938) found that for younger children these tendencies did not operate and the figures were reproduced in a manner quite different from that postulated by Wertheimer. Thus the easiest figure could be reproduced correctly at 7 years, but the most difficult not until 11 years. However, it is difficult to classify the types of error systematically, although this has been attempted when the test is used in connection with reading achievement. In general it appeared that for younger children of 5–6 years there was a tendency towards 'primitivization'; that is to say, simplification, failure to integrate parts and rotation (Keogh, 1968). Errors were also made in size of angles and in substituting lines inclined angularly for curves (Snyder & Kalil, 1968).

Not only may the perception of parts of figures be inaccurate in young children; but in some cases they may be unable to perceive *parts within the whole*, because the former are so completely embedded in the latter. Simplified versions of the figures originally designed by the Gestalt psychologist Gottschaldt (1926) were presented by Ghent (1956) to children of 4–8 years who were asked to trace out each simple figure in the corresponding complex one (see Fig. 2). None of the 4-year-old children could perform this task correctly, and only a quarter of the 8-year-olds. It is true that

identical with it. Thus the children judged these to be the 'same' as the standard figure, differentiating only those which were strikingly dissimilar. At the later age, some children judged as 'same' only figures identical in every respect; but other children ignored orientation and judged as 'same' all those of the same or similar shape. Thus the apparent accuracy of form discrimination would appear to depend both on the nature of the comparison sets employed and also on the children's concepts of 'sameness'.

* For an illustration of the figures of this test, see M. D. Vernon (1957). The scoring of the test will be discussed on p. 31.

even for an adult it is quite difficult to extract a single part from a continuously outlined figure; but until a certain age it is impossible, for closely connected parts are not differentiated by young children.

On other occasions it may be difficult for children to *integrate* strongly differentiated parts within wholes, as in the Bender test. Elkind, Koegler & Go (1964) showed to children of $4\frac{1}{2}$–9 years pictures in which both the whole picture and also the parts possessed representational meaning. Thus pictures of different kinds of fruit

Simple   Complex

Fig. 2. Simple and complex figures. (After Ghent, 1956, p. 580.)

were grouped together to look like a man. When asked to say what they saw, the younger children reported the parts alone. With increase in age, an increasing number reported the wholes rather than the parts; and at 8–9 years, parts and wholes were integrated together, as for instance 'a man made of fruit'. However, the frequency of part perception by the younger children may have been due to some extent to the fact that the parts were better integrated internally than were the wholes, which were somewhat difficult to perceive as representations of whole objects. In another experiment, Elkind, Anagostopoulou & Malone (1970) compared two groups of 6–7-year-old children, the first consisting of children who reported only the parts on this test, the second of children who reported wholes and part–whole combinations. The former, in contrast to the latter, were unable to reconstruct the wholes from memory with cut-out parts; and also to report both the object and the material in composite objects such as a hat made from newspaper. It would appear therefore that at this age some children are less able than others to grasp the dual nature of configurations. Thus they might also have similar difficulty in recognizing words both as meaningful wholes and also as combinations of parts, the letters.

There may be tendencies, therefore, both towards global perception and also towards defective integration of whole patterns. This was also shown by Satterley (1968), who employed tests both of analysis, of the Gottschaldt figures, and of synthesis, in which partial cues were to be integrated to form wholes (details of this test were not given). There was an increase in analysis as age increased from 7–11 years, and some decline in synthesis; but considerable individual differences occurred, some children scoring better on synthesis, others on analysis.

Other difficulties in the accurate perception of complex figures may be caused by the *omission* or *obscuring* of parts of the outlines of figures. Piaget & Stettler-von Albertini (1954) presented forms to children such as those shown in Fig. 3, and, after a demonstration, instructed the children to complete and name the figure. About $\frac{3}{4}$ of a group of 6-year-old children could perform this task with simple forms such as that in Fig. 3 *a*; and about $\frac{3}{4}$ of a group of 7-year-olds could do the same with the more complex double figures such as that in Fig. 3 *b*. Even matching is more difficult for children than for adults in such impoverished conditions. Thus Munsinger & Gummerman (1967) required children of 7 and 9 years to recognize and match irregular silhouette shapes, presented tachistoscopically and obscured by grids of lines. The younger children found this task harder than did the older ones, and were almost as confused by grids of widely spaced lines as by the greater obscurity of lines placed close together. These findings suggest that younger children require optimal conditions of clarity for easy and accurate perception, and their perceptions are readily impaired by confusion or incompleteness of the figures shown.

Numerous studies have indicated that children do not remember accurately the *orientation* or position of forms in space. To them a shape does not appear to change its identity when it changes its spatial position, just as an object retains its identity whatever its spatial position. Differences of *inversion* are perceived at a fairly early age. Thus Wohlwill & Wiener (1964) required children to match forms which contained small shapes in their upper or lower parts (to indicate directionality) against one of a pair of forms, the first identical, the second inverted. Children of 3 years could not perform this task, but at 4–4½ years there were few errors. This task of direct matching was an easy one. Had the children been required to remember and identify a form as upright or inverted, they might have had more difficulty in making the correct choice.

(a)   (b)

Fig. 3. Incomplete figures. (After Piaget & Stettler-von Albertini, 1954, pp. 211 and 224.)

It is probable that children acquire some discrimination between upright and inverted forms fairly early in life, since the up–down position may be related to the gravitational coordinate. *Reversals* from left to right are far more confusing. Thus Wohlwill & Wiener (1964) found more errors of reversal than of inversion in their task. Again, Gibson *et al.* (1962) showed that rotations and reversals of their letter-like forms were common in the younger children though they largely disappeared by 7–8 years. Keogh (1968) also found that rotations of the Bender test figures, which occurred in 87 per cent of cases at 5 years, decreased to 27 per cent at 9 years. Again, memory and identification of reversed forms is undoubtedly harder than matching or direct copying. Indeed, it appeared that if they were allowed to compare shapes and their mirror images directly, only a small minority of children of 5–6 years were unable to differentiate these (Robinson & Higgins, 1967). What is difficult is to realize that reversed shapes may have different connotations.

18

Further inaccuracies and confusions may arise when a child endeavours to *explore a wide field of view* containing several different figures, in sequence or scattered at random. This involves direction of attention, and in infancy there is no voluntary direction of attention. Salapatek & Kessen (1966) showed that the attention of new-born babies may be caught and fixed upon a single aspect of a figure. Systematic direction develops slowly. When children of $3\frac{1}{2}$–6 years were required to match an irregular shape against a similar shape contained in a row of shapes, it was found that the younger children tended to look only at the bottom parts of the shapes (Kerpelman & Pollack, 1964). These observations agree with the hypothesis advanced by Piaget (1961) that children under about 6 years of age are incapable of exploring systematically an extended figure or field of view. Rather, they wander about in a random manner, glancing here and there, sometimes going outside the figure altogether. Or if some part of it attracts their attention, they gaze at it fixedly with what Piaget has termed '*centration*', ignoring the remainder of the field. Piaget & Vinh Bang (1961) obtained evidence of this by recording the eye movements made by children in examining figures of certain visual illusions. Mack-worth & Bruner (cited by Gibson, 1969) also found that the eye movements made by children in identifying blurred pictures were shorter and more restricted in coverage than were those of adults. Inspection was piecemeal, and there were numerous fixations on unimportant details. Again, Elkind *et al.* (1964) considered that the tendency in younger children to perceive parts only and not the whole was due to centration; and also their difficulty in extracting the simple from the complex Gottschaldt figures (Elkind, Horn & Schneider, 1965).

Piaget (1961) hypothesized that at the age of about 7 years children develop the capacity for systematic scanning and observation, which he termed '*perceptual activity*'. Elkind & Weiss (1967) presented children of 6–8 years with pictures of common objects arranged either at random or in a triangular structure. In naming the objects, scanning of the latter was fairly systematic at all ages. But systematic scanning of the randomly arranged pictures increased from the younger to the older children. With pictures of objects arranged in rows and columns, order of report became more systematic at 5–6 years than it was in 4-year-old children (Gottschalk, Bryden & Rabinovitch, 1964). It seemed that regular scanning of successive rows from left to right did not occur until the children had begun learning to read. In the early stages of learning, before children had acquired the capacity to scan regularly, it might well be that confusion would be caused by random and irregular scanning.

In viewing complex pictures, failure to scan systematically seems to be associated with inability to grasp what are the essential features of the picture. Thus even 9–10-year-old children may 'centrate' on quite unimportant and irrelevant details, while ignoring those parts of the picture which indicate its meaning (Vernon, 1940; Mackworth & Bruner, cited by Gibson, 1969). As Piaget suggested, effective perceptual activity is associated with intelligent understanding of the nature of the material, and hence appropriate direction of attention.

It is probable that associated with inability to extract the essential features of complex configurations is difficulty in appreciating the importance of *sequential pattern*. Children can perceive and remember shapes accurately before they can perceive and remember their *order* in a sequence. Piaget & Inhelder (1956) found that children under 6–7 years could carry out the task of reproducing the order of beads on a string only by direct copying; they had no grasp of sequential ordering as an independent property of a group of objects, and could not remember it. Direct correspondence of sequences may be perceived and remembered fairly readily. Kahn & Birch (1968) found that the matching of a sequence of groups of dots against one of three dot sequences presented subsequently was carried out adequately by about 7 years of age. But when a rhythmical sequence of flashes from a blinking light was to be matched against a sequence of dots, performance continued to improve up to about 8 years (Rudnick, Sterritt & Flax, 1967). Tasks such as these necessitate the abstraction of the spatial sequential pattern as independent of the particular stimuli employed, and its association with a temporal sequential pattern. This would appear to demand conceptual thinking rather than direct perception. As we shall see, such an activity may be highly significant in learning to read, where the order of letters in words is of paramount importance.

It might be supposed that the ability to perceive forms and patterns could be improved by *practice* and *training*. But on the whole the effects of these seem to be slight. In younger children especially, improvement in recognition would appear to be limited to the particular type of material which is practised, and there is little transfer of the effects to others. Young children are unable to generalize readily from one situation to another. However, Sokhina (cited by Zaporozhets, 1965) found that children of 3–7 years, who could not discriminate between and identify the elements of complex forms, could be trained in this by a series of practical exercises in constructing three-dimensional structures from their parts. The children were required to predict which parts they would need, and could then check for themselves if they were correct. Thereafter, from 4 years of age, they began to make purely visual analyses of the two-dimensional figures; and this ability was transferred to other tasks, such as that of extracting the simple from the complex Gottschaldt figures. It would seem possible that this technique is relevant to the construction of words from isolated printed letters, in learning to read.

Experiments on training in the perception of simple forms have shown however that this seldom has any effect on learning to read. Training at the pre-reading stage in visual discrimination between shapes did not improve word recognition in 6-year-old children (Gorelick, 1965). Rosen (1966) found that children of similar ages, trained on the Frostig tests which relate to figure–ground discrimination, perception of shape and spatial position, etc., were not superior on reading tests to children given an equal period of reading instruction; and the latter were superior in the understanding of word meanings. Beck & Talkington (1970) trained a group of 5-year-old deprived children over a period of 7 months with the Frostig–Horne visual perception materials. At the close of this period there was an improvement on the Frostig tests; but the superiority over a matched group, given other activities, was on the orientation test only. Both groups improved about equally on the Peabody Picture Vocabulary test, a test of verbal intelligence and visual recognition.

Goins (1958) found that a 10-week period of training in tachistoscopic perception of digits and geometric figures produced an increase in the number of digits and figures which could be perceived by 6–7-year-old children, but had no significant effect on reading performance. In some schools, children are required to perform what are termed 'reading readiness' activities which include practice in the discrimination and matching of shapes. It would seem improbable that this training has any useful purpose.

It is possible to train children to discriminate between the mirror images of shapes exposed simultaneously (Newson, 1955; Bijou, cited by Fellows, 1968). But such training does not produce improvement in the capacity to remember orientation and to identify figures in different orientations. Jeffrey (1958) found that 4-year-old children had great difficulty in learning the correct names, Jack and Jill, of two 'stick' figures facing right and left respectively. However, they succeeded when they were taught to respond by pressing one or other of two buttons corresponding to the two figures. Newson (private communication) found that her programme of training in discrimination between reversed shapes did not decrease letter reversal in learning to read. It seems probable again that there is no transfer effect from general training in perception of orientation. But children learnt to discriminate between the reversed letters 'b' and 'd' when they were specifically trained with these (Hendrickson & Muehl, 1962).

We have seen that the development in children of correct perception of form is uneven, proceeding at different rates with different types of task. Discrimination between figures similar to letters appears at a fairly early age, except that certain characteristics, notably orientation, are often perceived erroneously. The accurate perception of details in complex forms and configurations is difficult, still more the identification of these from memory. Young children may require material which is clear and unambiguous in appearance, to a greater extent than do adults. The children may fail to extract significant details and perceive them correctly; or they may be unable to integrate into wholes the parts of forms not obviously related to each other. It is possible that this is due in part to inability to direct attention systematically over the whole field, noting its significant features and ignoring the remainder. This inability may also affect the perception of sequential patterns. Spatial position is perceived and understood at a later age than is form, and failure in direction of attention may be involved here also. It seems possible therefore that development in the ability to organize reproduction of material effectively and to integrate parts within the whole is slower than development in immediate perception and memory.

All these difficulties may have considerable effect on learning to read in its early stages, especially in British children who go to school a year earlier than do most American children. It seems possible that reading might be facilitated by practice in simultaneous comparison of letters and words of similar appearance but with small differences, and especially of letters with inverted or reversed orientation, in such a manner that the child directly discriminates the differences. Indeed, Gibson (1965) has advocated this method in respect of letters. Reading might also be assisted if the child were made aware from the beginning that words are not global wholes but consist of separate identifiable letters; but at the same time that the letters must be integrated together to form words. Training in the discrimination of shapes other than letters is of little assistance; but training in the construction of words from isolated letters, in correct sequential order, might be valuable. However, the efficient performance of many of these processes would seem to be determined to a great extent by maturation.

(2) VISUAL PERCEPTION OF PRINTED MATERIAL

For the reasons outlined in the previous section, it would appear that when children begin to learn to read they might have considerable difficulty in perceiving printed material visually. However, before long children can usually begin to learn their *letters*. There has been some discussion as to the desirability of teaching children to perceive, name and sound letters before they begin the reading of words. Several experiments, however, have shown a close relationship between early reading achievement and ability to identify letters. Wilson & Flemming (1938) obtained a high correlation between reading achievement and both naming and sounding of letters. Extensive investigations by Durrell (cited by Chall, 1967) indicated that systematic formal teaching of letters at the beginning was more effective than informal teaching, and that the former should be independent of teaching the reading of words, though it benefited this.

In England it is usual to begin teaching reading by *whole word methods*. Goodacre (1967) found this in the majority of the 100 London infant schools she studied. The whole word method most frequently used was that of labelling pictures with the names of the objects and activities depicted, and requiring the children to learn the printed names. Now children do not always perceive correctly what is shown in pictures, except with simple outline drawings of common objects. Indeed a recent investigation by Keir (1970) showed that backward readers of 7–11 years were often unable to name correctly coloured pictures of objects specially chosen for use in word recognition. Often quite common objects were unrecognized or incorrectly identified, such as a plum, a peach and a pear. Or objects were recognized but named incorrectly, or given an alternative name, such as 'flash-lamp' for 'torch' and 'cooker' for 'stove'. Objects depicted in reduced size or in unusual perspective were often unrecognized. Thus it would appear to be necessary for the teacher always to name the pictures used in word recognition.

The argument for the use of whole word methods appears to be that children perceive wholes rather than parts. Diack (1960) published a highly critical discussion of the beliefs of educationists in the efficacy of whole word methods who sought to reinforce their beliefs by citing the tenets of Gestalt psychology. This theory holds that perception of the whole may be prior to, and indeed independent of, perception of the constituent parts, as for instance in the Gottschaldt figures. Hence it was concluded that children should first learn to recognize words as structural wholes before proceeding to analyse them into their constituent parts, the letters. Yet as we noted such global perception of wholes tends to be vague and inexact, and to produce adequate identification only with simple and easily identifiable forms of clearly perceptible structure. Printed words are certainly not of this nature; their structure is complex and neither clearly defined nor obviously discriminable.

It is also true that it is difficult for children to analyse such structures correctly into their essential parts. Yet it would appear that in perceiving and memorizing words attached to pictures, some *discrimination of individual letters* does take place. In certain circumstances, words of very different length are distinguished from each other through discrimination of over-all length. But more commonly they are identified from certain particular letters. Edelman (1963) and Marchbanks & Levin (1965) showed that, in the matching of 5-letter nonsense words by children of 5 and 6½ years, the first letter was the most important, and then the last letter. Some of the younger children who had not begun learning to read used the last letter more often than the first, probably because they had not learnt to scan from left to right. Williams, Blumberg & Williams (1970) found that in matching 3- and 5-letter nonsense words there was no consistent selection of particular letters by children below 6 years. At 6–7 years matching was mainly by means of the first letter, though sometimes by the last; but over-all shape was seldom employed. However, the matched nonsense words were of the same length.

It would seem therefore that ability to discriminate and identify letters is of major importance from the beginning. Undoubtedly some letters are easier to discriminate and recognize than are others. In the experiment of Gibson *et al.* (1962; see p. 13), the younger children, who had not learnt to read, were required to discriminate *capital letters* from transformations of the same kind as those employed for the letter-like forms. The real letters were less readily confused with their transformations than were the letter-like forms;

but the types of confusion were similar. A further study (Gibson, 1965) was made in which children were required to match each of the capital letters against one of six letters; that is to say, they had to discriminate each capital letter from five others. The greater the number of similar features in the letters, the greater the tendency to confuse them. Important differentiating features were straight *v.* curved lines and oblique *v.* vertical lines. However, combinations of oblique and vertical lines were easily confused, as in 'M' and 'N' and 'M' and 'W' (Gibson, Schapiro & Yonas, 1968).

An experiment by Pick (1965) appeared to show that learning to discriminate between different types of transformation of the letter-like forms, for instance from straight line to curve, was easier than learning to discriminate between different standard forms with the same types of transformations. Thus new standards with previously learnt transformations were learnt more quickly than were old standards with new transformations. However, Caldwell & Hall (1970) suggested that this result was an artifact of the experimental conditions, in that children required to learn old standards with new transformations were given insufficient information for discriminating the latter. Specifically, they were not told that transformations by rotation were not to be accepted as being the same as the standard; and such rotations are particularly likely to give rise to confusion. When Caldwell & Hall demonstrated clearly at the beginning of the experiment which transformations were not to be accepted as matches, there was no difference between the two conditions.

However, it must again be emphasized that it is not sufficient in learning to read for the child simply to discriminate between one letter and another. He must be able to remember the essential characteristics of letters as such, in order to identify them. Most of the evidence goes to show that this is the harder task. Thus it could be said that it was the standards which must be perceived and remembered, whereas transformations such as those which occur in different type faces must be disregarded. However, Neisser (1963) was dubious as to the importance of isolated distinctive features, and considered that it was the totality of features making up the whole form of the letters which was essential. These features he thought were simultaneously and multiply processed in the perception of total form.

In the *small lower case letters* distinctive features are probably less easy to isolate and observe; they are therefore more readily confused than are capital letters (Smith, 1928). Moreover, children may not find it easy to transfer from capital to lower case letters, and *vice versa*. The distinctive features of lower case letters were analysed by Dunn-Rankin (1968), who required children of 7–9 years to match each of the twenty-one commonest lower case letters against pairs of letters. He found that these letters fell into groups such that letters were readily confused with others in the same group, but not with letters in other groups. The groups comprised: (1) e, a, s, c, o; (2) n, u, m, w; (3) b, p, d; (4) h, f, l, t, k, i; though 'i' was less readily confused than were the other letters in the group.

However, it cannot be assumed that confusions between letters will be the same when they are contained in words as when they are isolated (Smith, 1928). Thus 'n' and 'u', inverted letters which may be confused in isolation, are seldom transposable in words. But there is a general tendency to confuse the reversible letters 'b' and 'd'; and to a less extent, 'p' and 'q'. This reversal is very common among young children, but tends to disappear at about 7 years (Ames & Ilg, 1951).

It would appear likely that *words* containing many confusable letters would be most difficult to differentiate from each other. But here other factors such as *order of letters* in words are important. Thus Ilg & Ames (1950) and Ames & Ilg (1951) found that transpositions of letters within words and complete word reversals persisted in reading and writing until 8–9 years, after letter reversals had disappeared. Wiley (1928) also found a tendency in 6-year-old children to confuse words containing some of the same letters but in a different order, such as 'dog' and 'girl', 'you' and 'boy'. But discrimination and matching in tachistoscopic presentations of pairs of words and pseudo-words with reversed letters was unrelated to reading in retarded and normal readers of 7, 9 and 11 years

(Bonsall & Dornbush, 1969). Thus direct matching of order seemed to be irrelevant in children of these ages. However, with younger children who had not begun to read, discrimination of order was related to perception of similarity of form of capital letters and to reading readiness (Nodine & Hardt, 1970). Though pre-reading test scores are by no means an infallible indicator of later reading ability, it is likely that discrimination of order as well as of form is an important factor in learning to read.

It is generally found that *familiar forms* are perceived more readily than unfamiliar, because the observer develops an expectancy as to what will appear; thus he is on the look-out for types of form structure with a high probability of appearance. Thus Payne (1930) found a tendency in the tachistoscopic perception of words by children of 7–10 years to substitute more familiar for less familiar words of similar structure. According to Bloomer (1961), the age at which words could be read was related to their familiarity as assessed from their frequency of occurrence in the English language. But Wiley (1928), who practised children of 6–7 years in the recognition of 60 words in a list, found that speed of learning was not correlated with word frequency. He argued that the child's vocabulary of familiar words does not correspond with their frequency in adult speech. But it could also be that in this task, which is dissimilar from ordinary reading, the children became thoroughly familiar with all the words. Ryan & Muehl (1965) presented frequent and infrequent nouns and verbs tachistoscopically to children of 8 years, and found that in general the more frequent were perceived more quickly than the less frequent, though some simple but relatively infrequent words were read without difficulty.

The factor of familiarity also operates in the ability to perceive words more easily than sequences of letters which do not make words. Though the speed of reading 3-letter sequences tachistoscopically increased considerably between 6 and 12 years of age, it remained substantially less than the speed of reading 3-letter words (Fraisse & McMurray, 1960). However, according to Levin & Biemiller (1968*a*), the difference in speed of reading between 5-letter words and 5-letter sequences was greater for older children of 9–10 years than for younger ones of 7–8 years, presumably because the former, but not the latter, had learnt to read long words easily.

Wallach (1963) exposed 6-letter sequences, with different degrees of resemblance to real words, tachistoscopically to 10-year-old children, and found that the closer the resemblance, the greater the number of letters the children could perceive. The increase in score with resemblance was related to spelling ability, indicating that the better spellers had become more familiar than had the poorer with the customary sequential order of letters in words. The fluent reading of older children and adults depends on their familiarity with this sequential structure.

However, it seems possible that in the reading of words *understanding of meaning* may have a function as significant as familiarity with word structure. Words may be easier to perceive than letter sequences at least in part because they are meaningful; and this effect is of course augmented when the words are presented in sentence context. Again, in the experiment of Ryan & Muehl (1965), it is possible that the children did not understand the meanings of the less familiar words. However, differences in meaning were not responsible for the results of Wallach (1963), since none of his letter sequences was meaningful. Meaning was also claimed to be less important than word frequency in the experiments of Bloomer (1961), who found that even real words which the children did not understand were sometimes read quite quickly. Rudishill (1956) presented phrases such as 'two red trains' tachistoscopically to 8-year-old children and instructed them to read half of the set of phrases, but with the other half to point to models of the objects described in the phrases. He found that the more backward readers, with reading ages about $1\frac{1}{2}$ years below normal, could in some cases verbalize the phrases more rapidly than they could understand their meaning as demonstrated by pointing to the relevant objects. The rate of understanding of meaning was more closely related to reading achievement than was verbalizing the phrases. From this experiment, and from numerous observations on backward readers, it would therefore appear that one of their characteristics may be that they do not make use of meaning in word recognition. The proficient reader may be one who is able to utilize meaning, firstly in word recognition, later in reading continuous texts.

(3) RELATION OF READING TO PERCEPTUAL DEFICIENCIES

We noted that whereas most children could perceive and remember simple forms by the time they went to school and began learning to read, they might have considerably more difficulty in analysing complex irregular structures such as words into their constituent parts, the letters; and in re-synthesizing these, in correct sequential order, to form whole words. In fact, it appears that children may differ in their capacity to perform these tasks, and that those who are notably deficient may have unusual difficulty in learning to read. However, several experiments have demonstrated little correlation between reading achievement and shape discrimination. Gates found only a small correlation of 0.3 at 6 years (1926) and no significant correlation at 8 years (1922). But the type of discrimination he tested was that of simple geometrical form. Thus the conclusion is reinforced that such discrimination has little significance in the perception and analysis of complex structures such as words. Moreover, it is possible that children who are notably deficient in the perception of complex shapes are not very numerous, and therefore do not stand out in large-scale reading surveys of unselected groups of school children. But a number of small-scale studies has been carried out in which various perceptual performances of backward readers are compared with those of average or good readers. The perceptual deficiencies of the former then become apparent.

Whereas simple immediate perception does not seem to be inferior in backward readers, the *ability to analyse complex* form may be related to reading. Ames & Walker (1964) found that children of 4–5 years who were able to analyse the Rorschach ink-blots and perceive correctly the form of details within them, subsequently became better readers than did those who perceived the blots globally as wholes. However, by the age of 8 years these differences were not marked, though good readers made better verbal responses to the ink-blots than did poor readers (Knoblock, 1965). Thus capacity for perceptual analysis was more significant at the earlier stages of learning to read. Goins (1958) obtained a correlation of 0.5 in 6–7-year-old children between scores on reading tests, and on a test of completing progressively more complex patterns, which had been administered some months earlier.

Numerous studies have been carried out on the relationship between reading achievement and performance of the *Bender test*. These results must be viewed with some caution, since it is difficult to assess and score errors on the test. In some cases, those for instance cited by Crosby (1968), children with severe reading disability exhibited such gross disorders in reproduction that it was obvious they were unable to grasp the manner in which the figures were constructed. Various experimenters have adopted different methods of scoring minor errors. Thus Galifret-Granjon (1951) selected, as criteria of successful reproduction, correct construction of angles, orientation of axes of figures and relative positions of the elements; and graded children's performances into categories of good, medium or poor. He then found that 32 per cent of normal readers of 7–10 years made poor performances, but none of 10–13 years; whereas 70 per cent of children of 7–10 years with severe reading disability made poor performances, and 16 per cent of those of 10–13 years. Thus the latter showed some improvement in accuracy of perceiving and reproducing these particular characteristics of the Bender test figures, but they were still inferior to normal readers. Lachmann (1960) found that children of 8–10 years with an average retardation in reading of 17 months made significantly more of the following errors than did normal readers: inaccurate reproduction of angles and slant (orientation), rotations, separation of adjoining and overlapping parts.

Koppitz (1958) selected twenty types of error in the Bender test which appeared to relate to achievement in reading, writing and spelling. Scoring these as either present or absent, she found that seven of them were significantly more frequent in children of 6–10 years who were graded by teachers as below average in achievement than in those graded as normal. These errors fell into two main categories: incorrect reproduction of shape and direction of lines, and failure to integrate parts into wholes.

The Bender test has also been used with young children who have not begun reading, to predict future reading achievement. Thweatt (1963) gave the Bender test at 6 years, on entry to school, and assessed reading vocabulary and comprehension at 8 years. He found that 77 per cent of one group and 55 per cent of another who made above average numbers of errors in the Koppitz categories became reading problem cases by 8 years; whereas none of those with few Koppitz errors did so. Both Koppitz, Mardis & Stephens (1961) and Smith & Keogh (1962) obtained significant correlations between scores on the Bender test administered on entry to school at 6 years, and scores on reading tests given a year later. Wedell & Horne (1969) found that children who scored well on the Bender test at $5\frac{1}{2}$ years were superior in spelling at 7 years to those who scored badly. De Hirsch, Jansky & Langford (1966) also employed the Bender test predictively, using as the main criterion perception of essential form and degree of differentiation. They found that performance with six of the Bender test figures by children of 5–6 years correlated significantly with reading achievement two years later. They considered that the test was one of the best predictors of subsequent reading achievement. However, somewhat conflicting results were obtained by Keogh (1965) and Keogh & Smith (1967). They found that when the Bender test was administered as a group test at 5–6 years, the correlation with reading achievement at 8–9 years was almost insignificant; whereas at 11–12 years it was greater. Only good performance on the test was predictive at 8–9 years, but both very good and very poor scores were predictive at 11–12 years.

Bender (1970) disapproved of scoring individual items on the test, as in the Koppitz method, considering that reproductions of all the test items should be judged together as an integrated Gestalt. De Hirsch et al. seem to have adopted such a procedure. Bender distinguished certain stages of maturation in test performance, the arrangement of items on the page being included as well as the separate items. The stages were: control of circular movement, figure–ground differentiation, horizontal, vertical and diagonal orientation, differentiation of figures and their parts and relation of parts to the wholes. The later stages in particular tended to show 'primitivization' in backward readers. When there was improvement in repeated performances of the test, improvement in reading was likely to occur also.

Some of the discrepancies in the results of the Bender test might be due to differences in sampling, test procedures (individual and group testing) and scoring criteria. However, the results probably warrant the following conclusions: young children just beginning to learn to read who exhibit excessive errors in reproduction of certain general characteristics such as differentiation and integration of parts and wholes, or certain particular characteristics of shape and orientation, may have difficulty in learning to read. These errors are of the type associated with immaturity in perception, but are more frequent and persist longer in backward than in normal readers. The disability involved, whatever its nature, may be less significant in older readers, but may be associated in certain cases with severe reading disability. However, dyslexic cases are comparatively uncommon, and may not appear in all samples. In other backward readers the disability has disappeared.

Other forms of deficiency in the perception of complex forms do persist in older backward readers. Walters & Doan (1962) found that severely retarded readers performed less well than did good readers in discriminating the Gibson & Gibson 'scribble' figures (1955). Whipple & Kodman (1969) required children of about 10 years, retarded in reading by 8–24 months, to learn to discriminate these figures correctly, and found that they made more errors than did normal readers, and took more trials to learn. Leader (1968) obtained a correlation of about 0.6 in children of $8\frac{1}{2}$–$10\frac{1}{2}$ years between the scores on a word recognition test and in figure completion – drawing the missing lines in progressively more complex patterns. Thus it would appear that deficiencies in both analysis and synthesis of more complex patterns persist to a considerable age in backward readers, at least in some types of perceptual task.

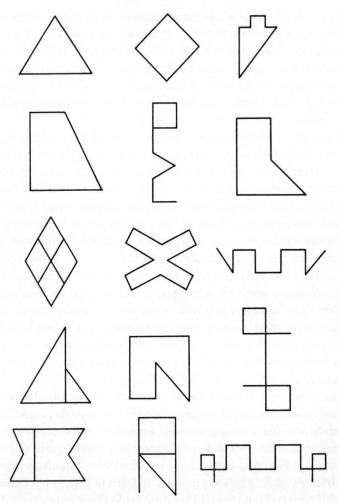

Fig. 4. Memory-for-Designs test. (After Graham & Kendall, 1946, p. 305.)

One might expect that *visual memory* would also be deficient in backward readers – as indeed it was in the experiment of Whipple & Kodman (1969). The remembering of designs in a graded series gradually increasing in difficulty, the Graham–Kendall Memory-for-Designs test (Graham & Kendall, 1946; see Fig. 4) was unrelated to reading achievement in a large unselected sample of children aged 6–8½ years (Kendall, 1948). Lyle (1968) found that children of 7–12½ years, none of them able to read effectively, were significantly inferior to normal readers on this test. Again, Lyle & Goyen (1968) required children of 7 and 9 years, retarded in reading by an average of 0.9 years at 7 years up to 1.9 years at 9 years, to recognize tachistoscopically presented line drawings from among groups of similar drawings shown them subsequently. These children, and especially the younger ones, were significantly inferior to normal readers. Thus although there may be no general relationship between reading achievement and visual memory in large unselected groups, it would seem that certain backward readers are deficient in this.

There are undoubtedly differences in ability to perceive the *orientation* of forms which are related to reading achievement. Children judged by teachers to be poor readers were significantly less accurate than good readers, both at 6–7 years and also at 8–10 years, in discriminating from its reversed form an irregular figure resembling a 'lamb chop' (Wechsler & Hagin, 1964). This was found with both simultaneous and successive comparison. Leader (1968) required children of 8½–10½ years to detect where the whole or some part of one of a pair of patterns was reversed; and obtained a correlation of about 0.6 between scores on this test and on a word recognition test. Among the Frostig tests, which have been claimed to differentiate good from poor readers (Maslow *et al.* 1964), only the sub-test for discrimination of spatial orientation in shapes was found by Olson (1966) to correlate significantly with word recognition at 7–8 years.

There are also differences in the ability to perceive and remember *order* in sequences of shapes which relate to reading achievement. There may be reversal of order even in immediate perception. Thus Monroe (1928) found that 4.7 per cent of a group of severely retarded readers aged 6–10 years named rows of pictures in reversed order, as against 0.9 per cent of a matched group of normal readers. As a predictive test administered to children of 5–6 years who had not begun to learn to read, De Hirsch *et al.* (1966) pre-

3-2

sented the Horst Reversals test. In this test two- and three-letter combinations had to be matched against combinations in the same or reversed order. Performance showed a significant correlation with reading achievement at 8 years. Doehring (1968) also found a deficit in boys aged 10–14 years, retarded in reading by 3 years or more, in visual sequential processing. Thus they were inferior to normal readers in the rapid reproduction of letter and number series; and also in a task of joining up circles numbered consecutively but scattered at random over the field.

⤸ Lyle (1969) carried out a factorial analysis of measures of letter and sequence reversals in reading and writing, the Memory-for-Designs test, the WISC and certain other tests, with a group of children aged 6–12 years, half of whom were normal readers while the other half were retarded by from $\frac{1}{2}$ year at 6 years to 3 years at 12 years. From this analysis he extracted two factors related to reading retardation, the first of letter reversals, which also correlated with the Memory-for-Designs test; and the second, of sequence reversals, related to capacity for verbal learning. The first appeared to be a visual disability which declined with age. The second, which did not decrease with age, may be of fundamental importance in learning to read; it will be discussed in subsequent chapters.

It would appear therefore that there are several types of perceptual and associated cognitive processes in which readers may be retarded or basically deficient. Analysis of whole patterns and integration of parts into wholes are clearly significant. So also are the correct perception of orientation and the comprehension of sequential order. Exact perception of certain details such as size of angles seems to be inferior in backward readers. This deficiency would not in itself appear to be of great importance in reading; but it is possible that it is related to general failure in accurate perception of detail. In all these cases it may be that accurate memory is of greater importance than immediate perception. We noted that backward readers appeared to grow out of some of these deficiencies as their age increased; thus the differences in performance between normal and backward readers were less in the older children of

10–12 years than in the younger ones of 7–8 years. This suggests that the backward readers may have matured more slowly than the normal readers in certain types of perception, making errors characteristic of younger children. They were particularly deficient perhaps in the ability not so much to perceive and image what was shown them as in the perceptual activity necessary to reproduce spatial complexities and sequences correctly. Birch (1962) has suggested that perception may operate at different levels: in the youngest children, in recognition of objects; later, in the perceptual analysis of parts within the whole of a complex figure; and finally, in the resynthesis of parts into wholes. In backward readers, perception would appear to function normally at the lowest level, but not at the levels of analysis and synthesis. It is possible that thought processes are involved here which mature more slowly than does immediate perception.

Finally, it should be noted that other studies, mainly of a clinical nature, have demonstrated that not all backward readers, even the severely retarded, exhibit deficiencies of the kind discussed here. Furthermore, it must not be concluded that, where there is an association between these deficiencies and reading disability, the deficiencies necessarily *cause* the disability. Indeed, it might be that lack of expertise in reading was responsible for inadequate perception, the perception of the normal reader having been improved by practice in reading. However, if the deficiency were due to prolonged reading failure, it might be expected to increase with age. But in fact, as we have seen, the tendency is for many perceptual deficiencies to decrease with age even in backward readers. It remains possible that perceptual deficiencies are neither causes nor effects of reading disability, but are accompanying symptoms of an underlaying disorder.* We shall consider this matter in Ch. VII.

* No discussion is included in this chapter of the effects on reading of sensory disorders of vision. There is no reliable evidence that such disorders affect the capacity to learn to read (see Vernon, 1957), provided that the child is not suffering from such gross refractive errors or diseases of the eye that he is unable to see the print. This conclusion was substantiated by Gruber (1962), who obtained no correlation between reading ability in retarded readers, and binocular coordination, eye muscle balance and ability to fuse the binocular images.

CHAPTER IV

AUDITORY AND LINGUISTIC FACTORS IN READING

(1) AUDITORY AND LINGUISTIC DEVELOPMENT IN CHILDREN

It is often assumed that by the time they go to school children can hear speech sounds clearly and correctly. It is certainly true that from early infancy children listen and respond to voices, and attend to them to a greater extent than to other types of sound except sudden loud noises. Turning the head towards the direction of a human voice was shown to occur at 2 months (Piaget, 1955); and smiling in response to a voice at 2–4 months (Hetzer & Tudor-Hart, 1927). Infants are aware of and respond to the emotional significance of voices as demonstrated in patterns of intonation before they perceive the phonemic pattern. Towards the end of the first year of life, infants appear to hear the phonemic pattern, at least in part, since they gradually adapt their own babbling sounds to resemble it more closely. However, the child imitates the intonational pattern before the phonemic pattern.

In recent years it has become possible to record sound patterns electronically and convert them into visual spectrograms.* It has then become apparent that the acoustic characteristics of the *phonemes*, the basic sounds of speech, are extremely complex and far more variable than might be supposed from ordinary listening in which minor variations are disregarded in identifying familiar word sounds. In fact the acoustic constituents of one and the same phoneme may vary in different contexts. Those of a consonant differ according to the vowels with which it is associated and with its position in the word, as well as with the voice of the speaker. Vowel phonemes are somewhat steadier, but they also vary with variation in the preceding and following consonants. Moreover,

---

* Much of this discussion is based on that given by Lefevre (1964) and Liberman *et al.* (1967).

the acoustic characteristics of different vowel phonemes are not discontinuous, but modulate gradually from one phoneme to another. Again, successive phonemes in continuous speech are not temporally distinct; there is no sudden break as one succeeds another. Finally, acoustic variation is produced by variations in intonation which fluctuates, not only according to the characteristics of the speaker (emotional mood, accent etc.) but also with the syntactic structure of sentences, as in statements, questions, etc. When spoken in isolation a word may have a pattern of intonation different from that of the same word spoken as part of a sentence.

Clearly therefore what is actually heard consists of a complex pattern extracted with considerable modification from the acoustic pattern. Gibson (1969) considered that the acoustic features common to each particular phoneme are discriminated as *invariants* from features which vary in different contexts and with different speakers. Thus each phoneme possesses an essential acoustic structure, although with many minor variations. The invariants form complexes or Gestalten which are independent of absolute stimulus value (Cooper *et al.*, cited by Gibson, 1969). But it has also been suggested (Liberman *et al.* 1967) that the sounds are integrated into patterns in accordance with the articulatory movements of the lips, tongue, vocal cords, etc. in speech. Thus the individual comes to associate the auditory pattern of each phoneme, which he hears in his own speaking voice, with a synthesized kinaesthetic pattern derived from articulatory movements. The auditory patterns and the associated kinaesthetic patterns are gradually modified as the infant learns to match his speech sounds to those he hears in the speech of others. Whether or not this hypothesis is correct, it is clear that the language which the child understands is very closely related to that which he speaks, although the vocabulary of the former exceeds that of the latter.

Gibson (1969) also stated that the initial stage for the infant in the understanding of speech is the discrimination, from the total phonemic pattern, of contrasting phonemes. Vowel–consonant contrast is discriminated first, and then labial *v.* dental contrasts, and breaks in the continuous sound pattern are apprehended at an early stage. Consonants within words and consonant clusters are learnt later. Discrimination of phonemes improves with increase in age; and those phonemes which possess the most distinctive features are most accurately discriminated. Even at 7 years, pairs of words were most often confused in auditory discrimination when there was a difference of only one phoneme feature between them (Tikofsky & McInish, 1968). Auditory discrimination was closely related to articulation in children up to 8 years of age (Wepman, cited by Robinson, 1966). Consonant sounds are articulated properly later than are vowel sounds. Poole (cited by Robinson, 1966) stated that 'v', 'sh' and 'l' were not correctly articulated until 6½ years, and 's' 'r', 'th', 'wh', 'ch' and 'j' not until 7½ years. In general, phonemes which are difficult to articulate are more difficult to hear correctly.

Until fairly recently it was supposed that children learnt to speak by direct imitation of the speech sounds of others. Indeed some imitation must be involved; thus the particular pronunciation of the child tends to resemble that of the mother (Fry, 1966). Moreover, it is true that the child's early attempts at language are frequently reinforced by the pleasure and encouragement expressed by adults on hearing him speak. Also he soon finds that he is able to satisfy his wishes more effectively by naming or describing them in intelligible words than merely by crying.

Nevertheless, recent investigations of *linguistic development in children* have suggested that, contrary to behaviorist theory, the child's early utterances are not directly copied from adults. When, during his second and third years, he begins to produce sentences of two or three words, these have a characteristic structure, but it differs from the structures of adult speech. The first sentences consist typically of certain 'pivotal' words in the initial position (Braine, 1963). These recur frequently, with a variety of other words attached to specify the situation. This construction differs from those of adult speech, for instance by reversal of order as in 'allgone shoe', 'allgone egg', 'allgone lettuce'. Thus it has been hypothesized that these short sentences are unitary structures of meaning, expressing the child's wishes to his parents or his comments on events and situations; and that their particular grammatical construction is a spontaneous production, not a direct imitation of adult speech (McNeill, 1966). It has indeed been supposed that children have an innate linguistic capacity for producing such constructions. Even the earlier one-word utterances may imply the additional words necessary to make sentences. For instance, 'dog' may mean 'there is a dog' or 'the dog is barking'. The linguistic ability continues to operate in the later spontaneous production of more complex sentences consisting of subject–verb–object, together with qualifying adjectives, etc. Such constructions are said to occur in all languages.

But it would appear that although these constructions possess a characteristic grammatical structure, the child employs the utterance as a unitary whole, and cannot analyse it into separate parts, the individual words, grammatically related to each other. This tendency to agglomerate words in sentences appears in word association test performance (Brown & Berko, 1960). Adults tend to give as associations similar parts of speech, synonyms, opposites, etc., but children tend to produce phrases, for instance 'send – away'. Huttenlocher (1964) also found that children of $4\frac{1}{2}$–$5\frac{1}{2}$ years had some difficulty in separating the two words of familiar phrases, such as 'red' and 'apple'. Thus they might not be able to repeat these correctly in reversed order; or even repeat the second word correctly after a slight delay. On the other hand, they had little difficulty with reversal and delayed report of pairs of digits, letters and even words not commonly paired such as 'table' and 'goes'. This difficulty in analysis of phrases and sentences may have some importance when the child is required in learning to read to associate the printed shapes and sounds of words.

Imitation of adult speech must operate in the development of more complex grammatical constructions, as also in the acquisition of a wider vocabulary. This is clear from the frequently observed linguistic retardation of children brought up without close contact with adults, for instance in institutions; and indeed in those whose parents' speech is simple and primitive. It would appear, however, that the child may learn the *general patterns of language* rather than specific constructions, as for instance with certain irregular inflexions. Thus there is a tendency for children to use the suffix 'ed' for the past tenses of all verbs. It would seem also that children begin to understand the significance of inflexions before they can employ them correctly. Fraser, Bellugi & Brown (1963) presented pairs of contrasted sentences to 3-year-old children, together with pairs of appropriate pictures. The contrasts were: singular–plural, active–passive and present–past. In some cases the children had to select which picture in the pair corresponded to which sentence, to demonstrate that they understood the grammatical inflexions of the sentences (comprehension). In other cases, they had to select the sentences appropriate to the pictures to show that they could use them correctly to indicate meaning (speech production). It appeared that comprehension was superior to production. But Osser, Wang & Zaid (1969), using a similar technique of matching sentences to pictures, showed that children of $4\frac{1}{2}$–$5\frac{1}{2}$ years had some difficulty in matching sentences in the passive voice. Negro children made significantly more errors than did white children, substantiating the effects of unfavourable environmental influences on language development.

The understanding of grammatical construction develops rapidly between the ages of 3 and 5 years. Thus Brown (1957) showed that children of these ages could in most cases apply nonsense syllables having the functions of verbs, particular nouns and mass nouns to pictures indicating actions, objects and substances. Again, Berko & Brown (1960) presented pictures of objects, labelled with nonsense syllables, to children of 5–6 years, and by means of suitable questions asked them to provide the plurals, possessives and other inflexions of these. Even the younger children showed considerable proficiency in this task, though the older were more correct than the younger, and neither were as proficient as adults. The commonest inflexions, such as 's' for plurals and 's' for possessives, were supplied before the less common.

Although understanding the meaning of grammatical constructions develops before the ability to use these correctly in speech, nevertheless even the latter appears surprisingly early. At about

3 years, children produce sentences of 3–4 words in which order of words, phrase structure and grammatical inflexions are approximately correct, although the structure of these sentences is not exactly the same as that of adult speech (Lennenberg, 1966). The actual stages of development are comparatively unaffected by environmental influences and occur normally even in children with deaf parents. It is interesting to note, however, that when children of 5–6 years, beginning to learn to read, are required to construct sentences from words printed for them, they frequently put them in the wrong order; for instance, 'schools to go children little' (Mackay, Thompson & Schaub, 1970). Thus it would seem that imparting of correct order may be learnt as a habit of speech which cannot be used in other forms of linguistic manipulation.

Children also begin at an early age to grasp the syntactic structures known as 'transformations'. Chomsky hypothesized that in the generation of grammatical constructions, a simple declarative sentence could act as 'kernel' from which variations were generated to form negative, passive, past tense and interrogative sentences with of course the appropriate grammatical inflections.* Menyuk (1963 a) investigated the occurrence of such transformations in the spontaneous speech, in various conversational situations, of children aged 3–4 years and 6–7 years. All the children used the simpler transformations correctly, but the more complex ones were used more correctly by the older than by the younger children, and were not always completely accurate even in the former. Thus the successive parts of a transformation did not always agree grammatically with each other. Slobin (1966) required children of 6–12 years and adults to match affirmative and negative, active and passive transformations against pictures demonstrating these relationships. The time taken to perform these matchings and the number of errors made decreased with increase in age. But the order of difficulty was much the same at all ages, indicating that the system employed in making transformations was well established by

* It is impossible to discuss here the full scope and details of Chomsky's generative grammar, but his hypotheses have had great influence on the work of psycholinguists and psychologists.

6 years. Nevertheless, the hierarchical structure of transformations does not develop with rigid and complete regularity. Francis (1969) recorded samples of speech in different situations uttered by a child of $2\frac{1}{2}$ years, and found that the structure of these varied considerably with the nature of social situations and the type of activity in which the child was engaged. He concluded that the child acquired first those language structures which were meaningful and useful to him. But in such a young child a stable system may not have been fully established.

Menyuk (1963 b) also found that the understanding of transformational grammar preceded its use in speech. She selected from her speech samples examples of correct and incorrect transformations, and spoke them to the children, who were required to repeat them after her. The transformations were repeated correctly by most of the children in both age groups, though there were some errors, for instance in the use of the auxiliary 'have', and in replacing subordinate clauses by separate sentences linked by 'and'. The ungrammatical transformations were frequently corrected in repetition, but more frequently by the younger than by the older children. More children were able to repeat transformations correctly than could use them correctly in speech; and also children could correct ungrammatical transformations which they themselves had uttered.

This discussion of linguistic development may not at first sight appear altogether relevant to learning to read, though as we shall see in section (5) reading achievement is related to early linguistic ability. It does suggest, however, that children may have comparatively little difficulty in understanding the language of teachers and of reading books. But though they may comprehend the meanings of whole sentences, they may find it more difficult to break these up into words, since they are accustomed to hear and understand complete phrases in speech rather than separate words (see Carterette & Jones, 1968). Thus it is not surprising that numerous investigations have shown that children even of school age do not accurately perceive words in isolation, as we noted above. Thompson (1963) found that auditory discrimination between words was often inadequate in children of 6–7 years. About a quarter of the children tested at 8 years still showed poor discrimination between like-sounding words; and half of these children were poor readers. On the other hand, the majority of those who became good readers had adequate auditory discrimination for words on entry to school, at 6 years.

In learning to read the child must realize that the sequences of printed shapes represent the linguistic patterns which he hears and utters. Moreover, the linguistic patterns are not simply continuous structures of phonemes, but must be broken up into discrete units – the words – corresponding to the visual structures separated by empty spaces. To do this, he must understand that the teacher's continuous speech pattern is made up of separate words, some of which, in whole word teaching methods, can be used singly as names attached to objects and pictures of objects. Furthermore, it is necessary for him to hear the phonemic patterns of words clearly and accurately. But many children may not hear these patterns exactly. Moreover, the phonemic patterns vary considerably in different English accents. Thus Sheridan (1948) noted how difficult it was for Lancashire children to hear correctly some of the words she spoke in standard English. However, it would seem dubious practice for a teacher to attempt to 'translate' her speech into the phonemic patterns current in the local accent.

The accurate perception of words is in part a function of *selective listening*, that is to say, the extraction of separate word sounds from continuous speech and from background noise. The capacity for selective listening may be poor in young children. Maccoby & Konrad (1966) required children to listen to two voices, a man's and a woman's, speaking words simultaneously, and to report the words spoken by either the man's or the woman's voice. The ability to do this improved from 5 years up to 9 years. The number of intrusive words reported from the unselected voice decreased, but they were not entirely eliminated, as occurs in adults. Siegenthaler & Barr (1967) also found that the capacity to hear words against a background babble of speech improved from 4–7 years. It would appear that when the words of a message are partly drowned by irrelevant noise, the missing words must be guessed by inference, which is easier for older than for younger children.

The ability to perceive isolated words depends also on their *familiarity*. Words which children commonly employ in their own speech or are accustomed to hear spoken to them are easier to hear correctly than are relatively unfamiliar words, because they are expected. Total vocabulary of known words increases rapidly during the early years of life from about 20 words at $1\frac{1}{2}$ years to about 1000 at 3 years (Lennenberg, 1966). Watts (1944) estimated that 2000 words were understood at 5 years and 4000–5000 by 7 years. It is difficult to estimate accurately the size of the child's spontaneous vocabulary; and indeed it varies greatly among different children. Those with cultured and educated parents commonly have a much wider vocabulary than have children of working-class parents. It is particularly important that in early reading teaching, both in reading books and in the speech of teachers, words familiar to such children should be employed. Again a valuable feature of pre-reading teaching may be the inculcation of a wider vocabulary.

The effect of familiarity also operates in hearing phrases and sentences of words frequently associated together. Thus Maccoby & Konrad (1967) found that the ability to listen to single words and two-word phrases spoken by one voice, and to disregard words and phrases spoken simultaneously by another, varied with familiarity. Common words and phrases consisting of commonly associated words, such as 'dark night', were heard increasingly more correctly by the older children in a group aged 5–11 years. These effects they attributed to increasing familiarity both with particular words and also with phrase associations between words. It is probable that such familiarity is important even in younger children in the early stages of learning to read.

One may therefore conclude that children when they first go to school *can* hear reasonably correctly and understand the normal speech of adults, but may not always listen sufficiently carefully to do so. But, just as in visual perception they perceive complex shapes inexactly with little observation of detail, so also at this stage they may not hear single words clearly if these are spoken in isolation and not in the context of sentences. Even if single words are heard and understood, for instance as names, their exact phonemic structure may not be discriminated.

(2) PHONIC ANALYSIS AND SYNTHESIS OF WORDS

It was shown in Ch. III that even when taught by whole word methods, children tended to pick out certain letters and recognize words by means of these. Thus from the beginning they carried out a kind of word analysis, though it was unsystematic and inexact. Before long, a more efficient type of *word analysis* becomes inevitable. Reading cannot proceed very far through whole word methods. The child learns to recognize and enunciate only those words which he has been specifically taught, and as we have noted these may not always be heard correctly. Moreover, memory for the shapes of isolated words is limited. In order to be able to read new words, the child must learn to break these down into their alphabetic constituents; attach appropriate sounds to the printed letters; and combine the letter sounds together to form the sounds of whole words. Yet it appeared in the discussion in the last section that the analysis of continuous phonemic patterns into words might be a matter of some difficulty for children. As we shall see, the detection of isolated letter sounds within words is even harder.

In order to enable children to proceed satisfactorily in learning to read, some such '*phonic*' *teaching* is commonly introduced during the first or second year in the infant school. Goodacre (1967) found that although in the infant schools she studied phonics were introduced gradually, the majority of children were receiving some phonic instruction by the end of the first year at school. In the study by Kellmer Pringle *et al.*, cited in the Plowden report (1967), it was shown that in a group of over 10,000 English children the peak age for the introduction of phonics was 5½–6 years; though in 700 Welsh children and 1400 Scottish children it was between 5 and 5½ years.

Until some ten or fifteen years ago, phonic teaching was unpopular, probably because of the unsuitability of the particular methods employed, and also because of the obvious difficulties encountered by children in the analysis of word sounds. But *modified phonic methods*, such as that introduced in the 'Royal Road Readers' by Daniels & Diack (1954), appeared to be more effective.* Letter sounds are taught through the discrimination of similar sounding words with different initial letters, presented in sentences with illustrative pictures. Thus the child is not confronted with a phonic drill of meaningless letter groups. Nor is he required to attempt to sound letters in isolation. This method was found to be more effective than were mixed phonic and whole word methods in teaching the early stages of reading (Daniels & Diack, 1960). Thus 7-year-old children who had been taught by the modified phonic method were significantly superior to those taught by mixed methods in both word recognition and comprehension. The modified phonic method was also successful with 8-year-old backward readers in the first year of the junior school (Daniels & Diack, 1956).

The teaching of reading, even by phonic methods, is stated to be most effective when it is preceded or accompanied by the teaching of letter names and sounds (Chall, 1967). It would appear that the children were helped to understand that printed material was based on an alphabetic code that determined which of the printed letters they saw corresponded to those sounded in spoken words. But here a difficulty immediately arises. Unless the selection of words is carefully controlled in the initial stages of teaching, con-

* Phonic methods of the old type are still taught; as for instance a method designed by Woolman (Edwards, 1966). The child is taught: (1) to discriminate features of capital letters in a target word; (2) to remember their shapes; (3) to give the letters their associated sounds, even if they are consonants; (4) to combine consonants and vowels in the correct order, to produce single sounds even though these may be meaningless; (5) to read whole words, regularly spelt words being employed at first; (6) to read short prose selections. Thereafter, the different possible sounds for certain printed letters are learnt. This method is claimed to be successful because the learner must at each stage make an active response, which is immediately confirmed or corrected by the teacher.

fusion may be caused by the variability in the *association* between printed and sounded letters. Each printed vowel corresponds to a large number of different phonemes which vary according to the word in which it occurs; and each vowel phoneme can be produced by a number of different printed letters and letter combinations.* Similar though less extensive variations occur with consonants. In many cases vowels or consonants may be silent; or they may modify the pronunciation of other vowels or consonants within the word though they are not themselves sounded. Although in most phonic methods irregularly spelt words are introduced only gradually, it is difficult to construct sentences which do not contain some such words, and children may be required to learn them by rote, as exceptions.

In order to obviate irregularities, Sir James Pitman designed the '*initial teaching alphabet*' (i.t.a.), which consists of forty-four characters. Many of these resemble the ordinary letters of the alphabet, though some are slightly more difficult to perceive; others are new characters. They cover the majority of phonemes used in reading, including certain common vowel and consonant digraphs (fused pairs of letters such as 'th'). It should be observed that not only is the alphabet expanded in such a manner as to provide printed characters for all the principal phonemes; but also spelling is simplified and regularized. Thus many silent letters are omitted. Downing (1969) claimed that there is increased regularity of grapheme–phoneme correspondence; and that spelling indicates the correct order and number of phonemes. Hence it is possible for the child to perceive clearly the correct structure and pronunciation of words. Though there has been much controversy as to the value of this alphabet, it appears from most enquiries that children do indeed learn to read the i.t.a. more easily than the traditional alphabet. But when they reach the stage of transfer from the former

* It has been pointed out by Peters (1967) that in English spoken with a Scottish accent the phonemes associated with different vowels and combinations of vowels are more clearly and precisely differentiated than in standard spoken English. Also certain consonants, 'r' for instance, are accentuated. This should make it easier for Scottish than for English children to grasp the variations in letter-sound correspondence.

to the latter, some difficulty may be encountered, and reading progress is delayed. Thus finally there may be little difference in achievement between those taught by the two media (Warburton & Southgate, 1969).

Other media have been used for signalling to the child the sounds to be associated with particular letters in particular words. Thus in Gattegno's *Words in Colour* (1962) there is a complete colour code for phonemes, such that each phoneme is printed in a different colour, and this colour is the same no matter how the phoneme is spelt. A more complex code designed by Jones, in *Colour Story Reading* (1967), was claimed to produce better reading than did the i.t.a. and less difficulty in transfer to ordinary un-coloured letters (Jones, 1968). A subsequent experiment (Jones, 1970) demonstrated the superiority in both reading and spelling of children taught for one year with *Colour Story Reading* to those who had used ordinary reading material.

But as we noted the great difficulty with all methods that involve the association of phonemes with single letter shapes lies in the isolation of the former and their subsequent combination to form whole word sounds. Young children may be simply incapable of *analysing into phonemes* the sounds of whole words which they themselves utter and which they hear in the speech of others. Phonemes are integrated together in phrases, which are unitary patterns of sound possessing characteristic structures associated with their syntax and meaning. Hence phonemes are not perceived as discontinuous entities in a temporal sequence, nor heard separately like the notes of a tune, for instance; but each word or phrase is a unitary unanalysed event. Thus the task of perceiving the phonemes is comparable in difficulty to that of extracting the simple Gottschaldt figures embedded in the complex ones. And not only are phrases unitary phonetic structures; they are also units of meaning. Broken down into phonemes, the meaning is lost. Although in phonic analysis single words are frequently presented rather than phrases, it would appear that the inclusion of words in meaningful phrases and sentences would be advantageous in the teaching of reading.

The difficulty of isolating phonemes was demonstrated in an experiment by Bradford (1954), in which children of 6–8 years were presented with pictures and required to pick out those the names of which contained a phoneme which had previously been sounded. The older children were fairly successful in performing this task, and the younger ones could select correctly picture names which contained the easier consonants. They were less successful with vowels and double consonants. Thus the ability to isolate phonemes from whole word sounds was apparently still developing at about 7 years of age. A study by Bruce (1964) indicated that certain types of word analysis might be even more difficult. Thirty familiar words were presented orally to children of 5–7 years with mental ages of 5–9 years; and they were asked what word (also a familiar one) would remain if a particular letter sound was omitted from the beginning, middle or end of the word; for instance, B-EAR, PIN-K. The proportion of words which could be broken up correctly at various mental ages was as follows:

Mental age in years	5	6	7	8	9
Per cent correct	0	6	29	55	89

The younger children, even those who had received some phonic teaching, could not analyse the words at all; though those with mental ages of 7 and 8 who had received phonic teaching performed rather better than those who had not. At 6 years there was a tendency to substitute rhyming words for the original words. After this, there was some elision of letter sounds, but it was frequently incorrect, particularly with letters in the middle of the word, indicating that the children were beginning to analyse, but did not hear the letter sounds sufficiently exactly to omit them correctly. Certain digraphs, such as 'fr', 'br', 'st' and 'sp', were particularly difficult to break up.

It is possible that this type of analysis is more difficult than any which the child is required to perform in phonic analysis in reading. But we noted that the child had not only to analyse word sounds, but also *reconstruct word sounds from their constituent phonemes*, thus matching the blended phonemes against spoken words. But he could not do this unless he was able to hear the separate phonemes within the whole word sound. It may be that the process of synthesis is inherently more difficult than that of analysis. Indeed, Leroy-Boussion (1963) found that the younger children in a group of 5–8 years could not even combine a consonant and a vowel sound into a syllabic unit. And Conners, Kramer & Guerra (1969) showed that the ability to blend separate sounds, presented by a loud speaker, to form words increased steadily from the age of 7–12 years. Clearly synthesis is likely to become harder as the words increase in length; and correct accentuation may create further difficulty in synthesizing polysyllabic words.

It has appeared possible that the difficulty in analysing word sounds and re-synthesizing letter sounds might be avoided, or at least reduced, if in the early stages of reading *groups* or *clusters* of letters were utilized rather than single letters. Thus Jeffrey & Samuels (1967) found that kindergarten children, presumably aged about 5 years, related consonant–vowel pairs to meaningless shapes more quickly and correctly if they were first taught to associate consonant–vowel pairs with shapes than if they were first taught the association of single vowels or consonants with shapes. It might be that children taught groups of three letters, for instance consonant–vowel–consonant (*CVC*), would acquire some knowledge of the letter combinations in monosyllabic words and syllables from which longer words could be constructed. Gibson, Shurcliff & Yonas (1968) considered that letter clusters within words operated as relatively invariant units. Though they did vary somewhat in pronunciation as the vowel or consonant sounds varied, this variation was governed by rules which they suggested children grasped relatively easily as they learnt to read.

Children also begin to identify certain simple letter clusters as such at a comparatively early age. To children of 7 and 9 years, Gibson, Osser & Pick (1963) presented tachistoscopically, one at a time, 3-letter words and pronounceable and unpronounceable trigrams, such as SUN, NUS and NSU. Although the words were always perceived more accurately than the trigrams, the pronounceable trigrams were reported more correctly than were the unpronounceable. Pronounceable and unpronounceable 4- and 5-letter pseudo-words were also presented, such as DINK and NKID, GRISP and SPIGR. The younger children could read hardly any of these; but the 9-year-olds read more pronounceable pseudo-words correctly than unpronounceable ones. In a later study, Biemiller & Levin (1968 a) graded monosyllabic words for pronounceability, from DINK to DRIGHK, and presented them to children of 9–10 years, measuring the time they took to read them. There was a high negative correlation between this time and pronounceability, even when variation in length of words was allowed for. And for the longer words there was a high negative correlation between pronounceability and number of errors.

It would seem that what was happening here was that the pronounceable trigrams and pseudo-words were being processed as single unitary structures, whereas the less pronounceable and unpronounceable had to be perceived letter by letter before they could be reported. Thus the letters in the pronounceable pseudo-words were being assimilated in '*chunks*'. Miller (1956) showed that a 'chunk' of information could be processed as rapidly as a single item. The 7-year-old children were able to 'chunk' the trigrams; and the number of letters which could be combined in this way increased with age. Unfortunately we do not know if younger children, such as the 5-year-old beginners in British infant schools, are capable of performing this process. To them groups of letters, even if less variable in sound than single letters, may be no more like their customary speech sounds than are isolated phonemes. This requires further investigation.

It is also true that the pronounceable trigrams and pseudo-words were made up of combinations of letters occurring quite frequently in the English language, though of course with modifications from real words. Thus the children may have been assisted by familiarity with that type of letter combination. It seems likely that the trigrams were read less easily than the 3-letter words because they were less familiar; though meaningfulness may have been an additional factor in reading the latter. However, it appears that it is not the frequency with which the pronounceable combinations are

53

used in actual speech which is important. For Gibson, Shurcliff & Yonas (1968) found that when they required deaf adult students to write down pronounceable and unpronounceable pseudo-words presented to them tachistoscopically, they made significantly more errors with the latter. Moreover, Doehring & Rosenstein (cited by Gibson, Shurcliff & Yonas, 1968) obtained the same result for pronounceable and unpronounceable trigrams with deaf children. Thus it was inferred that familiarity was acquired with commonly occurring spelling patterns, whether heard in speech or not; and this made it possible to 'chunk' frequently occurring combinations of letters.

Further light was thrown by Thomas (1968) on the importance of familiarity, which might in some cases have more effect than pronounceability. Thomas observed that in the experiment of Gibson et al. (1963) all the pronounceable trigrams were of the form CVC, whereas the unpronounceable were all CCV. Now in children's reading books words with the structure CVC outnumbered those with the structure CCV by 15:1. Thus children would be less familiar with the latter type of structure than with the former. In support of this argument, Thomas found that when he presented CCV pronounceable trigrams to 6–7-year-old children, these were perceived less easily than were CVC pronounceable trigrams, and no more readily than were CCV unpronounceable trigrams. Thus there would appear to be some doubt as to the extent of the effects of pronounceability, at least in young children.

Another commonly occurring type of letter grouping is the digraph. Digraphs may also be processed as units in which the letters are so closely associated that they are difficult to separate. Thus Biemiller & Levin (1968a) presented tachistoscopically words each of which was separated into two parts, either in the middle of a digraph, as in 'c-hip' and 'c-lip'; or between the digraph and the remainder of the word, as in 'ch-ip' and 'cl-ip'. Children of 7–9 years were slower in reading the former than the latter. However, the splitting of digraphs in the middle of the word, such as the vowel digraphs in 'fail' and 'boat', had no such effect.

It seems possible that these must be analysed into their constituent letters.

The importance of letter grouping had been emphasized by Bloomfield (1942) and Fries (1963). In the first place, they pointed out that the phonemes of letters vary less when the letters are associated in trigrams than when they are sounded singly. Single printed letters cannot be exactly matched with single phonemes; it is patterns of phonemes which are the functional units of speech sound. The basic speaking patterns of English consist of regularly spelt trigrams, which may be monosyllabic words or the syllables making up longer words. Fries listed the simplest regularly sounding trigams, followed by more complex ones involving less common vowel sounds, digraph vowels and consonants. In the so-called 'linguistic' methods of teaching reading, the child, after learning the alphabet, is presented with lists of simple 3-letter words, in which each letter has only a single sound. He discovers the sound values of the printed letters himself, and, it is said, phonic analysis and re-synthesis are avoided. New letter sounds and more complex combinations are introduced gradually. A linguistic approach was provided in material designed by C. M. Gibson & I. A. Richards (1957). This began with a succession of simple sentences consisting of easily read phonically simple words, constructed from ten letters only. The sentences were so arranged that the children could proceed logically to learn new words by comparing their similarities with and differences from previously learnt words. The efficacy of this method was investigated by MacKinnon (1959). Five-year-old children, who had been learning to read for 5 months by a traditional method, then progressed more rapidly with the Gibson & Richards method than did children who continued to be taught by the traditional method. The latter method utilized books containing a high proportion of phonically irregular words which the children, through lack of phonic knowledge, were unable to recognize. Hence the superiority of the Gibson & Richards method. Unfortunately no comparison was made with children taught systematic phonics, which might have produced an equally good result. Again, linguistic methods have

have been criticized by Southgate & Roberts (1970) in that although they provide logically structured material in graduated stages of increasing difficulty, this material is not of a kind likely to appeal to children. We shall consider later the importance of children's interest in what they read.

It cannot be assumed, also, that the use of letter groups will automatically overcome all the difficulties of phonic analysis and re-synthesis. The child must at some time learn the sounds of single letters, the manner in which these vary in different word contexts and their relation to the different types of letter combinations. Levin & Biemiller (1968b) demonstrated that difficulties due to variation in sound may arise even with consonants. Thus they presented to children of 7–9 years lists of words in which the pronunciation of the initial consonant was contingent on the following vowel, and found that consonants with the less common pronunciation, such as 'c' in 'cent', were read more slowly and with more errors than were those with the more usual pronunciation, such as 'c' in 'colt'. Moreover, whereas normally there are fewer errors at the beginnings of words than in other positions, with the less common pronunciations there were more initial than other errors. But Lee (1957), grading regularity and irregularity of spelling of words from the frequencies of their phonemes, found that there was no great difference in the errors made in oral reading of these words in a continuous text by children of 6–11 years. However, when the words were read orally in isolation, the relatively regular words were on the whole read more easily than the less regular. There were numerous errors in which letters were sounded as they sounded in other words; for instance 'o' in 'most' was sounded like 'o' in 'hot'. Lee concluded that spelling irregularity was not a major cause of reading difficulty. But it did appear to be one cause of confusion in reading isolated words, where meaning could not be derived from the context.

Thus it would seem that even if frequently occurring combinations of letters are quickly recognized because they are 'chunked' as units and because their spelling patterns are familiar, yet recognition must be constantly checked and confirmed or confuted in the light of the whole word context, and in some cases of the sentence context. This occurs with words which are pronounced in one way as nouns or adjectives and in another as verbs, for instance 'close' (adjective) and 'close' (verb). Thus from the early stages the child must learn the variety of sounds associated with particular letter shapes. It is certainly possible that the difficulty of synthesizing words from individual letter sounds may be obviated by utilizing simple, common and regular letter combinations whenever possible, provided that the child does not become so habituated to these that he is unable to recognize the manner in which they may vary in different word contexts. Nor is there any satisfactory evidence that linguistic methods are superior to that of learning single letter sounds in word contexts, as in the modified phonic method of Daniels & Diack (see Chall, 1967).

Children have to learn not only the associations between printed letters and their sounds, but also that the *order* of the former in printed words corresponds with the order of the latter in spoken words. It is likely that young children may not perceive correctly the order of phonemes in spoken words. It is not uncommon for them to utter these in the wrong order, especially in long and unfamiliar words. Ingram (1960) found that older children with certain language disorders mispronounced syllables and combined them together in the wrong order. It has also been found that young children have difficulty in perceiving and remembering auditory sequences as such. Thus Birch & Belmont (1965) showed that ability to match a rhythmical sequence of taps, perceived auditorily, to a series of dots subsequently presented visually, increased rapidly from $5\frac{1}{2}$–$7\frac{1}{2}$ years, and thereafter more slowly until $10\frac{1}{2}$ years.

But the sequential order of letters in words forms a temporal pattern of great complexity, and not a simple rhythm. Therefore, *a fortiori*, one might expect it to be difficult for young children to grasp. These patterns, when they are associated with printed material, are governed by the rules of spelling. Ahlstrom (cited by Peters, 1967) tested children's ability to predict the pronunciation of written nonsense words and the spelling of spoken nonsense words, and found that achievement in these tasks was closely related to spelling ability. He concluded that knowledge of sequen-tial probabilities as determined by the rules of spelling was involved.

It has been claimed, as we noted, that children begin to learn these rules at an early age. Some writers have maintained that even young children are capable of grasping rules of spelling, not by learning these formally, but through acquiring habits of responding to frequently occurring grapheme-correspondences and generaliz-ing these to classes of correspondence (Carroll, 1964). However, these classes must be presented to children in a rational order of difficulty, and they must be taught to expect variation and even ambiguity in the application of rules. It must be realized that this procedure is difficult for young children since, as we shall discuss in the next chapter, they are not capable of performing accurately the processes of abstraction and generalization which are involved in comprehending and defining general principles. At most they can grasp certain simple correspondences, provided that the teacher explains these clearly to them. Many rules are not easy to under-stand and apply; exceptions are numerous, and the spelling of some words appears to follow no rule. The irregularity of English spelling has indeed instigated many movements for its reform (Pitman & St John, 1969). Moreover, it is well known that certain children have such difficulty in learning to spell correctly that they never achieve it successfully. It is possible, as we shall discuss in Ch. VII, that this inability is the most characteristic feature of dyslexia.

(3) READING OF CONTINUOUS PROSE

The ultimate object of learning to read is of course the understand-ing of meaning of continuous texts. Now we have noted that the essential units of normal speech are *phrases* and *sentences*, which have characteristic grammatical constructions and convey meaning. The object of reading is to reconstruct these units from the printed text. Single words undoubtedly possess some meaning, but this may not be clear unless they are contained in sentence context. This is particularly obvious with words of variable meaning. Thus it has been advocated by many educationists that the '*sentence*' *method* is the most effective method of teaching reading. By this is meant the direct recognition of words in sentences, without any phonic analysis. But as with whole word methods, the child cannot proceed far with sentences alone. He must be able to analyse and identify the individual words, or he will merely resort to guessing. Chall (1967) found that in general methods which depended almost entirely on the understanding of meaning were less successful in the early stages of learning to read than were those which employed some kind of phonic approach. However, she considered that throughout some attention to meaning was essential, and that it should be emphasized more and more as word recognition through phonic analysis and synthesis improved.

Indeed, it is likely that this phonic analysis and synthesis is best taught with words presented in sentence context. The child is then helped to recognize the words from the meaning and the syntactic structure of the context. Moreover, he is encouraged from the first to aim at understanding the gist of what he reads. Ruddell (1968) investigated the effects of teaching reading with phonics and controlled regularity of letter-sound correspondence from the beginning, as against introducing phonics later, with no control of regularity; and also of supplementing both with special teaching aimed at stressing meaning and linguistic structure. Testing various aspects of reading 6 months later, he found that achievement was greatest with the beginning phonics together with supplementary linguistic teaching. But even without the latter, those who began phonics earlier, with controlled letter-sound correspondence, read both regularly and irregularly spelt words better than did those who began phonics later.

We have noted that children quite early acquire the capacity to understand and formulate *sentences* with correct grammatical construction, provided that this is not too complex, as in long sentences containing subordinate clauses. Of course spoken sentences increase in length with increases in age, from an average of 4 words at 3 years to $5\frac{1}{2}$ words at 5 years (Templin, 1957). The latter are more complex than the former; prepositions and conjunctions appear, and there is a fair mastery of inflexions. Compound sentences begin to occur at 6–7 years, but structurally incomplete sentences are still numerous, even at 9½ years (McCarthy, 1960). However, these developments vary greatly in different children, and are less advanced in those of poor intelligence and social status, as we shall discuss in Ch. VI. Although the simpler types of language construction may develop spontaneously (see p. 41), the more complex are unlikely to do so unless the child is accustomed to hear them spoken. Thus disadvantaged children may have difficulty in understanding the material in reading books, unless the syntax is very simple. Indeed, it has been claimed that even older children, of 9–10 years, showed better comprehension of material formulated in accordance with the grammatical constructions used in their own speech than with less familiar constructions (Ruddell, cited by Weber, 1968).

Because the length of sentences uttered in speech increases with increase in age, it has been suggested that the comprehensibility of continuous prose varies with the length of its sentences. However, Bormuth (1968) believed that the length of independent clauses, between conjunctions, was more important, presumably because these were natural units of meaning. He measured the comprehensibility of passages with clauses of different lengths by requiring children of 9–13 years to fill in words deleted in various places, and found that this performance did indeed vary with independent clause length, both in good and in poor readers. However, the majority of these children had presumably reached the stage of fairly fluent reading.

For beginners, the use of '*language experience*' methods has been advocated, employing material formulated in the children's own words and syntax, and therefore supposedly easier for them to understand. The material may be obtained by recording what the children themselves say, for instance in discussions with the teacher. However, it is probable that such recorded speech would contain many words which are difficult to spell and read; certainly the words are unlikely to form a sequence of gradually increasing difficulty in phonic association. Therefore it seems unlikely that this method would be successful if utilized alone; it would require extensive supplementation by systematic phonics. Moreover, it should be possible to prepare material, graded in phonic difficulty, which nevertheless appeals to children's interests and employs their natural vocabulary, although it is not written in their own words. Anderson (cited by Smith & Dechant, 1961) claimed that although a method in which the children make their own selection of reading material may produce less rapid reading at the start than does systematic phonic teaching, children taught by the former method catch up and equal those taught by the latter by eleven years. But this is rather late.

In the most recent example of individualized learning by a language experience method, *Breakthrough to Literacy*, which has been promulgated under the auspices of the Schools Council (Mackay, Thompson & Schaub, 1970), the child begins to learn by constructing sentences from words printed for him, but forming part of his own vocabulary and in many cases chosen by himself. In arranging these in sentences he presumably learns to recognize them as wholes; he observes their meaningful continuity within sentence structures; and he acquires the ability to formulate simple sentences of correct grammatical structure. When he is fairly adept in this procedure, he begins to construct words from printed letters and digraphs, starting with groups of familiar phonetically simple words in the main, differing only in their initial consonants. Some of these are words which were used in the sentences. It appears that in this way many difficulties of sounding and blending are avoided; and it is claimed that children can acquire the rudiments of word structure, though additional practice later in spelling the more difficult constructions is necessary. However, although the authors state that this method was worked out through practice with teachers and children, it has not been submitted to experimental validation. The early stages of word recognition, sometimes of quite long and difficult words, might produce some confusion.

We have noted that it is an advantage to introduce the use of *context* at an early stage. Although children may at first be inclined to guess words incorrectly from their context, they make increasing and good use of this as word recognition improves. It has been stated that it is the five words immediately preceding and following an unfamiliar difficult word which have the greatest effect in enabling children to read it. However, the content of a whole paragraph may have some effect also (Weaver, cited by Spache, 1968). The better readers among a group of children of 5–6 years, who had learnt for only a short period, showed that they were able to predict from the context in identifying words (Clay, 1969). Levin & Turner (1968) measured the eye–voice span of children aged 7–8 and upwards; that is to say, the distance of the eyes ahead of the voice in oral reading. This was done by turning out the light at various points in the reading of continuous prose and asking the children to continue as far as they could; thus it was shown how far ahead of the voice the eyes had reached. It was then found that the better readers were able to read in phrase units, finishing off the whole phrase when they were stopped. But the younger children and the poorer readers among the older children read word by word.

The reading of continuous prose in phrase and sentence units is assisted both by the meaning, or *semantic structure*, of the material and also by its *syntactic* or grammatical structure. The meaning of a prose passage establishes an expectancy on the part of the reader, defining the contents of the material. Thus Weaver (cited by Spache, 1968) found that when children were asked to fill in words deleted from a prose passage, the words supplied were determined by semantic rather than syntactic constraints. In children of 5–6 years, about 70 per cent of the errors made in oral reading were substitutes for words of similar meaning (Clay, 1969). However, we have noted that by the time they begin learning to read, children are familiar with at least the simpler forms of syntactic structure, which apply constraints to the manner in which language is formulated, both in speech and in written material. Thus in reading, knowledge of the syntactic structure will affect expectancy as to what types of word are likely to appear, and in what order, and will enable the child to read correctly. Weber (1968) showed that the mistakes made in oral reading by 6–7-year-old children were, in about 90 per cent of cases, grammatically acceptable, agreeing with the preceding context. Only a small proportion were words resembling in form the words for which they were substituted, but not grammatically correct. The children were often unaware that they had made grammatically congruent mistakes. But if the mistakes were not grammatically congruent with the remainder of the sentence following the substituted word, they were frequently corrected, especially by the better readers. Thus these children could make efficient use of the syntactic structure of the sentence. However, in many cases it is probable that the semantic effect, that is to say the preservation of meaning, was operating additionally, and was as important as, if not more important than, the syntactic. It was not possible in Weber's experiment to differentiate between the two effects.

(4) RELATION OF READING TO AUDITORY DEFICIENCIES

Since many different types of linguistic deficiency are encountered in children learning to read, it is not surprising that reading achievement may be retarded in children whose linguistic ability is in some way impaired. This impairment may take place through hearing loss; through retarded development, both in articulation of speech and in understanding the speech of others; through deficiencies in the more advanced language functions; and through lack of ability to perform certain processes involved in reading such as phonic analysis, synthesis and sequential auditory–visual association.

Deaf children are usually retarded in the acquisition of every type of language function, including reading and writing (Myklebust, 1964); and there is no clear-cut method of overcoming this retardation. It would appear that reading is acquired most readily through the operation of lip-reading, and that therefore reading achievement in the deaf depends on lip-reading ability, which is extremely variable. It seems also that it is more difficult for the child to associate printed words with his visual perceptions of lip movements made by other people in sounding words than with the word sounds themselves, as in hearing children. In any case, these visual perceptions are seldom as accurate and as highly developed as is the hearing child's auditory perceptions of speech sounds. Myklebust cited test results indicating that a retardation in reading vocabulary of 3 years in children of 9 years of age increased to one of 7–8 years at 15 years of age; that is to say, the deaf children increased their reading vocabulary at a much slower rate than did the hearing. However, it would not appear that a retardation of such magnitude is inevitable. Thus Ewing & Ewing (1954) found that some deaf children they tested had learnt to read adequately as early as about 7 years of age; though some were still severely retarded at 11 years. In deaf children who employ manual communication extensively, the language used in writing may be very primitive and inaccurate. This may well affect their capacity to understand what they read.

Reading may also be retarded by *partial hearing loss*, in proportion to the amount of loss. Partially hearing children of 8–16 years were found by Hine (1970) to have a mean R.Q. of only 79, as against WISC Verbal and Performance I.Q.s of 82 and 98. Moreover, the R.Q. decreased with increase in age, that is to say, the children became more retarded. The low R.Q. may have been caused to some extent by the rather low Verbal I.Q. It may also have been affected by emotional maladjustment which, as assessed by the Bristol Social Adjustment Guide, was considerably above normal in these children. The effects of emotional maladjustment on reading will be discussed in Ch. VI; it is possible that it may be a factor of importance in the deaf also.

Perhaps more relevant to linguistic deficiency in general is the case of children in ordinary schools with *minor degrees of hearing loss* such that they can hear speech but cannot hear it clearly and exactly. It might be expected that the difficulties mentioned in earlier sections would here be exaggerated. Words spoken in isolation would be more readily confused with similar sounding words. Phonemes are presumably even harder to identify correctly. A number of studies has been made in which a general relationship was established between reading achievement and poor auditory acuity for pure tones. Thus Henry (1947) tested the auditory acuity of 288 children aged 5–17 years, and found that reading achievement was on average slightly less in children with 17–65 *dbs.* hearing loss at high frequencies than in those with normal hearing. Reading performance in the former was extremely variable. Thirty-five per cent were well below normal, but 18 per cent were above normal. Therefore it would seem that some children are able to compensate for a considerable degree of hearing loss. Hamilton & Owrid (1970) found that a group of children with variable amounts of hearing loss, attending ordinary schools, were retarded in reading with a mean R.Q. of 87. This lay between the R.Q.s of matched controls, one set selected as average readers, the other as poor readers. But the children with impaired hearing had an average I.Q. of only 88.6 on a non-verbal test of intelligence, and reading achievement was highly correlated with scores on this test. Thus it may be that impaired hearing affects reading to a lesser extent than has been supposed. This may depend on the detection and remediation of the hearing defect.

Sheridan (1948) found that reading achievement in 11-year-old children decreased steadily from a hearing loss of under 10 to over 40 per cent. But high frequency loss affected reading to a greater extent than did low frequency loss, because the former interferes more than the latter with the hearing of speech sounds. Sheridan described five cases of severe high frequency loss, three of whom were grossly retarded in reading; one girl of 8 years could not read at all, but two had learnt to read fluently. Thus again it appears that hearing loss, even for high frequency tones, does not preclude learning to read efficiently, though it may make this more difficult especially when other factors are also operative to produce retardation.

Cases have been reported of children suffering from what has been called 'central deafness' or 'congenital auditory imperception' in which the sensory capacity for hearing sounds is normal but there is a peculiar difficulty in hearing speech, attributed to some disability in the central nervous system. However, the nature of this disorder is obscure, and also its effect on reading.

But also there are children with no gross incapacity in the hearing of speech, but a subnormal ability to *discriminate speech sounds.* A number of experiments have claimed to demonstrate an association between word-sound and letter-sound discrimination and reading achievement (see Vernon, 1957). But in the earlier experiments it was found that both the sound discrimination and the reading achievement also correlated highly with intelligence test scores; and when the effect of these was removed, little relationship remained, at least in older children. Nevertheless, more recent experiments appeared to show that in some cases auditory discrimination between words was poorer in retarded readers, independently of intelligence. This was found by Blank (1968) in children of $6\frac{1}{2}$–$7\frac{1}{2}$ years and by Clark (1970) in children of 8 years. Wepman (cited by Flower, 1965) showed that early reading ability was related to performance on the Wepman Test of Auditory Discrimination, which assessed discrimination between similar sounding words such as 'cab' and 'cad', 'sake' and 'shake', 'year' and 'beer'. And De Hirsch *et al.* (1966) found that poor performance on the Wepman test at the age of 5–6 years was one of the best predictors of subsequent inability to learn to read normally. Johnson & Myklebust (1967) considered that in some severely retarded readers, discrimination of short vowel sounds was particularly poor. Again, Silver (1968) found that 50 per cent of a group of severely retarded readers aged $8\frac{1}{2}$–14 years were deficient in perceiving auditorily the differences and similarities between words and in matching letter sounds at the beginnings and ends of words.

It was also observed by Johnson & Myklebust, Silver, and Bruininks (1969) that *auditory blending of letter sounds* to form whole words was inefficient in backward readers. Chall, Roswell & Blumenthal (1963) studied the blending ability of a group of Negro children aged 6–10 years by requiring them to say the whole word when the experimenter uttered separate phonemes consecutively, such as 'c-all' and 'r-ug'. Blending performance showed a correlation of 0.64 with reading ability, even when I.Q. was held constant; though blending ability itself correlated with I.Q. from the age of 7 years, and children with I.Q.s below 100 tended to have poor blending ability throughout. However, Chall *et al.* were not certain whether inadequate blending was caused by inaccurate auditory perception of the phonemes, or inability to synthesize them. A small study by the author (Vernon, 1957) of nine backward readers of 7–8 years suggested that synthesis caused difficulties additional to those of phoneme perception. Thus it was found that children could sound correctly about 50 per cent of single letters and of two-letter combinations such as 'la' and 'ed'; but could blend these into simple three- and four-letter words in only 35 per cent of cases. Again, they could often match words correctly from a number of alternatives, but could not read them. It seems probable therefore that the difficulty in blending is not due simply to failure in auditory perception and discrimination, but to inability in synthesis as such.

(5) AUDITORY AND VISUAL SEQUENCES

We noted in section (2) that young children had difficulty in matching temporal rhythms of taps against visual sequences of dots. The same type of difficulty appears with backward readers. Birch & Belmont (1965) obtained a significant correlation between reading achievement and scores on a test of matching various temporal rhythms of taps against series of dots, up to 7 years of age, but not thereafter. It would seem therefore that the ability to associate auditory and visual sequences may be important during the stage of learning to read, but not at later stages. Again, Muehl & Kremenak (1966) found that ability to match rhythms of brief tones against series of dots, when tested before the children began to learn to read, was related to their subsequent reading achievement. But reading was not related to the matching of two visual sequences. Sterritt & Rudnick (1966) required children of about 9 years to match subsequently presented series of dots against: (1) sequences of taps, visible to the observer; (2) rhythms of tones; (3) sequences of flashes of light. Only performance on the second test correlated with reading achievement; and it was concluded that the effect might be due to poor auditory memory for rhythms in backward readers. However, these children may have been too old to show the effects of inability to associate the other visual and auditory sequences. For in a subsequent experiment, Rudnick et al. (1967)

showed that there was no relationship between matching of visual and auditory sequences and reading achievement at 8–10 years. Ford (1967) found that any correlation of this kind at 9 years was due to the correlation of both with intelligence. When intelligence was partialled out, the correlation of matching and reading achievement was reduced to zero. However, Beery (1967) showed that 11-year-old children, retarded in reading by at least $2\frac{1}{2}$ years, were inferior to normal readers in matching both visual to auditory sequences and auditory to visual sequences. It would seem therefore that although both visual and auditory sequences may be difficult to remember, an additional difficulty may arise in the matching of these which is significantly related to learning to read. Older children who have learnt no longer experience such a difficulty; but it persists in those who have not. Thus Clark (1970) found that 9-year-old children, two years or more retarded in reading, scored significantly lower than did normal readers on matching tapped and dotted rhythms.

It is also possible that backward readers may have peculiar difficulty in *cross-modal association* itself. Thus Katz & Deutsch (1963) found that the reaction times of backward readers, aged 6–10 years, to a light preceded by a sound signal, or *vice-versa*, were significantly slower than those of normal readers. When signal and stimulus were in the same mode, there was no significant difference. Thus it appeared that the backward readers were unusually slow to integrate stimuli of different modes.

Blank & Bridger (1966) and Blank, Weider & Bridger (1968) obtained evidence which showed that the deficiency in backward readers might be principally in the verbal labelling of rhythms. In the first study, it was shown that 9-year-old backward readers were inferior both in matching a temporal sequential pattern of light flashes against dot patterns present subsequently; and also in reporting verbally the nature of the sequential pattern, that is to say, describing the number of lights in each group when there were pauses between groups. In the second study, 6–7-year-old children, backward in word recognition, were inferior to those with superior word recognition in matching groups of light flashes in temporal sequence against dot patterns, but not in matching groups of light flashes presented simultaneously in different spatial positions to dot patterns. Nor were the backward readers inferior in reproducing tapped rhythms directly. All the children reported using some type of verbal labelling of the visual sequences; but the backwa˙ d readers were less efficient in labelling temporal sequences, though not spatial groupings.

Corroborative evidence for this conclusion was obtained in an experiment by Fearn (cited by Cashdan, 1970). He presented tasks of auditory–visual sequence matching to normal and backward readers of 9 years, the latter retarded by $2\frac{1}{2}$ years on the average. With half the children, each auditory sequence was followed by a verbal description, before the visual sequence was presented; for instance, 'that was two taps and then two taps'. No such instructions were given to the other half. The normal readers performed the task better than the backward readers, and there was no difference between the instructed and the uninstructed. The instructed backward readers performed significantly better than did the uninstructed. Thus it appeared that even if cross-modal matching was deficient in the backward readers, inability to label verbally was also important. This labelling would involve abstract conceptual reasoning rather than immediate perceptual identification and association.

If conceptual reasoning is involved in grasping the correspondence between temporal auditory sequences and visual spatial sequences, at the stage of word recognition, it is possible that it is even more essential in the comprehension of sequentially related ideas at the later stages of reading a continuous text. In a recent investigation by Doehring (1968), it appeared that there was a general deficit in *sequential processing* which affected ability to grasp the sequential contents of continuous reading material. The children studied were aged 10–14 years, retarded in reading by at least 2 years but in the majority of cases by a greater amount. Intelligence was within the normal range. Presumably they had some ability in word recognition; but were greatly inferior to normal controls on most verbal tests. Performance on visual tests was normal in most cases, except that there were deficits in spatial ordering: for instance, in the perception of sequences of forms and in connecting up scattered circles in the order in which they were numbered. The matching of auditory rhythms and the naming of verbal sequences were also inferior. It was concluded that, although these cases were limited in linguistic ability, the main disability was in sequential processing; that is to say, in dealing with a chain of associated events, keeping in mind the characteristics of the whole sequence. Such a conceptual disability might well affect the capacity to assimilate the contents of continuous texts.

(6) RELATION OF READING TO DEFICIENCIES IN SPEECH AND LANGUAGE

It is not surprising that learning to read is particularly difficult when, whether or not there is auditory impairment, language is inadequate, either in simple speech or in the more highly developed linguistic functions. The relations between auditory, speech and language functions seem very complex. In the first place, speech is frequently impaired in cases of hearing loss, even in children who are not completely deaf. Sheridan (1948) found that 57 per cent of a group of school children aged 8 years with impaired hearing showed *articulatory defects*. The greater the hearing loss, the more defective the speech; and in those with the most severe loss, speech was sometimes unintelligible. Even with a slight hearing loss of less than 10 per cent, speech might be appreciably impaired. Pronunciation of the consonants 's', 'z', 't' and 'th' was particularly affected; but also speech in general tended to be flat, monotonous and lacking in variation of intonation. Moreover, whenever a speech defect was present, achievement in linguistic subjects, including reading, was seriously retarded.

Other studies have demonstrated a relationship between articulatory defects and poor auditory discrimination. Clark (1960) found that children aged 4–6 years with articulatory defects performed less well than normal speakers on tests of discrimination between vowel and consonant sounds; and of memory for digits and tapped rhythms. Thus both auditory discrimination and memory were affected. By contrast Lennenberg (1962) has cited the case of an 8-year-old boy whose acquisition of motor skill in speaking was so severely impaired that he was unable to speak; yet he appeared to understand speech normally.

It is common to find that articulatory defects are associated with *slow development of speech.* Thus Morley (1957) showed that in a group of 162 children with defective articulation there had been a general delay in the early development of the language functions, such as the first appearance of words, sentences, etc. However, by the age of 3–4 years these language functions had in most cases become normal. But in older children, Templin (1966) found that those with defective articulation also showed some retardation in the production of correct inflexions in spoken language. An extensive investigation was carried out by Ingram (1959a, b) of a group of children aged 2–7 years with defective articulation. This was caused by hearing loss in only 4 per cent of cases; but it is possible that no cases with severe hearing loss were included in this group. About 40 per cent of the children suffered from functional speech disorders, of whom half had shown slow speech and language development. Thus the first intelligible word was not spoken until 18 months or after, and the first combination of two words not until 30 months or after. Speech was not fully intelligible before about 6 years, mainly through defective articulation of consonants. Understanding of speech was also delayed. In some cases other language functions were impaired: vocabulary growth was slow; there were reversals and alternations of syllables in words and omissions and substitutions of words in sentences; and grammatical construction of sentences was faulty. However, the incidence of these defects was variable; many children grew out of them by about 7 years, and difficulties in comprehension disappeared before errors in speech. Some cases of severe linguistic disorder were classed as suffering from 'auditory imperception'. Of fifteen children who were aged over 5 years, eight had difficulty in learning to read and write, making errors which were similar to those in speech.

Crookes & Greene (1963) studied a group of twenty children aged 5–11 years, referred to a clinic for speech defects. In eight of these, the disorder was primarily motor. Articulation was defective and motor maturation late and poor, but auditory perception and memory, and language development, were normal. In the remaining twelve children, motor maturation had been normal, but speech was confused and auditory memory, especially for language, was poor. Reading achievement was greatly below I.Q. for both groups. Thus apparently reading was impaired both by defective articulation of speech and also by purely linguistic deficiencies. Cohn (1961) found that forty-six children aged 7–10 years with severe reading backwardness showed poor language ability in almost all cases, and also impaired muscular control of speech.

It would appear that inadequacy in the simpler speech functions may be less significant in reading than are the more complex and highly developed linguistic functions, which are not disordered in all articulatory cases. Evidence as to the different nature and causes of these simple and complex functions was given in a study by De Hirsch, Jansky & Langford (1964) of children of $5\frac{1}{2}$ years who had been prematurely born. These children were of normal intelligence and not inferior to full-term children in auditory discrimination and memory, and in articulation. But they were significantly inferior in vocabulary, understanding of questions, naming of familiar objects, length and elaboration of sentences in spontaneous speech. When they began to learn to read and write, their achievement was significantly poorer than that of full-term children.

Again, Martin (1955) found no relationship between facility in oral language, as measured by the total number of words used, the number of different words and the length of sentences; and reading readiness test scores on entry to school and reading achievement after one year in school. But Sampson (1962) obtained a significant correlation between reading comprehension, measured at 8 years, and amount of correctly phrased speech, assessed at $2\frac{1}{2}$ years. There were also correlations between reading comprehension at 8 years, and vocabulary and language development, as measured by the Watts English language scale, at 5 years. Ravenette (1968) also obtained a significant correlation at 7–8 years between reading achievement and vocabulary as assessed on the Crichton Vocabulary scale and the N.F.E.R. Picture Vocabulary test. And De Hirsch, Jansky & Langford (1966) found that useful prognostic tests for subsequent failure in learning to read were: memory for words, giving generic names to groups of objects, and numbers of words used in telling a story. In contrast to these results, Silver (1968) found that there were no defects in severely backward readers in the understanding of word meanings as assessed by ability to pick out pictures to match spoken words. It must be concluded that the relationship between reading backwardness and other linguistic functions depends on the sample tested and the degree of backwardness. It is possible that there is a continuously varying degree of linguistic skill which correlates with reading achievement within the normal range. But in severely backward readers, linguistic difficulties may operate somewhat differently, and not appear in all cases, as we shall discuss in Ch. VII.

The nature of linguistic ability and the differences which may occur in different types of linguistic activity have been investigated by means of the *Illinois Test of Psycholinguistic Abilities*, designed by McCarthy & Kirk (1961). This consists of six sub-tests intended to assess the representational level of language organization, involving the use of symbols; and three sub-tests of the automatic use of language. The first set covers the understanding of spoken words and of pictures (decoding); ability to express oneself in words and gestures (encoding); and the meaningful relation of words to pictures (association). In the second set are tested ability to match grammatical inflexions of words to pictures; immediate memory for rapidly presented digits; and reproduction of correct order in series of shapes and pictures. Now it was claimed by McCarthy & Kirk that each test assessed a different ability. However, Mittler & Ward (1970) found that a large part of the variance in test scores made by 4-year-old children was attributable to a *single general factor of linguistic ability*. There were some additional factors involved in particular sub-sets of tests, but it was difficult to establish their nature. It would seem, however, that the more or less automatic linguistic processes tested in the second set of sub-tests ought to be differentiated from those operative in the first set, in which understanding and reasoning are involved. Nevertheless, as we saw in section (2) these functions seemed to develop in close conjunction with each other. However, according to Spache (1968), reading achievement was related to performance on the second set and not on the first. A somewhat similar finding was obtained by Kass (cited by Ravenette, 1968), with children of 7–10 years severely retarded in reading; though there was also a deficiency in meaningful associations between words. Naidoo (1970) observed that backward readers performed the sequencing test badly, a finding which agrees with those of Doehring (1968). However, Clark (1970) found that 9-year-old children, retarded by 2 or more years in reading but within the normal range of intelligence, were significantly lower on the whole scale than were normal readers; there were no significant differences between sub-test scores.

Obviously there is considerable disagreement as to which types of linguistic skill may be impaired in cases of reading backwardness. Indeed, an enquiry by Ingram (1960) indicated that several types might be affected, in 78 children aged 6–9 years with severe reading difficulties. Three types of linguistic impairment were found: (1) in relating written to spoken letters or groups of letters and *vice-versa*; (2) in constructing words from letters which had been correctly sounded; (3) in comprehending the meanings of words and sentences. Some children whose performance in (1) was adequate failed in (2); and some who were successful with (1) and (2) failed in (3). But failure in (1) was the most common. Many who were deficient in (1) and (2) had shown slow speech development; and the slower the development, the greater the deficiency. There had been slow speech development in all who were deficient in (3).

Finally, Rabinovitch & Ingram (1968) described cases of severe reading backwardness who were unable to formulate precise answers to questions. For instance, to the question, 'Why is it better to build a house of bricks than of wood?', the reply by a 9-year-old child was: 'Well just in case a hurricane the house can break down, but you put the brick on, it can just hit it but break nothing down.' Here apparently the child could understand the meaning of the question and reason out the correct answer, but was unable to formulate it coherently in correct syntax. Thus these cases differ again from those described by Ingram (1960).

It is obvious that there is much variation between the findings of different experimenters as to the relation of linguistic processes to reading achievement. It is clearly difficult to specify, differentiate and measure exactly the different types of linguistic skill. Possibly learning to read by younger children is affected by poor auditory discrimination of speech sounds, and by inability to analyse phrases into words and word sounds into phonemes. Also the synthesis of sequences of phonemes into the integrated structures of word sounds may be inadequate. Some or all of these defects may be related to a fundamental linguistic disability, as we shall consider in Ch. VII. Environmental restrictions may limit children's vocabularies, but the consequences of these depend on the vocabularies of the reading materials employed. Difficulties in comprehending the meanings of sentences and continuous texts are likely to have greater effects at the more advanced stages of reading.

It is difficult to decide whether there exist basic constitutional differences in auditory and linguistic ability (other than those resulting from hearing loss and defective articulation); or whether variations are caused only by differences in environmental conditions. In so far as linguistic achievement is acquired, it should be possible to improve it by special *training*, and in this manner to promote reading achievement. Now it would seem that simple auditory training in word discrimination may have little effect. Thus Feldman, Schmidt & Deutsch (1968) gave special training in auditory discrimination, recognition and memory for speech sounds, to backward readers of low socio-economic status, aged 8–9 years, and obtained little improvement other than that due to improved motivation and attentiveness. Again, Denmark & Guttentag (1969) found that 4-year-old Negro children improved in auditory discrimination and ability to tell a story in their own words to much the same extent when they were given a general education in close contact with children possessing high linguistic ability, as when they were specially trained in cognitive skills. Elkind & Deblinger (1969) obtained a favourable effect on word recognition by training in various experiences connected with language usage, or perhaps with verbal reasoning. These were: understanding anagrams and sentences with scrambled words, and coding of words to visual symbols. This effect was greater than that of ordinary reading teaching; and the experimenters claimed that the training encouraged the children to re-organize the material systematically, rather than merely repeating what they had learnt. It may therefore be that the important factor in improving linguistic expression is the inculcation of linguistic skill either through direct teaching or through spontaneous imitation. But for linguistic ability to function effectively in reading, there should be some training in the use of language in verbal reasoning. This we shall consider in the next chapter.

NOTE, 1973 Bakker (in Bakker, D. J. and Satz, P. (Eds.), *Specific Reading Disability*, Rotterdam University Press, 1970) has drawn attention to the importance in learning to read of the capacity to remember *temporal order* as such in verbalized sequences. In children of seven years, those who made below average performances in recalling the order of pictures and letters, presented sequentially, made many more errors of order in reading than did those with above average performances – though not other types of error. Severely backward readers of 7–12 years were inferior to normal readers in recalling the order of pictures and letters presented sequentially, though not the order of meaningless stimuli; indicating that verbalized order was the important factor.

CHAPTER V

THE RELATION OF READING TO REASONING, AND TO INTELLIGENCE AND OTHER ABILITIES

(1) CONCEPTUAL REASONING

It has become apparent that reading involves not only the perception and memory of visual shapes and sounds, but also more complex cognitive processes such that the child is obliged to organize his visual and auditory perceptions and to reason about the relationship between the printed symbols of the text and the verbal symbols of language which indicate its meaning. Little study appears to have been made of children's capacity to understand this *symbolization*, though it may well be of great importance. Children have had little experience of visual symbols before they begin learning to read; for pictures are representational rather than symbolic. Thus Reid (1966) found that 5-year-old children, when they first began learning to read, sometimes completely failed to understand what reading was; that print must be handled differently from pictures; that reading and writing were related to each other; that words were composed of letters; and that letters differed from numbers. This suggests that they did not understand the symbolic nature of written language. Although Reid found that within three months they learnt that there was a direct relationship between printed and spoken words, and even some simple phonics, it is possible that the prolonged difficulty of some children in acquiring the visual-auditory associations of letters and words may be due in part to a failure of clear understanding of the nature of symbolism. Rabinovitch (1962) and Kucera, Matejcek & Langmeier (1963) noted that severely backward readers appeared to have unusual difficulties in realizing that forms such as those of printed words were symbols of spoken words and of their meanings. They might also experience other difficulties in the use of symbols.

It would appear that *conceptual reasoning* is involved in learning to read, in particular in abstracting the essential characteristics of printed and spoken words and in generalizing these to cover a wide range of minor variations. Now Piaget has shown that children do not develop the ability for conceptual reasoning until they reach the 'concrete operational' stage of intelligence at 6–7 years and upwards. Younger children are deficient in the capacities of abstraction and generalization necessary for the conceptual grouping of objects; that is to say, grouping similar objects into mutually exclusive categories (Inhelder & Piaget, 1964). Problems of 'conservation' also require an understanding of the more abstract concepts of number, volume, weight, etc., such that it is realized that these may remain constant when the location and distribution of objects is altered. Children under 6–7 years of age do not grasp this, but base their judgments on the perception of certain prominent but irrelevant characteristics. For instance, the child sees that when water is poured from a wide to a narrow jar, the level of the water rises, and then says that there is more water in the narrow than in the wide vessel.

Now Anisfeld (1968) pointed out that at first sight it seems surprising that children can understand and operate the complex processes of grammatical construction at such an early age, whereas they are so much slower to understand conservation, which to adults seems simple enough. It would seem that the confusion in the latter may be due to the necessity to extract the relevant from the irrelevant features of the situation. Anisfeld demonstrated that the same type of difficulty might occur in other conceptual classifications. Children of $5\frac{1}{2}$–$6\frac{1}{2}$ years were presented with two series of pictures, one in which a picture of a single object was paired with a picture of several of these objects; and a second in which a picture containing a single detail within an object was paired with the object containing more than one of such details. For instance, a single paned window was paired with a window containing sixteen panes. The children were required to sort the pictures into groups of singular and plural, after this distinction had been demonstrated to them. Whereas 74 per cent of the first series were sorted correctly, only 60 per cent of the second series were correct. It was concluded that classification was more difficult when the characteristics on which it was based were 'embedded' in the perceived material, as with the details, than when they stood out clearly.

It would seem that in learning to read it is essential for the child to realize and understand the fundamental generalization that in alphabetic writing all words are represented by combinations of a limited number of visual symbols. Thus it is possible to present a very large vocabulary of spoken words in an economical manner which requires the memorizing of a comparatively small number of printed symbols and their associated sounds. But a thorough grasp of this principal necessitates a fairly advanced stage of conceptual reasoning, since this type of organization differs fundamentally from any previously encountered by children in their normal environment.

Moreover, the child has to realize that the shapes and sounds of letters and words possess certain essential features which do vary according to context, but in a lawful manner, and these he must learn to recognize. At the same time, he must ignore certain other *irrelevant variable characteristics.* The latter include minor differences of shape in different printing faces, and the more noticeable differences between printed and hand-written letters. Early reading books are sometimes printed in a type face resembling handwriting. It will then be necessary for the child to learn the correspondence between such letters and those of normal printing types; and the differentiation of the essential features of the latter. Klapper (1968) stated that backward readers often had difficulty in recognizing the identity of graphic symbols which remained constant despite changes in their form, size and spatial position. Indeed, we noted in Ch. III that children generally find it harder than do adults to perceive and identify shapes which are obscured or deformed in any way; and this might apply to unusual printing types or hand-writing.

The irrelevant features of letters and words sounded in speech are more difficult to specify. Variations in phonemes with local accent are irrelevant and possibly confusing intrusions in word recognition; and variations with intonational pattern, though important to general significance in reading aloud, must not intrude on the grasp of the phonemic pattern of words. Some of these variations are important in reading, as when letters and digraphs are differently pronounced at the beginnings and endings of words, for instance with 'gh' in 'ghost' and 'through'. Again there are minor variations, especially in vowel phonemes, in isolated words and words in sentence context which are of no importance, and which must be disregarded if confusion is to be avoided.

As we have already noted, the differences especially in vowel phonemes which occur in different words must be thoroughly learnt by the child before he can attain any proficiency in word recognition. It was pointed out that in the linguistic methods of teaching reading it was customary to give the child a thorough grounding in the common vowel sounds before he proceeded to the less common variants. However, it has been shown in experiments using other material that in some circumstances it is better that from the first children should realize the existence of lawful variations. Otherwise they become rigidly set in one type of response, and have great difficulty in acquiring other variants. Levin & Watson (1963) hypothesized that for reading new words it was better to learn certain certain alternative letter–sound associations simultaneously, though possibly not the whole range, rather than to learn the simplest first and then proceed to the others later, as Bloomfield recommended. They attempted to test this hypothesis by requiring children of 8–9 years to learn lists of words written in artificial letter shapes. One group of these children learnt a list with constant correspondence between the shapes of vowels and their sounds, followed by a list with variable correspondence in which each vowel shape had two or three different sounds. A second group learnt two lists with variable correspondence. Finally, both groups learnt the same list with a new set of letter shapes and variable associated sounds. The second group, which was 'set' for variability, learnt the original lists more quickly than did the first group, and with fewer errors. But there was no significant difference on the final task. Thus either there was no transfer of the variable 'set', or transfer was equal in both groups; and the evidence for superiority of teaching alternative shape–sound associations was ambiguous. Moreover, it cannot be assumed that even if 8–9-year-old children benefited by learning the variable correspondence, the same would be true for younger children just beginning to learn to read, who might easily be confused by variability. It might be best for young children to learn single simple associations for a short time before they were gradually introduced to the alternative associations; but not to spend long enough on the former to become rigidly set in their use. However, here, as so often, the problem of individual differences is encountered. Children with different degrees of linguistic and intellectual ability may well require different periods of practice with simple shape-sound associations before they proceed to the more complex. Variations in association are not random, but are governed by rules. Yet as we noted, it is doubtful whether young children possess sufficient conceptual ability to grasp and operate rules of spelling, except perhaps of a very simple kind.

It would seem therefore that ability to reason conceptually may be of greater importance in learning to read than ability merely to learn by rote. Various studies have suggested that reading achievement may be related to the ability to form concepts. Thus Goins (cited by Smith & Dechant, 1961) found that poor readers had difficulty in selecting the common elements from among a group of different objects, and in noting the essential differences between similar objects. Braun (1963) presented to children of 8–13 years a test of concept formation consisting of paired sets of four words each. The children had to detect the one word in each set which had something in common with one word in the other set; that is to say, they had to conceptualize the common factor. The concepts varied in abstractness. Scores on the concept formation test correlated more highly with reading test scores than did scores on the WISC; and also more highly than did concept test scores with WISC scores. 'Under-achievers', whose reading age was below their mental age, performed significantly worse at all ages than did 'over-achievers' whose reading age was above their mental age. Moreover, the latter continued to improve their performance as age increased, through ability to form the more abstract concepts. The under-achievers could not do this, and improved little between 10 and 13 years. Again, Rabinovitch *et al.* (1954) found that some of the severely backward readers, aged 10–16 years, whom they studied had difficulty in abstract and conceptual thinking, and particularly in formulating abstract concepts of size, number and time.

Lovell, Shapton & Warren (1964) investigated the relationship between reading achievement and certain of Piaget's spatial–conceptual tasks, in judging: the level of water in a tilted vessel; the relation of a ship and its mast to the sides of a tilted flask; and the orientation of objects on a sloping hillside. They compared the performance on these tasks of 50 children of normal non-verbal intelligence but R.Q.s below 80 to that of normal readers. The oral language of the former on the Watts language test of formulating sentences was not significantly different from that of the latter, who were however significantly worse on the Piaget tasks. But it is possible that they experienced difficulty in judging orientation.

Kagan (1965) distinguished between children who were impulsive in making perceptual and conceptual judgments and jumped rapidly to conclusions from those who were more reflective and deliberate. He assessed the ability of 6-year-old children to analyse a complex design into figure and ground and the former into its constituent elements; and to produce a name previously attached to a whole design for one of these elements presented singly. The reflective children were slower in doing this and made fewer errors. Though performance was unrelated to intelligence test scores, the reflective were more skilled in reading than were the impulsive.

The employment of reasoning is almost certainly involved in understanding the variable associations between printed and sounded letters. It might appear that certain writers suppose that these associations may be acquired through rote learning. But even if this is possible with very simple letter–phoneme associations, the more complex associations and the correct application of the rules of spelling necessitate intelligent comprehension. Moreover, as we have seen, correct sequential processing of spatial visual sequences and temporal auditory sequences demands even more complex reasoning processes. We noted in Ch. III that Piaget had postulated the employment of intelligence in the development of perceptual activity of a comparatively simple nature. In comprehending phoneme sequences and relating them to printed letter sequences, which as we noted in Ch. IV appeared to be defective in backward readers, it would seem that a higher order of reasoning would be essential.

It is clear that when children become sufficiently fluent in learning to read continuous texts of a complex nature, their capacity for verbal reasoning is increasingly employed in understanding the gradually developing meaning of the text and the implications of its contents. Thus the more difficult the text is to understand, the greater the intelligence required in the reader. We must consider therefore the relation of intelligence to reading achievement and to reading difficulties.

(2) INTELLIGENCE AND OTHER ABILITIES

It is often difficult to determine at all exactly the relationship between intelligence and reading achievement, since this relationship varies with the type of intelligence test employed. In particular, it has commonly been found that correlations of reading achievement with *verbal intelligence tests* are higher than those with non-verbal tests. Naturally, backward readers perform group verbal tests badly because they are unable to read the test material easily. It has been stated that a typical group intelligence test for 11-year-old children requires for full understanding a reading age of over 9 years (P. E. Vernon, 1960). Moreover, correlations between such tests and reading tests may be increased in so far as the latter are comprehension tests which, as we noted on p. 6, may depend on verbal intelligence as well as on reading ability for their performance. But also tests administered orally, such as the Terman–Merrill (Stanford–Binet) test often show high correlations with reading achievement. It is true that Malmquist (1958) obtained the not very high correlations of 0.50 and 0.42 between Terman–Merrill scores and scores on silent reading tests of word recognition

83

and paragraph comprehension in children of 7 years. But the mean I.Q.s of below average and above average readers were 96.6 and 123.4 respectively. Again Ravenette (1961) obtained a correlation of 0.75 between scores on the Schonell Graded Word Reading test (a test of word recognition) and on the Crichton Vocabulary scale, in children of 8–11 years. Thus there would appear to be good evidence that reading achievement is associated with intelligence as assessed by verbal tests.

By contrast, the relationship of reading achievement to performance on *non-verbal tests of intelligence* is usually found to be less close. Phillips (1958) quoted correlations of reading achievement with group non-verbal tests as 0.5–0.65; with group verbal tests as 0.6–0.75; and with individual verbal tests such as the Terman–Merrill as 0.65–0.8. Kellmer Pringle & Neale (1957) obtained correlations of only 0.3–0.5 between the Moray House Picture Intelligence test and the reading tests of Schonell and Gates, in children of 8 years. These results suggest that a specific verbal or linguistic ability operates both in reading achievement and also in verbal intelligence tests. Nevertheless, Douglas (1964) obtained correlations of 0.56 and 0.53 between the N.F.E.R. Picture test of intelligence, and reading comprehension and word recognition respectively. Morris (1966) found a mean score of 87–88 in her sample of backward readers on a non-verbal test of intelligence, as against a mean score of 114–115 for the good readers. But the non-verbal intelligence test employed items such as similarities and analogies, which would appear to require a type of reasoning similar to that of many verbal intelligence tests, though the linguistic factor was absent. It may be therefore that the relationship between intelligence test scores and reading depends to a considerable extent on the type of reasoning employed in the former.

It could be argued that reading achievement must be related not only to intelligence but also to ability to learn. It would appear that two types of learning ability may be involved. The first operates in rote learning, and seems to a considerable extent to be specific to the kind of task involved (P. E. Vernon, 1969). We have already noted that visual memory is poor in some backward readers, and verbal memory in others. The second and more important type occurs in the learning of meaningful material, and involves conceptual reasoning and the acquisition of what Harlow (1949) termed 'learning sets'. These include the principles governing particular procedures such as the spelling rules which enable children to establish correct sequential associations. Undoubtedly this type of learning depends to a great extent on general intelligence.

It is certainly true that children of low intelligence learn to read at a later age than do those of better intelligence. Anderson, Hughes & Dixon (1956, 1957) obtained a correlation of 0.55 between the Stanford–Binet I.Q. and age of learning to read. Those with I.Q.s of 130 and over learnt to read at about $6\frac{1}{2}$ years of age; those with I.Q.s below 100, at about 8 years. The less intelligent began later and learnt more slowly.

It is likely that good intelligence is even more necessary for the attainment of fluent reading and understanding of continuous texts than in the early stages of word recognition. Bliesmer (1954) showed that intelligent children with I.Q.s of 116–138 and dull children with I.Q.s of 72–84 with the same mental age, $10\frac{1}{2}$–$12\frac{1}{2}$ years, were similar in attainment on tests of word recognition. But the more intelligent were significantly superior to the less intelligent in grasping the main ideas of the text and in drawing inferences from these.

Although children of low intelligence may never attain the most advanced stages of reading, yet high intelligence does not guarantee successful reading achievement. Thus Malmquist (1958) found that 36 per cent of his poor readers had Terman–Merrill I.Q.s of over 100, and 23 per cent of 110 and over. As we shall see in Ch. VII, many children with specific dyslexia have I.Q.s within the normal range. It would therefore appear that the noegenetic processes assessed by most intelligence tests are not necessarily the same as the processes of conceptual reasoning involved in learning to read. Although in the majority of children these may be closely associated together, there appears to be a specific deficit in the latter in dyslexic children.

Since reading achievement is therefore not necessarily determined by tested intelligence, it is unwise to assess a child's backwardness in reading in terms of discrepancy with his mental age; still less to calculate an '*achievement quotient*' in which mental age is the denominator. These measures suggest that any child whose reading achievement is less than that normally obtained by children of his mental age is an 'under-achiever' in reading. Thus many children of high intelligence may appear to be 'under-achievers'; and it is inferred that it is they who require remedial reading teaching, rather than children of lower intelligence and equally low achievement (P. E. Vernon, 1958). Curr & Hallworth (1965) distinguished between 'backwardness' in reading, the discrepancy between the child's reading performance and that normal at his chronological age; and 'retardation', which was the discrepancy between his reading performance and that expected at his mental age. They found backwardness to be associated with a number of variables such as social class, parental treatment, emotional stability, freedom from hearing and speech defects. But retardation was unrelated to these variables; and Curr & Hallworth considered it to be a measure of little importance.

P. E. Vernon (1950) has shown that the factorial analysis of correlations between test scores demonstrates that reading achievement is related to performance on verbal intelligence tests not only through '*g*' (noegenetic reasoning ability) but also through a factor of *verbal ability*, '*v*'. This factor operates in most verbal tests, though it is of less importance than is g; for instance, a vocabulary test of intelligence showed a loading of 0.8 on g and of 0.5 on v. A later study of 100 11-year-old boys (P. E. Vernon, 1965) employed a great variety of tests of verbal and non-verbal intelligence, including some modelled on Piaget's conservation and spatial tests. The main general factor g ran through all these, and also functioned in the performance of a test based on Gottschaldt's embedded figures and of the Bender test. A second, educational, factor correlated with all the verbal tests; and a small verbal factor covered additional variance in vocabulary, concept formation and reading tests. But neither of these factors was correlated with the Piaget tests. These results would seem to indicate that learning to read

86

involves both g and v. However, in a factorial study reported by Reed (1958), early reading ability, not tested in Vernon's study, did not appear to be related to Thurstone's verbal factor (V) in 6–7-year-old children. But achievement in reading at more advanced levels, in children of 12–13 years, was closely related to V.

Some disagreement between the results of factorial analyses may then be attributed to differences in age, and some to variability in the nature of the verbal factor. As in all factorial studies, this is based on the contents of the tests with which it correlates most highly. Thus it may enter into extensiveness of vocabulary and proficiency in the use of words, formulation of sentences, and verbal reasoning. Or in some studies some of these processes may be tested, but not all. According to P. E. Vernon (1950), the abilities to perform these processes are highly correlated. But a correlation demonstrates only a general group relationship, and there may be many individual exceptions. We noted in the last chapter that Mittler & Ward (1970) extracted a general factor of linguistic ability from correlations of scores of 4-year-old children on the Illinois Test of Psycholinguistic Abilities. These tests were designed to cover language comprehension and verbal reasoning ability as well as the simpler automatic linguistic functions. Thus it may be that in young children there is a single main linguistic factor varying continuously from the least to the most linguistically skilled. But in older children linguistic skills may be more specialized; and in dyslexic children linguistic disabilities may be specialized also, as was suggested by the findings of Ingram (see p. 74).

Again, some writers have argued that there is a close relationship between reasoning ability and linguistic skill, and indeed that the development of the former depends on the adequacy of the latter (Lewis, 1968). Piaget, however, considered that the concrete operational stage, at which conceptual reasoning developed, was independent of linguistic ability (Furth, 1969), a hypothesis which agrees with the results of Vernon's factorial analysis. Furth himself (1964) concluded from studies of deaf children that their intellectual development was not retarded directly by their deafness, though it might be affected by lack of adequate cognitive stimulation. They did give inferior performances in tasks depending directly on linguistic skill. Thus it would seem that verbal intelligence and linguistic skill may be independent abilities, although they are often intercorrelated. Probably both are involved in performing verbal intelligence tests; and at some stages in learning to read.

It might be supposed that the ability to learn to read would be correlated with another factor frequently appearing in factorial studies of abilities, namely the so-called k factor. This factor is often termed 'spatial ability' (MacFarlane Smith, 1964), but in fact it usually operates in tests of perceiving and memorizing shapes and patterns, and in reproducing them as in formboard and Kohs Blocks tests. There has been much argument as to whether this factor covers immediate perception of shape and pattern, analysis of complex forms, memory for forms and capacity for manipulating these imaginally; or whether certain of these processes are more important than others. MacFarlane Smith stated that the perception of whole patterns and their contours was more significant than the perception of their details. However, P. E. Vernon (1965) found in his study of 11-year-old boys that two separate factors could be distinguished: (1) 'Perceptual', functioning in the Gottschaldt embedded figures (see Fig. 5),* Bender test, Draw-a-Man and Picture Recognition tests; (2) 'Practical', in a formboard test, and to a lesser degree in Kohs Blocks test. Though Jamaican boys of the same age showed less clear differentiation between the two factors, they did perform better on the Perceptual than on the Practical tests. Thus it appeared that the latter required some ability, deficient in the Jamaican boys, additional to perception and memory for visual form. But in Eskimo and Uganda boys the two types of ability were scarcely differentiated (Vernon, 1969); except that the latter were deficient in understanding the representation of distance in the Picture Recognition test.

* These figures were in the main derived from those employed by Witkin (1950), though with certain additions such as that shown in Fig. 5, but Witkins' colouring was not employed. They are more difficult than those of Ghent (1956); and in addition the simple and complex figures were presented on different pages of the test booklet, to prevent matching of the simple to the complex forms.

Presumably the performance on the Perceptual tests, though it might not be related to reading ability in older children, would correlate with ability to learn to read in younger ones. Thus the data cited in Ch. III demonstrated such a relationship. But perceptual discrimination of visual form does not correlate with intelligence even in younger children, as was shown by Gaines (1969). No relationship between reading achievement and the Practical tests appears to have been demonstrated. Bond & Clymer (1955)

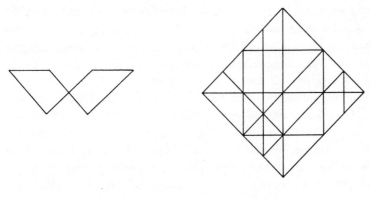

Simple   Complex

Fig. 5. Simple and complex figures. (After P. E. Vernon, unpublished.)

found that reading comprehension in children of 7–11 years was unrelated to the Primary Mental Abilities test of 'Space', a test of form construction. However, there is evidence, discussed in Ch. VII, that severely backward readers are deficient in this respect, as shown by their poor performance on Kohs Blocks test.

Attempts have been made to differentiate the abilities involved in learning to read by relating reading achievement to scores on the different sub-tests of the WISC, and particularly to differences between the WISC Verbal and Performance sections. It was claimed, for instance by Graham (1952), Neville (1961), Paterra (1963), McCleod (1965), Belmont & Birch (1966), Huelsman (1970) and Clark (1970) that on the average backward readers scored better on the Performance than on the Verbal tests. However, in 30–40 per cent of Huelsman's cases, Verbal scores were higher than Performance. Other experimenters, Altus (1956), Beck (1968) and Lyle & Goyen (1969), found no over-all difference between Verbal and Performance test scores. Lyle & Goyen also stated that there were no sub-groups of children with, respectively, Verbal scores superior to Performance, and Performance superior to Verbal. We shall see below that other studies have shown that such sub-groups may be distinguished in clinic cases of backward readers; but it would seem that a large unselected sample does not naturally divide in this way. This is not surprising in view of the fact that the Verbal and Performance sections possess overlapping factors. Thus Maxwell (1959) submitted the correlations between the scores on sub-tests obtained by normal children to factorial analysis, and found that the principal factor, which he termed verbal intellectual, had high loadings on several of the Performance sub-tests as well as all the Verbal sub-tests. A second factor appeared in the Block Design and Object Assembly tests. These factor loadings did not vary with age between $7\frac{1}{2}$ and $13\frac{1}{2}$ years. Clearly there is only a partial dichotomy between Verbal and Performance test ability, which can hardly be applied effectively to the abilities of large samples of backward readers.

Numerous studies have also been carried out to ascertain if there is any specific association between reading achievement and any of the individual sub-tests of the WISC. These appear to assess a heterogeneous range of abilities which Wechsler (1939) considered to involve samples of intelligent behaviour. In relating them to reading achievement, various hypotheses have been advanced as to the psychological processes involved in their performance, but with considerable disagreement.

Several studies showed that backward readers scored relatively badly on the Information, Arithmetic, Digit Span and Coding sub-tests; whereas they performed relatively well on the Picture Arrangement, Picture Completion and Block Design sub-tests. Graham (1952) and McLeod (1965) obtained low scores for backward readers on the Vocabulary test. But Altus (1956) and Robeck

(1964) found that Vocabulary test scores were adequate. Lovell *et al.* (1964) showed that backward readers performed badly on Vocabulary, Coding and Block Designs, in which rotations were frequent. On the other hand, Clark (1970) found no significantly low scores on any sub-tests among 8-year-old children with R.Q.s of 85 and below.

Huelsman (1970), summarizing the results of other experimenters and also those he himself obtained with 300 children aged 9–10 years, concluded that there was a tendency among backward readers as a group to score badly on Information, Arithmetic and Coding; and that although many individual children scored below their own mean on some of these tests, it was exceptional to find anyone who scored badly on all three. However, taken individually, more poor readers than good readers scored significantly below the mean on Information, Arithmetic, Coding and Vocabulary; whereas more scored above the mean on the Performance tests other than Coding. Now it has been suggested that Information and Arithmetic in particular are related to school work, and that any child retarded in reading might be expected to do badly in school work. In other words, low scores on these tests were the result and not the cause of reading backwardness. Lyle & Goyen (1969) argued that this could not be so, since the discrepancies of scores on these tests did not increase with increase in age; whereas if poor scores were due to reading failure, the effect should have increased.

Whether or not this argument is correct, poor performance on Information and Arithmetic gives little assistance in discovering the defects associated with reading backwardness. However, it has been fairly generally held that the Coding test, which requires the child to write down rapidly a series of signs corresponding to letters, is performed badly by backward readers. This might indicate that they are deficient in the ability to utilize symbols. Nevertheless, Huelsman found that many backward readers did not do this test badly; and indeed it would appear that the type of symbolism employed in the Coding test is very different from that which functions in reading.

The varying results on the Vocabulary test are surprising, since as we noted other experimenters, such as Ravenette (1961), found a high correlation between reading achievement and Vocabulary. One would certainly expect considerable interaction between reading capacity and knowledge of the meanings of words. Again, several experimenters found that backward readers performed quite well on the Similarities test, which is the only WISC test based on conceptual reasoning.

We must conclude that the administration of the WISC to large groups of backward readers does not provide much information as to the abilities in which they are deficient. Indeed, Koppitz (1958) and Brenner & Gillman (1968) found the relationship between reading and WISC scores to be less than that between reading and Bender test scores. However, the disagreements between different investigators and the anomalies we have noted may have been due at least in part to the fact that different investigators tested children of different ages, with different degrees of backwardness, often not severe, and correlated WISC scores with different types of reading activity, for instance measures of word recognition in the early stages of reading, or of comprehension of words and sentences in the later stages.

But there are studies which show that some severely backward readers score relatively better on the Verbal than on the Performance tests, others better on the Performance than the Verbal. Ingram & Reid (1956) found that out of fifty-two such cases, twenty-three obtained an average Verbal score 21 points above the average Performance score, whereas thirteen obtained an average Performance score 16 points above the average Verbal score. The first group was markedly inferior in tests involving the analysis and synthesis of patterns, and discrimination between patterns and their mirror images. The second group was inferior on tests of comprehension and vocabulary. Similar results were obtained by Kinsbourne & Warrington (1963 a). They selected two small groups of clinic cases severely backward in reading. In the first group, of five children aged 9–15 years, Performance I.Q. exceeded Verbal I.Q. by 23–45 points. Scores on the Vocabulary and Digit Span tests were particularly low, whereas those on Similarities and A. `hmetic were fairly normal. In the second group, of seven children aged 8–15 years, Verbal I.Q. exceeded Performance I.Q. by 20–35 points, and scores on the Block Design and Object Assembly tests were especially low. From these and other tests, they concluded that children in the first group were suffering from linguistic retardation and those in the second from some kind of disability in sequential ordering. In neither case did there appear to be any deficiency in verbal reasoning.

In a later study, Warrington (1967) studied the frequency of these two types of case among 108 children, aged 7–17 years, referred to clinics for reading difficulties. In 70 per cent of these cases, reading age, as measured by Schonell's Graded Word list, was retarded by 2 years or more below chronological age. Their Full Scale WISC I.Q.s were 80 and over. The distribution of cases in this sample with Verbal I.Q.s greater or less than Performance I.Q.s, as compared with that obtained by Seashore (1951) in a normal population, was as follows.

	Clinic sample (Per cent)	Seashore's sample (Per cent)
Verbal > Performance 20 points or more	5	6
Verbal > Performance 0–19 points	12	44
Verbal < Performance 0–19 points	51	44
Verbal < Performance 20 points or more	32	6

Thus there was an excess over the normal population of cases with Verbal below Performance I.Q., but not of those with Verbal better than Performance I.Q.; and a considerable number showed no significant difference, as with sixteen of the cases of Ingram & Reid (1956). The incidence of a number of developmental factors in the twenty-four children (32 per cent) with Performance I.Q. exceeding Verbal I.Q. by 20 or more points was compared with that in the remainder of the cases. Among the former, 46 per cent had a history of slow speech development, as compared with 19 per cent of the latter. All other factors showed insignificant differences between the two groups. Thus it would seem that there is some form of linguistic deficiency affecting verbal intelligence test performance in an appreciable proportion of backward readers.

In conclusion, it would appear that the relationship of reading to the intellectual abilities is not well understood, and much further investigation is required to determine what particular types of intellectual process are essential in learning to read. Clearly some degree of g and v are necessary for normal learning. But in certain cases there may seem to be a normal degree of g, in that ability is adequate to perform the noegenetic operations which are the main feature of so many intelligence tests, verbal and non-verbal. At the same time there is marked disability in learning to read. It may be that the abstraction and generalization involved in verbal concept formation constitute the essential types of intellectual process involved in reading. Further experimental study is needed to substantiate this. Moreover, it is necessary to discover whether some general ability or disability in concept formation is involved; or whether only certain particular types of conceptual reasoning are operating, such as those concerned with the abstraction and generalization of characteristics of visual and auditory configurations, the association of visuo-spatial and linguistic sequences and the apprehension of sequential meaning.

The exact nature of the verbal abilities essential to reading is not clear. Although it would appear that in some severely backward readers verbal processes in general are impaired, yet certain types of language function may be more affected than others. Ingram's work suggests that these may vary in different cases. Similarly with the visual abilities: in some cases analysis of complex forms may be deficient, in others it is the directional component of spatially extended forms which causes confusion. It seems probable that many severely backward readers are deficient in the performance of both these processes. But again the nature of the basic ability involved is doubtful.

CHAPTER VI

THE EFFECT OF MOTIVATIONAL AND EMOTIONAL FACTORS ON LEARNING TO READ

(1) CONDITIONS IN THE SOCIAL ENVIRONMENT

Difficulties in learning to read are often associated with children's social background. However, we are concerned here not so much with social factors as such, as with their relationship to cognitive and motivational differences in children which appear to affect reading achievement. Thus differences in socio-economic status would seem to be related both to differences in intelligence, knowledge and linguistic competence; and also with variations in motivation. These variations stem at least in part from the different types of parent–child relationship occurring more frequently in certain social classes than in others.

One of the few facts connected with variation in reading achievement on which there is little disagreement is that it is highest in the upper *socio-economic classes*, and decreases steadily as social class declines. This is well illustrated in Eisenberg's (1966) distribution of reading achievement (see Fig. 6), in which socio-economic status is lowest in the ordinary schools in the Metropolitan area and highest in the independent schools. In the three areas, the percentage of children retarded by two or more years in reading was 0, 3 and 28 respectively. Similar data have been obtained in British studies. Kellmer Pringle *et al.* (1966) grouped the reading achievements of 11,000 7-year-old children into three categories, good, medium and poor, on the basis of their scores on the Southgate test of word recognition. It then appeared that 7.1 per cent of those with parents in Occupational Classes I and II (Registrar General's classification), 18.9 per cent in Class III and 26.9 per cent in Classes IV and V were poor readers. Douglas (1964) found significant differences in word recognition and sentence completion among over 5000 8-year-old children between those in upper-middle, lower-middle, upper-working and lower-working classes. These differences increased slightly in the same children by 11 years, the middle-class children improving more than the working class.

Goodacre (1967) obtained a somewhat different result with 3000 children in infant schools, on the N.F.E.R. test of sentence completion. The mean test score of children in lower working-class

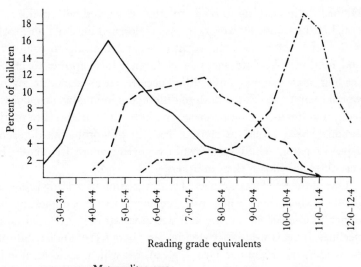

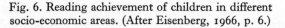

————— Metropolitan area
— — — — Surrounding suburban area
— · — · — Independent schools in Metropolitan area

Fig. 6. Reading achievement of children in different socio-economic areas. (After Eisenberg, 1966, p. 6.)

areas was significantly lower than that of all other children. But there was no significant difference between children in middle-class city schools and those in upper working-class schools. However, for such young children a written sentence completion test might not give very reliable results.

It should be noted that the effects of differences in socio-economic status are so generally accepted as sometimes to be exaggerated, even by teachers. Thus Goodacre (1968) found that teachers in infant schools expected that middle-class children would reach a substantially higher level of reading achievement than would working-class children, whereas as we noted the difference in tested achievement was sometimes small. The teachers over-estimated the reading ability of middle-class children and under-estimated that of working-class children.

There is a variety of factors associated with differences in socio-economic status which may affect school achievement, including achievement in reading. Wiseman (1964), studying the variations in different areas of Manchester of various indices of social dis-organization such as overcrowding, infant mortality, illegitimacy, etc., found significant correlations of 0.3–0.7 between these and reading achievement. However, these were lower than those ob-tained in London by Burt (1937), indicating a decrease of differences in the effects of poverty indices since that date. Though extreme poverty, malnutrition and disorganization in the home still exist, and may have a direct effect in depriving children of the physical energy essential for adequate school achievement, other factors in the home such as maternal care have begun to assume more im-portance (Wiseman, 1964). It should be noted that Wiseman found 'lack of home care' to be associated with absence of superior at-tainment in reading rather than with backwardness. However, Ingram & Reid (1956) obtained a high incidence of broken homes and parental disharmony in seventy-eight cases of severe reading disability, although the proportion of cases in social Classes I and II was relatively higher than that in Classes IV and V.

There may be genetic factors which vary in different social classes and which affect reading achievement, of which the principal is *intelligence*. There is little doubt that the average intelligence of the lower social classes is less than that of the higher. There is of course extensive disagreement as to whether, and to what extent, these differences are the consequence of genetic endowment or of environmental pressures, or of both; and it is impossible in this book to discuss this controversy. We have noted that some associa-tion is commonly found between intelligence and reading ability.

However, the evidence as to the association between class differences in intelligence and in reading achievement is somewhat more doubtful. Thus the investigation of Morris (1959) of over 7000 Kent school children aged 7–11 years gave a correlation of 0.68 between socio-economic class of schools and children's performance on the Watts–Vernon sentence completion test. But there was an even higher correlation of 0.71 between socio-economic class and non-verbal intelligence test scores; and when reading test scores had been adjusted for differences in intelligence, the correlation of reading with socio-economic class decreased to the non-significant figure of 0.20. Douglas (1964) showed that the variation with social class of scores on reading tests and on a non-verbal intelligence test were very similar. Morris, in a later study (1966), investigated three schools with high average reading scores in socio-economic catchment areas classed I or II, and two schools with low scores in areas classed V. A group of 100 children from these schools who were 'poor' readers was compared with a group of 100 who were classed as 'good' readers. The majority of those in the first group (80 per cent) were children of manual workers; whereas 63 per cent of those in the second group were children of non-manual workers. Again, the mean score of the latter on the non-verbal intelligence test was much higher than that of the former. But the overlap was considerable; many of the poor readers had high non-verbal intelligence. Lovell & Woolsey (1964) studied the performance on the Watt–Vernon reading test and the N.F.E.R. non-verbal intelligence test of 1800 children aged 14–15 years. Among those with I.Q.s of 90 or above who were backward readers with R.Q.s below 80, 8.9 per cent were in Classes I and II, as compared with 11.1 per cent of children of these classes in the total group; whereas in Classes III, IV and V the proportion of backward readers exceeded the proportions belonging to these classes in the total sample. It appeared therefore that lower social class was associated with backwardness in reading independently of intelligence. But Lovell & Woolsey considered low social class to be a pre-disposing factor rather than a causal factor in reading backwardness.

Clearly homes in different socio-economic classes show marked *cultural differences* which are likely to affect the children's linguistic ability, and this in turn is related to reading achievement. We noted in Ch. IV that even if the child's early speech developed spontaneously, his vocabulary and more complex language patterns were closely related to the language of the adults with whom he was in contact. The differences of language patterns between middle- and working-class parents were dramatically described and emphasized by Bernstein (1958). He hypothesized that working-class parents employ a 'public language', consisting mainly of short grammatically simple sentences, often unfinished. Syntax is rigid, sentences are mainly in the active voice, there are few subordinate clauses, adjectives and adverbs are limited. Phrases are often repeated, and strung together in a disconnected manner by conjunctions. There are no overtones of finer meaning, though these may be indicated in part by gestures and intonational pattern. By contrast, the 'formal language' of the middle classes is not only more subtle and complex, but also more logical and individual. Thus middle-class children become aware of a wide range of interpretations, meanings and precise discriminations in speech. This is the language mainly used by school teachers and in school books other than very early ones. The working-class child is not only unfamiliar with this language, and finds it difficult to understand; but he may even feel that it threatens his basic ideas. Bernstein himself showed that boys of 15–18 years, with unskilled and semi-skilled parents, scored within the normal range on a non-verbal intelligence test, Progressive Matrices, but were in most cases below normal on the Mill Hill Vocabulary test.

Again, Whipple (1961) found that American children of low socio-economic status employed in their spontaneous utterances a smaller and less variable range of words than did children of higher status; and used words which differed from those considered normal for 6–7-year-old children and from those appearing in these children's reading books. The children of low socio-economic status used shorter sentences, often incomplete; fewer compound and complex sentences; and more ungrammatical constructions.

7-2

Deutsch (1965) found that Negro and white children of low socio-economic status were particularly deficient in the more advanced uses of language, in abstract categorizing. As the level of language complexity increased, the negative effects of social disadvantage were enhanced. Moreover, these effects appeared to be cumulative; they were more marked in children of 10–11 years than in those of 6–7 years. A similar accumulating deficit on the Illinois Test of Psycholinguistic Abilities was found by Schwartz, Deutsch & Weissman (1967) in young socially disadvantaged children who were not given 'enriched' schooling, by comparison with those who did receive such schooling. Jensen (1967) also noted the inability of the severely culturally deprived, such as many American Negro children, to use language in conceptual reasoning; they were inferior even in the verbal labelling of objects.

Newson & Newson (1968) showed that it was not only the linguistic structure of speech which varied in different social classes, but also the manner in which speech was employed. They observed that conversation between mothers and 4-year-old children played a vital part in furthering the children's intellectual development. Such conversation did occur in all social classes. But middle-class mothers employed speech to a greater extent than did working-class mothers in controlling their children, explaining, persuading and reasoning with them, and formulating general principles of behaviour such as: 'If you tell lies, no one will ever believe you.' The working-class mothers, especially those in Occupational Class V, more often gave brief specific commands and prohibitions and reinforced these with smacking when the children disobeyed. Therefore the middle-class children were better able than the working-class children to become aware of the use of language as an integral factor in understanding and directing their behaviour in accordance with general concepts of socially accepted behaviour. This in turn would tend to bring home to them the nature and value of verbal conceptualization.

There are other cultural characteristics and uses of language which may affect reading. Fraser (1959) obtained correlations for 12-year-old children between school achievement and the education of parents and their reading of books and magazines, which were in general greater than were correlations with I.Q. Malmquist (1958) found a significant relationship between backwardness in reading and the education of both father and mother. The fathers and mothers of poor readers had in most cases received only elementary education, whereas those of a high proportion of good readers had reached matriculation standard. Morris (1966) showed very marked differences between good and poor readers in the number of adult books and newspapers in the home, and in the frequency of parental membership of public libraries. The parents' education and reading are of course likely to affect the type of language they use.

Another influential factor is parents' reading aloud to their children. Thus Durkin (1966) found that mothers of children who could already read by the time they entered school at 6 years read aloud to their children and read much to themselves. Often the children had been given books. This tends to happen more frequently in middle-class than in working-class families. Again, Newson & Newson (1968) found that middle-class parents, fathers as well as mothers, more often told their children stories at bedtime than did working-class parents.

The deleterious effects of various environmental factors on intelligence and on school achievement were studied by P. E. Vernon (1965, 1969), in an investigation of the variations in performance of intelligence and of other tests. Not only were differences in socio-economic status of British boys investigated, but also the much greater degrees of *deprivation* experienced by boys living in other cultures, Jamaican, African, Canadian Indian and Eskimo. The information on deprivation was obtained through interviews with the boys. It was quite clear that both intelligence (g) and verbal ability (v) were lower among these children, all of them to a greater or less extent economically and culturally deprived, than among British children. However, some groups, for instance the Jamaicans and Uganda Africans, were relatively less retarded in spelling and on memory tests than on tests of reasoning and vocabulary, because they had been drilled in rote learning at school.

Vernon analysed and assessed the following environmental factors as contributing to good intelligence and, in some cases, educational achievement.

(1) Reasonable satisfaction of biological needs.

(2) Stimulating environment and encouragement of exploration and experiment.

(3) Linguistic stimulation, encouragement of linguistic and conceptual development.

(4) Demanding but democratic family atmosphere, showing tolerance and lack of rigidity, and emphasizing self-control, responsibility and interest in school work.

(5) Cultural stimulation in the home; parents' education; books, etc. in the home; parents' cooperation with the school and aspirations for the child.

(6) Regular and prolonged schooling, also emphasizing individual initiative and responsibility and discovery methods rather than rote learning.

(7) Wide and adventurous leisure activities.

There was a general correspondence between the total number of adverse conditions and the inferiority of test performance, though particular factors affected some test performances more than others. The cultural stimulation supplied by the home was most closely related to all-round ability. But in children like the Uganda Africans from homes where little English was spoken, or where it was largely a form of pidgin English, as with many of the Jamaican children, all tests involving the use and understanding of language were badly performed. However, performance on the Piaget type of test was affected also. And it was difficult to differentiate the effects of different adverse factors at all precisely, since in most cases so many were operating. In all these groups the majority of children were living in conditions of insecurity and want.

Werner, Simonian & Smith (1967) carried out an investigation of the reading achievement and performance on Thurstone's tests of Primary Mental Abilities of 10–11-year-old children living in Hawaii. Many of these, and especially those of low socio-economic status, were brought up in homes in which pidgin English was spoken. The children of low socio-economic status were inferior to those of higher status in reading achievement and in most of the Primary Mental Abilities. A correlation of 0.71 was obtained between reading grade and the total score on the Primary Mental Abilities tests; and of 0.69 between reading grade and V (verbal ability). Lower correlations were obtained with P (perceptual speed) and S (space); and with Bender test scores. Thus Werner *et al.* concluded that when there were gross language deficiencies, these produced much more effect on reading than did perceptual deficiencies. However, it is possible that in this group also poor living conditions were partly responsible for reading backwardness.

Jensen (1967) considered that children's intelligence was not greatly affected by environmental factors within the normal range; though their effect on school achievement was greater. But severely adverse environmental circumstances, such as those suffered by many American Negro children, caused considerable impairment of intelligence, and even more of school achievement. Their cultural deprivation particularly affected their language abilities.

(2) EFFECTS ON CHILDREN'S MOTIVATION OF THE HOME ENVIRONMENT

Up to this point we have considered the relationships between environmental conditions and school achievement, particularly in reading, as if the effect of adverse conditions on school progress were a direct one. And so indeed it may be in the case of great poverty and malnutrition. The children are too weak, too lacking in energy and too prone to disease, to be able to work well. But except in circumstances of such physiological deprivation, the main effect of environmental factors may be upon the children's own cognitive abilities and on their *motivation to learn*. Of course poverty, hunger and insecurity impair motivation, as well as physical energy. No individual whose mind is dominated by craving for food or by fear of danger, illness or homelessness can take much interest in school activities, or make much effort to work hard.

Though we are inclined to believe that the effects of poverty described by Burt are no longer operative in this country, they may in fact be more persistent than we suppose. Indeed, recent reports by 'Shelter' confirm this.

But in default of these circumstances, or even in addition to them, as in some of the children studied in P. E. Vernon's investigations, there are many aspects of home life, and particularly of the relationship between parents and children, which may stimulate or inhibit school progress through their effects on the children's motivation to work and learn. One factor here would appear to be the closeness of the relationship between parents and children. The inferiority in reading achievement in the lower social classes may be due in part to the fact that the parents seem less close to their children, and do less to stimulate them to learn to read, than do parents in the higher social classes. Thus Milner (1951) found that among a group of 6-year-old children, the majority of those who showed the best language ability came from middle-class homes, and of those with the poorest language ability from lower-class homes. The difference was due partly to the lack of books and of reading aloud in the latter, and of opportunity for frequent conversation with adults in adequate speech patterns. But also the middle-class children had closer, warmer and more affectionate relations with their parents, who were permissive and encouraging to them.

The significance of *parental encouragement* was perhaps first noted by Fraser (1959) in relation to the general school achievement of 12-year-old Scottish children. She obtained a correlation of 0.66 between parental encouragement and school achievement, a higher correlation than with any other aspect of home life. However, parental encouragement was estimated by the teachers; and it is possible therefore that these estimates were affected by the teachers' observations of the children's school behaviour. Thus Goodacre (1968) found that infant teachers tended to derive estimates of differences in home background from the children's desire to learn to read, and from whether or not the parents provided their children with books. Their actual contacts with the parents were rather slight. There was also the tendency, noted on p. 97, to over-estimate the attributes of middle-class homes and under-estimate those of working-class homes.

Douglas (1964) also studied the effects of parental interest and encouragement, though the same doubts must be felt as to his findings since these were based on teachers' assessment of parental interest. However, the assessments had some objective basis, in, for instance, the frequency of visits paid to the school, by fathers as well as mothers; and general and medical care, and conscientious-ness in taking children to clinics when recommended to do so. The degree of interest was highest in upper middle-class parents, and decreased steadily down to the lower working class. But also, within each social class, the children with the most interested parents had the highest test scores; and this difference was greater for reading and arithmetic than for non-verbal intelligence. Indeed, there was an overlap in score between the children of the least interested parents in a particular class, and the children of the most interested parents in the class below it. Moreover, the children of the most interested parents improved their scores between the ages of 8 and 11 years, whereas children of the least interested parents did not. When the relationships of test scores to standard of home and size of family were allowed for, the relationship to parental interest was still considerable.

Kellmer Pringle, Butler & Davie (1966) attempted to make estimates of parental interest as objective as possible by asking head teachers: 'Have the parents taken the initiative to discuss the child, even briefly, with you or any member of your teaching staff?' The children were then classified according as to whether their parents had 'approached' or 'not approached' the teachers. The percentage of 'approached' among the 11,000 7-year-olds de-creased from 71 in Class I to 46 in Class V. Fourteen per cent of parents of poor readers fell into the 'approached' class; 41 per cent of medium readers; and 45 per cent of good readers. Moreover, in each social class there was a higher proportion of good readers in the 'approached' than in the 'not approached' class, although the differences were not significant in every social class. Incidentally, it should be realized that failure to make these approaches may be due in part to lack of interest and encouragement on the part of the teachers, probably more towards working-class than middle-class parents. But as we have seen parental interest and approaches are not governed solely by social class membership.

Douglas (1964) also investigated directly the relationship between parental interest and encouragement, and children's motivation and application to their school work. The teachers were asked to estimate whether the children were hard workers, average workers or poor workers. The frequency of hard workers varied with social class, from 26 per cent of upper middle-class children to 7 per cent of lower working-class children. Among children of interested parents, 70 per cent were hard workers, as against 33 per cent of those with uninterested parents. However, clearly a fair proportion of the latter did work hard in the absence of parental encouragement. Hard workers scored higher on the tests, and especially on those of school achievement, than did less hard workers. Moreover, the former improved their test performance between 8 and 11 years; whereas the poor workers decreased in score, whether they received parental encouragement or not. However, a later study (Douglas, Ross & Simpson, 1968) of some of the same children at 15 years showed that hard workers with interested parents had improved their scores since 11 years, whereas those with uninterested parents had deteriorated.

It is generally considered that reading achievement is increased by strong *achievement motivation.** Thus Zimmerman & Allebrand (1965) compared the Thematic Apperception test stories of 9–10-year-old backward readers, retarded by at least two years, with those of good readers. The stories of the latter stressed achievement and effort in work; but these themes were absent from the stories of the backward readers. Undoubtedly the motive to achieve is related to parental stress on achievement; and such encourage-

* It has been argued by critics of the author's book, *Human Motivation* (Vernon, 1969), that there is considerable doubt as to the existence of achievement motivation as an independent entity. This objection may be valid. Nevertheless, the term may be employed to refer to a class of behaviour which is frequent in and characteristic of Western civilization.

ment is more frequent in the higher than in the lower social classes. But parents of children with high achievement motivation, while advocating achievement and independence and rewarding children when they show these, are also permissive rather than authoritarian in their discipline. In other words, the child is attracted rather than forced by pressure to achieve; and this is reinforced by his identification with his parents and his desire to be like them. Thus if the parents are themselves well-educated and successful in life, the children are further stimulated to achieve by this identification. Moreover, educated parents tend to show greater encouragement to their children to work well in school than do less educated parents (Douglas, Ross & Simpson, 1968). Himmelweit (1963) compared the attitudes to school work of middle-class and working-class boys of 13–14 years, and found that the former were more concerned than were the latter with their school achievement and with higher educational and vocational prospects. They were more responsible, and possessed a higher and firmer system of values. Although the middle-class parents were more concerned than were the working-class with their sons' progress, and exerted more supervision over their work and leisure activities, they were also closer to their children in personal relationships. Any tendency to increase of anxiety in the children through parental pressure was relieved by this contact, and the feeling that they could talk to their parents about their aspirations and difficulties. The working-class children, less often urged by their parents to achieve in school, were left largely to fend for themselves without parental guidance. However, in this respect 'upwardly mobile' working-class parents were more like middle-class than other working-class parents. Now it is true that the interactions between parents and children are likely to be somewhat different at 13–14 years than at the age at which children begin to learn to read. But the findings of Milner (see p. 104) emphasized the importance of these interactions.

Further evidence was supplied in a study by Kent & Davis (1957). On the basis of interviews with the parents of 8-year-old children, they divided the parents into four classes: demanding, over-anxious, unconcerned and normal. These differences were unrelated to social class. The children of demanding parents, who put much pressure on the child to succeed, possessed higher Stanford–Binet I.Q.s than did those of normal parents, and tended to be higher on the WISC Verbal than Performance scale; but they were not significantly higher on the WISC mean I.Q. nor on reading test scores. It would appear that parental demandingness, which often caused the children to be emotionally disturbed and over-anxious to succeed, did lead to a greater development in verbal reasoning; but this did not affect reading. The children of over-anxious parents, though not significantly inferior generally to the normals, were somewhat deficient on the practical side; WISC Performance I.Q.s were lower than Verbal. Finally, the children of unconcerned parents, though too few in number to give entirely valid results, were inferior to the normals on the Stanford–Binet I.Q. and in reading age, which averaged only 6.4 years. The majority showed signs of emotional disturbance, which appeared in apathy, lack of effort and of spontaneity. Highfield & Pinsent (1952), in a study of difficult school children of 6–9 years, found that children of rigid punitive parents tended to be restless and distractible, and to need control in school. The children of lax indifferent parents were apathetic and listless, and required stimulation rather than control.

Other studies have indicated that children with relatively good verbal ability may have parents who afford them much verbal stimulation, but at the same time may be demanding and over-protective. On the other hand, children with parents who stimulate independence tend to have higher non-verbal than verbal ability. Bing (1963) carried out a study of the upbringing of and maternal behaviour towards 10-year-old children in two groups. In the first, verbal ability, as measured by Thurstone's Primary Mental Abilities tests, was significantly higher than non-verbal; in the second group, the reverse. Relatively higher verbal ability was associated with verbal encouragement in early childhood, a plentiful supply of books, punishment for poor school achievement, restriction on freedom and some degree of over-protectiveness. The mothers, when present while their children were being tested, tried to help the children, encouraged and put pressure on them to succeed, but discouraged them when they failed. Higher non-verbal ability was associated with opportunity for exploration and experiment. However, we cannot infer that the demandingness of the former parents and their emphasis on dependence necessarily promote good verbal achievement, including reading; or whether it is merely that the child is more proficient in verbal than in practical activities, practical ability being promoted by inculcation of independence. P. E. Vernon (1969) obtained some evidence that poor performance on tests of practical ability, such as Kohs Blocks, was associated with lack of encouragement of initiative in the home, which seemed to affect the capacity to act purposefully in performing such tests. But performance on purely perceptual tests such as Gottschaldt's embedded figures was unrelated to home circumstances, though deficient in some cultures. The causes of this deficiency were not clear.

However, it would seem that there is good evidence for the effect on reading achievement of lack of stimulation in the home. Again, Collins (1961) studied a group of primary school backward readers in whose homes maternal and cultural conditions were generally poor. The children lacked curiosity and vivacity, and interest in their work; and there was a general low level of value on culture and aspiration for success.

(3) MOTIVATION AND THE SCHOOL ENVIRONMENT

It would thus appear that interest and desire to achieve play an important part in stimulating children to learn to read. Those who inevitably find it difficult, through lack of intelligence, linguistic ability or favourable cultural influences in the home, may require *special stimulation in the school*. It is currently maintained that *free activities* in the school appealing to the child's natural interest, and methods of *discovery* and experiment, are more stimulating than are more formal methods emphasizing rote learning, in that the former improve the children's initiative, interest in school work and effort to learn. Indeed, we noted (see p. 102) that P. E. Vernon considered the former methods to constitute one of the factors favourable to intellectual development and educational achievement. Such methods appear to be employed successfully in the new discovery techniques of learning mathematics and science. On the other hand, their use in teaching reading would seem to be more difficult. Once the child has mastered basic reading skill, clearly he can discover much through reading. But in the early stages, there would appear to be little room for experiment or original thought, since the scope of these is limited by the necessity for learning printed letter shapes and their phonic associations. Thus Southgate (1970) considered that discovery methods were inappropriate to the teaching of reading because the irregularity of English spelling prevented children from generalizing phoneme pronunciation (as for instance from 'mat' to 'mate').* However, more regular schemes of grapheme–phoneme correspondence, such as those of the i.t.a. and Gattegno's *Words in Colour* (Gattegno, 1962) gave better opportunity for discovery. Indeed, it has been noted that one advantage of the i.t.a. is that children can learn from it themselves, with less instruction from the teacher than is necessary with the ordinary alphabet.

Though Southgate (1970) advocated the use of a carefully structured method of teaching reading such as she described, the results of experimental enquiries into the relative efficacy of *formal* and *informal methods* have been somewhat variable. Morris (1959) obtained a correlation of 0.4 between reading achievement in children of 7–11 years, and the employment of a formal approach and systematic instruction in reading in the infant school. But later (1966) she stated that this association was affected by other factors and was not significant. Anderson, Byron & Dixon (1956) showed that the average age of learning to read was lower in a school which employed early teaching of reading by formal methods than in a school which laid more emphasis on informal methods and encouraged individual activities. However, once the children in the latter school had learnt to read, they soon overcame their initial delay, and caught up those in the former. Gardner (1942, 1950)

* But see p. 58.

also found that children taught by progressive methods were able to read as well as those taught by formal methods at 9–10 years. Kellmer Pringle & Reeves (1968) compared the reading achievement of children in the second, third and fourth years at two junior schools, one in which they received a traditional formal education and the other in which a progressive approach was employed. Allowing for differences in intelligence between the two groups, there were no significant differences on the Neale Reading test. Curiously enough, the most able children profited more by the formal approach than by the informal.

Lovell (1963) gave the Vernon Graded Word Reading test and the N.F.E.R. non-verbal intelligence test to over 1300 children of 10–11 years in 11 matched pairs of schools. Each pair contained one school employing formal teaching methods with the traditional curriculum, and one school using informal teaching encouraging the children's interests and creative activities. There was no significant difference in average reading achievement between the children in the two types of school. But the spread of achievement was greater in the schools with formal teaching; 14 per cent of the children had R.Q.s below 80, as against 9.5 per cent in the informal schools. Thus it would seem that the amount of backwardness was greater in the schools using formal methods. Even if early reading teaching does not readily lend itself to informal teaching, this teaching may stimulate interest which may produce at least an adequate level of reading achievement. Morrison & McIntyre (1969) stated that studies had shown that children preferred the use of discovery methods, and were therefore presumably better motivated. These methods were less effective in the acquisition of routine skills than in more complex tasks where the employment of ideas is important. Nevertheless, the development of spoken language can well involve experiment and discovery, and in turn benefit reading.

The children's motivation may be particularly important in connection with what has been called '*reading readiness*'. It would appear that readiness to begin formal reading instruction depends in the first place on the child's level of development in conceptual reasoning, linguistic ability and visuo-spatial perception. We have presented evidence in previous chapters to show that a certain competence in performing these cognitive processes is essential, and without it children may experience great difficulty in learning to read. Indeed, it seems likely that many children do not attain this competence during their first year at school, and would profit from the postponement of formal reading teaching till the second year. Moreover, they would benefit from increased opportunity for free activity. However, children of superior intelligence and linguistic ability may well be able to understand and learn from formal reading teaching as soon as they enter school. This depends also on previous experience, especially in linguistic activities and in the use of books. We noted that Durkin (1966) found that children who could already read when they first went to school were accustomed to the use of books; and that their parents had read aloud to them and sometimes actually taught them.

Thus undoubtedly children vary considerably in the age at which they are ready to learn to read, and it may be difficult to estimate their readiness. In some schools in the U.S.A. children are given tests of 'reading readiness', adequate performance of which is claimed to demonstrate that the children possess the cognitive capacities necessary to enable them to learn to read. But these tests have not been standardized for British children. Goodacre (1970a) pointed out that their correlations with subsequent reading achievement were only of the order of 0.4–0.6. Indeed, tests other than those of actual letter discrimination and recognition appear to have little predictive value.

Moreover, it would seem that readiness depends also on the children's motivation, their interest in reading and their desire to learn, as is generally recognized by English infant teachers (Goodacre, 1970a). Interest may develop only slowly in those from un-cultured homes with uninterested parents. Desire to learn may be created by the example of other children; and in this connection Stauffer (1968) has suggested that group teaching may be superior to individual teaching in that children in a group stimulate one another. But in infant classes in poor neighbourhoods, particularly in the slums of large towns, the majority of children may have comparatively little desire to learn, and thus the effects of social conformity and imitation may be negative rather than positive.

Another factor of considerable importance is the child's capacity to attend to what the teacher says and does. Jensen (1967) noted that socially disadvantaged children were often unable to focus and sustain their attention on the teacher, and quickly became distracted and restless. He considered that middle-class children developed the capacity for sustained attention through their interaction with the mother, through observing and responding to what she did and said. This had not occurred in children who had not experienced a close individual relationship with the mother, as was frequent with socially disadvantaged children. Moreover, their capacity for attending might even deteriorate during their first year at school. They did not really understand what the teacher was saying and doing. The tasks she set were too difficult for them and they were unable to perform them successfully. Failure was negatively reinforcing, and the children became more and more confused, inattentive and discouraged, and might develop an aversion for school activities.

Clearly therefore readiness to learn to read may depend as much on the teacher's capacity to stimulate interest as on the children's cognitive abilities, and her task of arousing and maintaining interest as well as giving instruction may be exceptionally severe. She may find it best to postpone the difficult processes of phonic analysis, which require more concentration and energy than does simple look-and-say. The slow start in the early stages of reading which is almost inevitable in these circumstances may produce an apparent initial backwardness. But this is greatly preferable to a widespread failure among children who are not motivated to respond to this instruction, and therefore simply do not grasp what they are required to do. As we have noted, such failure has a negative reinforcing effect, decreasing positive motivation still further and even producing resistance.

It has been established by Morris (1966) beyond a peradventure that reading achievement is related to the *skill of the teacher*; and that children taught by untrained, inexperienced and unskilful teachers tend to be especially backward in reading. Now teaching skill obviously involves the knowledge of correct methods in all their details and variations and the ability to communicate these. But is some additional capacity necessary to stimulate and motivate? Perhaps this is relatively unimportant for normal, lively, curious and reasonably intelligent children. But for the apathetic and uninterested, the anxious and over-protected, constant encouragement and stimulation may be necessary, and above all the capacity to make reading materials and activities interesting. Teachers may regard these as truisms, but if as we noted reading is difficult to make the subject of discovery and experiment, it may not be easy to create interest.

A study by Sampson (1969) showed that teachers were well aware of the importance of incentives in learning to read. One teacher, fortunately exceptional, wrote: 'My children are not really interested in anything.' The majority thought that most children were eager to learn, but that success was the most important factor in encouraging effort, and that children were greatly disheartened when they failed. Thus encouragement and praise, even of small efforts, were important. But also frequent attempts were made to appeal to children's individual interests. Additional ways of stimulating interest were through provision of attractive books and of subsidiary games, for instance of word matching. The value of these for severely backward readers was strongly emphasized by Stott (1964). Morris (1966) found that the selection and supply of books and other reading materials was most inadequate in junior school classes in which there were many backward readers.

Several teachers in Sampson's enquiry noted the importance of good social relations between teacher and children. The ability to establish sympathetic, friendly and understanding relationships may be one of the most significant factors in teaching skill. Obviously this is more difficult in large classes of children, especially if many are apathetic and unforthcoming. Thus Morris (1966) showed that the junior school teachers of backward readers were less skilled in breaking up classes into small suitably occupied groups and in giving individual attention where needed.

Yet clearly the teacher must herself possess the ability to encourage and stimulate. Harvey *et al.* (1966) found that with teachers who were flexible in their ideas, perceptive of the children's needs and warm in their relations with them, the children were significantly more interested, active and higher in achievement than with teachers who were relatively rigid, authoritarian and intolerant. Washburne & Heil (cited by Morrison & McIntyre, 1969) showed that the interaction between teachers and children varied with the characteristics of the children as well as those of the teachers. In general teachers who were warm but also business-like and orderly in their treatment of the children were more effective than those who were conscientious but anxious. Children who in themselves were hard workers did comparatively well with all types of teacher; those who were docile conformers worked best with warm, exuberant and independent teachers. Children, however, who tended to oppose authority, though on the whole they performed badly whatever the type of teaching, were more responsive to the business-like and orderly than to the others. However, as Morrison & McIntyre pointed out, we need to know far more about the effects of social interaction between teachers and children, and how different types of children are best motivated. And if more information were available, then it might be possible to train teachers more effectively to exercise the most suitable treatment.

(4) EMOTIONAL MALADJUSTMENT

It is often found that children who are emotionally maladjusted are generally backward in their school work, including reading. Thus Chazan (cited by Sampson, 1966) found that when 9-year-old children were assessed by means of the Bristol Social Adjustment Guide, poor readers showed on the average many more signs of emotional maladjustment than did good readers. In the survey by Douglas (1964, see p. 105), children of 8 years reported by parents, school medical officers, etc. to show signs of maladjusted behaviour had poor scores on tests of achievement, including reading. Moreover, they tended to deteriorate between 8 and

11 years. They were often poor workers, lacking in concentration. Silverman, Fite & Mosher (1959) found that 35 children from a group of 151 children aged 8–10 years and of normal intelligence but retarded in reading by 1½–2 years, exhibited many emotional problems. Thus it would appear that about 25 per cent of the original group were emotionally maladjusted; and many of these were backward in all their school work. Indeed, it is probable that general school backwardness is more frequent in emotionally maladjusted children than is backwardness in reading alone.

It cannot be concluded that backwardness in reading is *caused* in all these cases by emotional maladjustment leading to lack of motivation and of the concentration and effort necessary to learn to read. Children who find learning difficult and hence fall behind their companions – still more those who fail to learn altogether – are not unnaturally frustrated, anxious and depressed by their failure. Hence even if the initial difficulty is due to some quite other cause, it is liable sooner or later to produce emotional disorders. Indeed, Ablewhite (1967) considered that most children are eager to learn in the early stages of reading, yet they may develop personality problems by their third year in the junior school if they have not learnt by then. Gates (1968) estimated that although about 75 per cent of cases of severe reading disability exhibited maladjustment – and the more serious the disability, the greater the maladjustment – yet in only a quarter of these cases was the maladjustment the cause of the reading disability. In an unselected school sample, these cases were small in number. Rabinovitch & Ingram (1968) stated that although reading retardation might be caused by emotional blocking in some cases, these were less common than was formerly supposed. Such cases were rarely totally illiterate, but could make some attack on words (Rabinovitch *et al.* 1954). Letter and word reversals, so common in many severely backward readers, did not appear in these cases, and there was no impairment of conceptual thinking. The basic capacity to read was intact; but it was not effectively utilized, and was blocked by lack of motivation and by anxiety, depression and negativism.

Malmquist (1958) found that although 40 per cent of the poor readers in his large unselected sample of children were reported by their mothers to exhibit 'nervous symptoms' at the pre-school age, only 23 per cent were reported by the teacher, at the end of the first year in school, to exhibit such symptoms. He concluded that only in the latter cases could the 'nervous symptoms' have contributed to the reading disability. On the other hand, a number of poor readers who lacked these symptoms did show deficiencies in personality qualities such as lack of self-confidence, persistence, concentration and emotional stability.

Numerous studies have demonstrated the frequency of *anxiety* and *depression* in certain backward readers. Silverman, Fite & Mosher (1959) found them to occur in about two-thirds of their emotionally maladjusted cases. Mussen (1965) considered that ability to learn to read was retarded by anxiety, especially in so far as this arose in more difficult and abstract tasks. However, once children had learnt to read, they might tend to withdraw from their anxiety and take refuge in reading. Scarborough, Hindsman & Harman (1961) found this to occur in highly anxious children of good intelligence. But those of low intelligence could not seek such a refuge. Other investigators have discovered *aggression* as well as anxiety in backward readers. Douglas *et al.* (1968) found that 15-year-old children assessed by parents and teachers as showing symptoms of emotional maladjustment scored less well than normal children on tests of school achievement; and the greater the number of symptoms of disturbance, the lower the scores. But there were two contrasted types: the 'nervous' who were well behaved and hard working but nevertheless poor in attainment; and the aggressive who were troublesome and negligent in work. Stewart (1950) compared two groups of maladjusted children of 8–12 years, the first of whom were retarded in reading, while the second was superior. The average difference in reading age was 2 years 4 months. The children in both groups were basically insecure, but the backward readers were more aggressive and self-assertive than were the good readers, who retreated into the phantasy world of reading. Spache (1957) showed that about 4 per cent of a group of children retarded in reading by 1–2 years were overtly aggressive and ego-defensive, as indicated by the Rosenzweig Picture Frustration test; aggressive both against adult authority figures and also against other children. By contrast, 10 per cent were below normal in aggression and showed excessive acceptance of self-blame.

Gates (1968) listed a number of conditions which might produce resistance to learning to read and blocking of the capacity to learn. These included: apparent indifference of parents or teachers to the child's welfare, causing feelings of neglect and insecurity; apparent hostility, if teachers or parents reacted by scolding, ridicule, encouragement of sibling rivalry, etc.; apparent anxiety of teachers or parents, indicated by constant fussing over the child's progress; over-protectiveness such that the child did not learn to work for himself; conflicts between parents, or between teachers and parents. But although teachers by their treatment of the child may aggravate tension and resistance, it seems probable that in most cases the primary cause is some inadequacy in *parental relationships*. Crane (cited by Bond & Tinker, 1957) found that 21 out of 23 backward readers referred to a clinic as problem cases suffered from disturbed parent–child relationships. Fabian (1955) showed that there was a high incidence of backwardness in reading in children referred to clinics whose parents were deprived, distraught or emotionally ill, and indeed often neurotic or even psychotic. Ingram & Reid (1956) found that in 24 per cent of 78 cases of severe reading backwardness the parents had received psychiatric help or were considered to need it. Ingram (1963a) stated that a high proportion of children retarded in speech development had a history of neglect by or separation from their parents in later infancy. Silverman, Fite & Mosher (1959) obtained evidence of frequent disturbed or deprived relationships with the mother during infancy, the father being indifferent. The parents were often maladjusted themselves, and marital discord was frequent.

But less severely disordered parents may adopt attitudes towards their children which give rise to emotional maladjustment. The type of disorder, aggressive or anxious and withdrawn, may bear some relationship to the type of parental treatment; though probably innate temperamental differences are involved also. Stewart (1950) considered that his aggressively maladjusted backward readers were directing hostility against parents who were either hostile to them, or over-indulgent or capricious. Harris (1961) pointed out that hostility towards parents or to a more favoured brother or sister, might be displaced on to the teacher, causing resistance to her teaching. In other cases there might be resistance to pressure exerted by over-ambitious parents. Ravenette (1968) also considered that backward readers might be prevented from profiting from remedial teaching by too great a parental demand for achievement and punishment for failure. In a later study (1970), he suggested that some children were inhibited from learning to read because they refused to experiment in an area in which dominating and over-protective parents were making demands which were too heavy for them. Mann (1957) considered that failure to learn to read might be a form of resistance against parents who tried to make the child unduly dependent; or it might be accompanied by anger against dominating parents. On the other hand, Vorhaus (1968) judged on the basis of their Rorschach responses that in the main severely backward readers were submissive, dependent, trying to withdraw from and avoid anxiety and insecurity; and that these effects were produced by inhibition caused by covert parental rejection and lack of warmth. However, there was sometimes concealed resistance to parents, and hence to learning to read. Other investigators have emphasized undue dependence in backward readers. Sperry et al. (1958) considered that children with reading difficulties tended to seek dependent love, rather than trying to achieve; indeed, they felt that they could be secure only through failure. The parents themselves believed that they could obtain security and social acceptance only through control and concealment of aggression.

Psychoanalysts have suggested that backward readers are children who are afraid to express openly their aggressive impulses and their curiosity, especially sexual curiosity. They are particularly afraid of the aggressive impulses arising through rivalry with the father at the Oedipal stage; and guilt and anxiety are especially likely if the father is perceived as a weak and unsatisfactory person. Upson (1968) found that in twenty-five cases of backward readers examined at the Tavistock Clinic, 88 per cent exhibited direct or indirect aggression; and in 72 per cent of cases the father figure was in some way unsatisfactory. However, a further study of the distortions in tachistoscopic perception by backward readers of pictures of family scenes did not seem to produce any supporting evidence.

P. E. Vernon (1969) compared the scores on a variety of tests of twenty-five delinquent boys and twenty maladjusted boys in a residential school; they were aged $10-13\frac{1}{2}$ years. Both groups were poor in scholastic attainment, including reading and spelling, the delinquent more so than the maladjusted. The delinquents, who were culturally deprived, were retarded in vocabulary and on some reasoning tasks, but the maladjusted were fairly normal, as also in visuo-spatial tasks such as Kohs Blocks. The delinquent boys performed badly on these tests, and it was suggested that this might be related to excessive dominance by the father or over-protectiveness by the mother. It would appear that motivation to learn was poor in both groups, but particularly in the delinquent.

Finally, the work of Kellmer Pringle and her colleagues (Kellmer Pringle, 1965) indicated that *parental deprivation*, the partial or complete severance in early childhood of the child from the parents, might have a marked effect on both the child's emotional stability and also his linguistic development. Studies were carried out of children who had been 'taken into care' by the Local Authority and placed in institutional homes. Kellmer Pringle found that those who had been taken into care at an early age, and those who now had little or no contact with their parents, were more retarded in intelligence, in linguistic development (both in vocabulary and in construction and understanding of sentences) and in reading achievement than were those who had entered institutions later and were less severely deprived of parental contacts. Reading comprehension in the former was inferior to word recognition; that is to say, the more advanced stages of reading were affected to a greater degree than were the early stages. Again, 80 per cent of the backward readers were maladjusted. In a selected group of 66 children, the maladjusted were found to have less frequent contacts with people outside the institution than did the stable; and twice as many maladjusted as stable were classed as 'illiterate', with reading ages below 7 years. An intensive study of 11 severely maladjusted and 5 stable children showed that the former were greatly retarded in language development, whereas the latter were normal. All the stable children experienced some lasting, dependable and loving relationship with an adult outside the institution, as against only one of the maladjusted.

It would appear from these studies that deprivation of the mother or any mother substitute produces maladjustment, which is associated with linguistic deficiencies, including difficulties in learning to read. Again, studies were made of the effects of remedial education, in which special reading teaching was combined with therapeutic treatment of emotional disorder. It appeared that increases of reading achievement went hand-in-hand with personality adjustment.

Nevertheless, it seems possible that in some cases parental deprivation may be related to linguistic development in the absence of emotional maladjustment. In another study, eighteen matched pairs of 4–5-year-old children were drawn half from day nursery schools and half from residential nurseries, after having been taken into care. Both groups had unfavourable home backgrounds. The residential children were not severely maladjusted, though they showed a constant craving for adult attention. Linguistically they were less mature than the day nursery children, though they appeared to be developing along normal lines. It would therefore seem that normal linguistic development and reading achievement are, as we have already suggested, closely linked to adequate relationships with adults, especially the parents. In children severely deprived of such relationships, emotional maladjustment may develop which may aggravate linguistic retardation. In any case, stimulation of achievement motivation is likely to be inadequate in institutionalized children.

These studies of the effects of interaction between parents and children suggest that in certain cases reading backwardness may be associated with a primary emotional disorder arising from disorganization of the relationship between the child and his parents. It would appear that the child may react to parental inadequacy by failure to learn to read, either as a form of aggression or resistance against dominating, demanding or over-protective parents; or as an expression of dependence or an appeal for help when one or both parents are missing or are rejecting, unaffectionate or merely passive and inadequate. The frequency of these different types of case as ascertained by different clinicians may vary with variations in sampling. Also clinicians tend to vary in their interpretation of the causes of the reading backwardness. It would seem however that in these cases the capacity to learn to read is not basically deficient, as it is in many of those described in the next chapter, but that they lack the motivation to attend, concentrate and work purposefully and energetically. Moreover, whereas in the children described in previous sections such motivation had not been aroused, in the emotionally disordered it is inhibited. Thus it is probably more difficult to stimulate them to learn than those whose motivation simply requires arousal.

Therefore it may be that therapeutic treatment is required to remove the blockage. Indeed, it has been claimed that in so far as such treatment is successful, the child may learn to read without further difficulty. However, it has been advocated, especially by Kellmer Pringle (1962), that what is required is remedial education, in which the specific teaching of reading is accompanied by creative and therapeutic activities, as well as case work with the parents when this seemed advisable. In a follow-up study of ten children aged 10–18 years who had received remedial education while in the junior school, parents reported in the majority of cases that there had been improvement not only in school achievement but also in social and emotional adjustment.

CHAPTER VII

SPECIFIC DEVELOPMENTAL DYSLEXIA

(1) GENERAL CONSIDERATION OF BACKWARDNESS IN READING

We have considered a number of disabilities and defects in cognition and motivation which appear to be associated with difficulty in learning to read; and also some of the causes to which these disabilities might be attributed. However, it has become clear that in the majority of cases the association has been only partial. Thus it cannot be said that reading backwardness is wholly or necessarily associated with any particular cognitive or motivational defect, except perhaps that in cases of severe intellectual subnormality it is inevitable. Nor does there appear to be any uniformity in relationship between the type of reading difficulty experienced and the cognitive or motivational defects. Some cases exhibit some defects, others exhibit others. Moreover, even when any defect does appear in a particular case, it cannot be inferred that it *caused* the reading difficulty. In some cases, indeed, as we have noted with some motivational deficiencies and emotional disorders, it may have been caused by the reading difficulty of failure. In other cases, the defect may, together with the reading difficulty, form part of a more general disability, the basic cause of which is extremely obscure. It also appears possible that there may be different types of reading disability, exhibiting different defects and with different causes.

It has been suggested by certain authors, notably Morris (1966), that backwardness in reading may be caused by a number of different predisposing factors; and that the greater the number of adverse factors, the more severe and lasting the backwardness. She calculated the number of unfavourable factors, including those in home and school conditions and individual attributes, operating in children who were good and poor readers; and found that the good readers exhibited on the average six unfavourable characteristics, whereas the poor readers exhibited twenty-one. The majority of the good readers, therefore, were subject to comparatively few handicaps, and of the poor readers, to many. Fig. 7 shows the distribution of unfavourable factors in good and poor readers respectively. Two things are apparent: (1) there were a few poor readers who were affected by only a small number of these factors; (2) there were some good readers who were subject to a considerable number. These findings suggest that a minority of

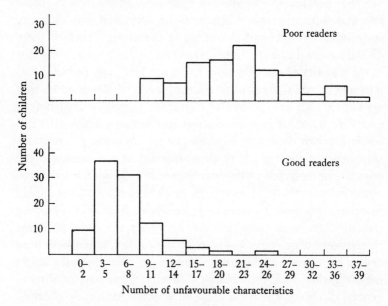

Fig. 7. Number of unfavourable characteristics of good and poor readers. (After Morris, 1966, p. 246.)

poor readers may suffer from few adverse circumstances in home and school; whereas some good readers manage to surmount the effects of several such handicaps.

This brings us to an important matter on which there has been and still is great disagreement: Whether or not there exists a condition of constitutional severe reading disability, a disposition, which may be innate, to encounter extreme difficulty in learning to read which is not the result of adverse circumstances in home or school, or of poor intelligence, or even necessarily of linguistic deficiency. It is this condition which has been termed *specific developmental dyslexia*.

This concept has been extant for many years, but it is unnecessary to present a detailed history here; it has been ably expounded by Critchley (1964, 1970). The term 'congenital word blindness' was applied to this disorder in the first instance apparently by Morgan (1896), but the first major exponent of the condition was Hinshelwood who discussed in it a series of medical papers and in a book entitled *Congenital Word Blindness* (Hinshelwood, 1917). This so-called 'word blindness' in children he attributed to a congenital defect in the cerebral cortex, apparently similar in nature to the acquired defect of 'alexia' which is caused by injury to the cortex. The term 'word blindness' has persisted to this day (see, for instance, Hermann, 1959), although clearly so-called 'word blind' children are not incapable of 'seeing' printed words. Hinshelwood was an ophthalmologist; and it is ophthalmologists and neurologists, on the continent of Europe as well as in this country, who have been the main advocates of the hypothesis that this is a condition *sui generis*, independent of other types of reading difficulty. It is now more commonly termed 'specific developmental dyslexia'; and according to Critchley (1970, p. 11) it has been defined by the Research Group on Developmental Dyslexia of the World Federation of Neurology as follows: 'A disorder manifested by difficulty in learning to read despite conventional instruction, adequate intelligence, and socio-cultural opportunity. It is dependent upon fundamental cognitive disabilities which are frequently of constitutional origin.' It is thus made clear that the condition is not associated with environmental handicaps or with poor intelligence. But it is generally considered to be severe and not easily remedied even by suitable teaching. Moreover, the reading deficiency is commonly accompanied by other defects, which we shall consider in the following sections of this chapter.

The condition was investigated extensively in the U.S.A. by Orton, who published a long series of articles which are summarized in his book, *Reading, Writing and Speech Problems in*

Children (1937). He also attributed to it a congenital defect in the cerebral cortex which he termed 'strephosymbolia'. This hypothetical disorder, which was associated with lack of hemispherical dominance in the cortex, is still cited today, for instance in the Plowden report (1967). We shall discuss below the significance of cerebral dominance in dyslexia.

But many educationists, including Morris (1966), have refused to accept that such a condition as dyslexia even exists, claiming that they have never encountered it in their investigations, and that it cannot be differentiated as an identifiable syndrome from other forms of reading backwardness. As we saw, Morris attributed severe backwardness to a multiplicity of unfavourable conditions. Moreover, she considered that since the achievement of her backward readers was improved by special remedial teaching, therefore their backwardness was not due to any constitutional defect. However, in some cases the improvement appeared to be minimal. Moreover, although dyslexia is hypothesized to be severe and resistant to treatment, it is not wholly impervious.

Although the existence of the condition of specific dyslexia has been denied by many educationists, it has long been recognized by the personnel of Child Guidance Clinics, to whom a considerable number of cases of severe and prolonged backwardness has been referred for diagnosis and treatment. Moreover, in recent years many parents, often themselves intelligent and well educated, have realized that their apparently normal and intelligent children are unable to read, or can do so only with extreme difficulty and inefficiency. Their dismay at this situation came to a head at a conference held in 1962 under the auspices of the Invalid Children's Aid Association (Franklin, 1962). As the outcome of the dissatisfaction expressed at the tendency of educationists to ignore the condition and their failure to provide suitable remedial treatment, a Word-Blind Unit was set up to investigate it and to give treatment. In other parts of the country Dyslexic Associations have been established, largely by parents of dyslexic children, to investigate and provide facilities for remedial treatment. Lastly, the condition has been recognized in special clauses in the *Chronically*

Sick and Disabled Persons' Act, Section 27, 1970, which enjoin local education authorities to provide special educational treatment in their schools for children suffering from acute dyslexia, and to inform the Secretary of State that they have done so.

Nevertheless, the nature and causes of dyslexia are still extremely obscure.* In the following sections the hypothesis will be discussed that dyslexia is a condition distinct from other forms of backwardness in reading. But it is difficult to draw any clear line of demarcation between constitutional dyslexia and reading difficulties due to environmental circumstances, which indeed in some cases aggravate the constitutional disorder. As we noted in Ch. II, the techniques employed for investigating reading backwardness have often been unsatisfactory, even in clinics, from which studies of dyslexic children are mainly obtained. Moreover, a wide age range is usually studied; and as we shall show symptoms of dyslexia may vary with age.

No reliable estimate of the *frequency* of dyslexia has ever been determined. Estimates of as high as 10 per cent of the total school population have been made by certain American authorities, and in England by Newton (1970). Rabinovitch (1968) gave a more conservative estimate of about 3 per cent. Though the number of 11-year-old illiterates in England may be only of the order of 0.5 per cent, as recent surveys suggest, not all these are dyslexic. On the other hand, not all dyslexics are illiterate, since by the age of 11 years they may have learnt to read, at least to some extent. But though dyslexics may be relatively infrequent in the ordinary school population, the numbers referred to clinics and remedial teachers are fairly considerable.

* Without prejudging the issue as to whether dyslexia is a condition distinct from other types of reading backwardness, it is convenient to use this term in the following discussion. Properly the word 'dyslexia' should always be preceded by the qualifying adjectives, 'specific developmental', in order to distinguish it from adult dyslexia acquired through organic impairment of the cerebral cortex. However, for the sake of brevity 'dyslexia' is used alone, since, unless otherwise specified, it is the children's disability which is under discussion.

(2) THE NATURE OF SPECIFIC
DEVELOPMENTAL DYSLEXIA

It cannot be claimed that there is any substantial difference in the nature of the reading performance of dyslexics and of other backward readers, apart from the severity of the former disability. Thus younger dyslexic children cannot read at all, or can read only a few simple words. They appear to have great difficulty with phonic associations; and even when able to sound printed letters and letter groups, they cannot blend these to form whole words. They are frequently characterized by the wild confusion of their writing and spelling. Fig. 8 shows an example obtained by Miles (1961),* and similar specimens have been presented by Hermann (1959), Crosby (1968) and Critchley (1970). Indeed in rather older children defective spelling may be more marked than reading disability. More intelligent children especially learn to utilize the contextual meaning in reading. But their continued inability to grasp phonic associations is notable in their spelling, which shows complete confusion in the sequential ordering of letters. A frequent, if not universal, feature, particularly in the reading and spelling of younger children, is the large number of reversals in the orientation of letters and in the order of letters in words. Sometimes the latter are completely reversed, in mirror reading and writing. These reversals occur with frequency even when the children have begun to read, and persist to a later age than in normal readers. Whether the reading and spelling disabilities are permanent, at least in a minor degree, or whether they can be entirely overcome by remedial treatment, will be discussed in a

* This figure shows the boy's attempts to reproduce from dictation the words of Burt's Spelling test (Burt, 1921, p. 382). It is difficult to match the reproductions against the words of the test, since the boy wrote the words all over the page. Thus he exhibited an incapacity to arrange material coherently, in a manner similar to that noted by Bender (1970) with Bender test reproductions by dyslexic children. It was hypothesized that 'toboot' was an attempt at 'table'; 'tades', 'today'; 'onree', 'only'; 'sare', 'sorry'; 'dut', 'doctor'; 'suntor', 'sometimes'. Other words could not be deciphered (Miles, private communication). The complete failure in spelling is obvious.

later section. It is also a moot point whether the disability appears in reading and writing only. Some dyslexic children seem to have normal ability in arithmetic; but Hermann (1959) found many dyslexics to be retarded in arithmetic also.

At first sight it is difficult to establish criteria for dyslexia apart from the characteristics just described, and from certain negative signs. Thus it is stated that there are no particular environmental handicaps, nor subnormal intelligence, nor emotional maladjustment. Some dyslexics have above average *intelligence* (see Miles, 1961; Rawson, 1968). Perhaps more commonly intelligence is within the normal range, but not high. Clark (1970) found in her

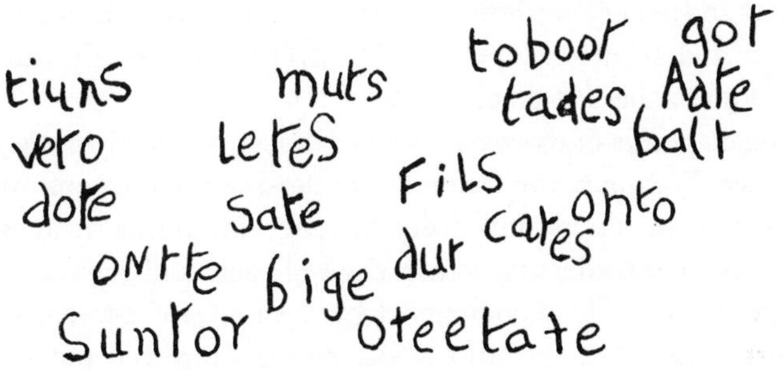

Fig. 8. Spelling of a dyslexic boy of 8 years, I.Q. 118.
(After Miles, 1967, p. 247.)

Dunbartonshire study that about 1·2 per cent of the 9-year-old children with intelligence in the normal range were retarded by two or more years in reading. The highest WISC Full Scale I.Q.s were 103, 101 and 100; the remainder were below 100. However, these children's WISC Performance I.Q.s were 112, 105, and 105. Thus Verbal I.Q.s were probably affected by linguistic deficiencies. In some of these cases poor home circumstances may have been contributory factors; therefore it is not certain that all were dyslexics. However, it is generally the case that reading achievement in dyslexics is much inferior to that expected from children of their intelligence.

The possibility of *emotional maladjustment* as a contributory factor is more difficult to check, since by the time the children are detected and examined, they are often extremely resentful or despondent as the result of reading failure. Therefore the non-existence of primary emotional disability can often be judged only from the parents' reports. However, they frequently affirm that their children showed no lack of eagerness to learn to read when they first entered school. Rawson (1968), whose study is described fully on p. 148, assured herself that none of her dyslexic cases were emotionally maladjusted; indeed in general they were highly motivated and showed great determination which enabled them to overcome the effects of their disability. Even in the cases of Ingram & Reid (1956), in whom a great many deficiencies in parent–child relationships were reported, it was also noted that anxiety and behaviour difficulties appeared in the children after they had started school. Moreover, the severity of their dyslexia was unrelated to the degree of anxiety.

The diagnosis of dyslexia does not in fact rest solely on negative evidence. We noted the frequency of persistent confusion over the orientation of letters and order of letters in words at an age at which normal readers no longer showed such confusion. And this is characteristically accompanied by a variety of perceptual and other defects which we must now consider. However, not all these defects occur in every case, which tends to make diagnosis more difficult. The defects are not in the main of the type which could be caused by environmental handicaps; thus their occurrence provides additional evidence for the constitutional nature of the disability.

In some children the principal deficiency appears to be visual, in others, linguistic; while many show both types of disorder. We noted in Ch. IV that Kinsbourne & Warrington (1963a) were able to select two small groups of dyslexics in one of which the WISC Verbal I.Q. exceeded the Performance I.Q. by over 20 points, whereas in the other group the Performance I.Q. exceeded the Verbal I.Q. by a like amount. But in a later study of an unselected clinic sample, Warrington (1967) found that the number with higher Verbal than Performance I.Q. was small.

(3) VISUAL DEFICIENCIES IN DYSLEXIA

Nevertheless, numerous studies have shown that some type of impairment in visual perception is frequent in dyslexia. According to Crosby (1968), defective visual perception is the most common cause of dyslexia, but this is doubtful. However, deficiencies in the *perception and reproduction of complex forms,* and also in the appreciation of spatial relations and sequential order, are often found. Some writers (Clements & Peters, 1962; Silver, 1968) have noted difficulty in discriminating the figure from the ground, particularly in rather complicated patterns such as those of the marble board test (Strauss & Lehtinen, 1947). A fairly general finding is poor performance on the Bender test (Galifret-Granjon, 1951; De Hirsch, 1954; Clements & Peters, 1962; Crosby, 1968; Clark, 1970). Crosby published numerous reproductions of the Bender test figures by dyslexics which varied from the fairly adequate to the highly incorrect. However, some of these were made by children of 7 years, who could not be expected to produce correct reproductions. A reproduction by a boy of $10\frac{1}{2}$ years, still reading at a 7-year level, is shown in Fig. 9. Though he showed some neurological symptoms, his disorder was stated to be mainly in visual perception. Crosby did not score reproductions by means of the Koppitz technique (see p. 31), but the errors resembled those listed by Koppitz. Failure to integrate parts was the most noticeable error. In addition some shapes were incorrectly or incompletely drawn; curves were reproduced as angles; and circles or lines were substituted for dots. However, Lachmann (1960) found that performance on the Bender test by dyslexics was inferior to that of normals only in his younger group of children of 8–10 years, and not in older children of 10–12 years.

Another visual perceptual test which has been employed is that of the Gottschaldt figures. Tjossem, Hansen & Ripley (1962) found poor performances by dyslexics on this. Clements & Peters (1962) also noted difficulty in perceiving the relationships between parts and wholes. Poor performance on Kohs Blocks test was noted particularly by Zangwill (1960), and on the similar Block Design

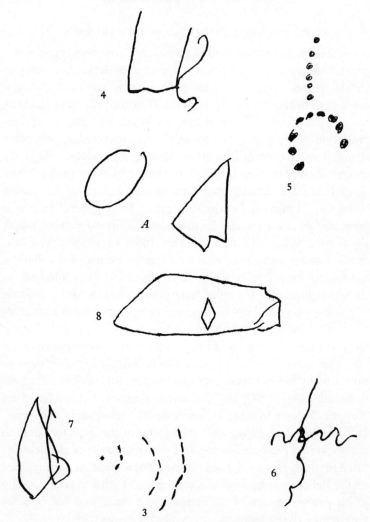

Fig. 9. Reproduction of Bender Gestalt test.
(After Crosby, 1968, p. 160).

test of the WISC by Kinsbourne & Warrington (1963*a*). Zangwill also observed complete inability to copy the Necker cube in two dyslexic girls of 15 and 11 years; the second was unable to copy a drawing of a bicycle (see Fig. 10). Critchley (1970) reported

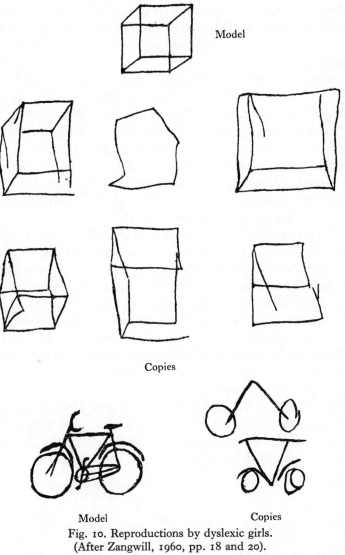

Model

Copies

Model   Copies

Fig. 10. Reproductions by dyslexic girls.
(After Zangwill, 1960, pp. 18 and 20).

confusions in perspective in drawings and plasticine models by
dyslexics. Some cases showed difficulty in the Goodenough test of
drawing a man, producing grossly immature figures (Shankweiler,
1964). Miles (1961) described a case of a 10-year-old dyslexic girl

133

whose drawings of a bicycle and a plan of her home were hope-
lessly confused; the same type of confusion appeared in her
attempts to reproduce from memory the Terman–Merrill design
for age 9.

In all these cases it would appear that it was not so much perception which was affected, but the capacity to reconstruct figures
in which the spatial dimensions and the relation of parts to the
whole were correctly copied. Though in some cases the constructions were direct copies of models, as in Fig. 10, more typical
perhaps were the cases in which the child had to design for himself.
If indeed certain types of dyslexia are associated with deficiency
in perceptual ability, it would seem that both the purely Perceptual
and also the Practical factor are involved (see p. 88).

There is another type of spatial disorder which occurs particularly frequently in dyslexics – failure to discriminate between *left
and right hand orientation*. The most common instances are those
of letter and word reversals. De Hirsch, Jansky & Langford (1966)
found that children tested at 6 years who subsequently failed to
learn to read were significantly inferior to those who succeeded in
ability to discriminate between reversed and unreversed letters.
The failure to discriminate orientation, sometimes termed *directional confusion*, appears also in confusions between the left and
right sides of the body, and of the bodies of others. Hermann
(1959) compared the performance of dyslexic children of 9–14
years with that of normal children of 9–11 and 12–15 years on two
tests, of touching the left ear with the right hand and the right
knee with the left hand. The results were as follows:

	Per cent making errors		
	0	1	2
Dyslexics	25	31	44
Normals, 9–11 years	57	24	19
Normals, 12–15 years	63	25	7

Thus errors were more frequent in the dyslexics than even in the
younger normal children.

Benton (1959) investigated extensively the development of left–

right discrimination and the relationship between errors in discrimination and dyslexia. He pointed out that left–right discrimination in children, and the evidence as to its failure in dyslexics, depended considerably on the children's age and on the type of discrimination tested. Thus normal 7-year-old children can usually say which is their left or right hand. But they are unable to say which is the left or right hand of someone facing them, or to perform the kind of crossed localization tested by Hermann. Even at 10 years, a normal child may be unable to perform more complex tasks such as placing his right hand on the left shoulder of a person facing him. Belmont & Birch (1963) found that accurate left–right discrimination of the child's own body parts and of someone facing him was established by about 7 years, though localization of objects in a series was not fully stabilized until 11 years. Shearer (1968) also showed that left–right discrimination improved with age between 8 and 11 years in both normal and retarded readers, though less in the latter than in the former. More of the normal readers obtained perfect scores, and more of the backward readers showed complete confusion even at 11 years.

Benton (1959) considered that the correct performance of his tasks depended on intelligence as well as on age. Left–right discrimination was particularly deficient in the mentally subnormal. However, some highly intelligent and literate individuals displayed weakness in left–right discrimination. Belmont & Birch (1963), on the other hand, found left–right discrimination to be unrelated to intelligence in children of 5–12½ years.

It would appear that deficiencies in left–right discrimination occur more frequently in dyslexics than in normal readers, but estimates of the extent and nature of this inferiority vary considerably, partly because the functions tested have varied. Benton (1959) found that poor left–right discrimination, especially of body parts in a picture, was more frequent in 8–10-year-old dyslexics than in matched controls. It was complete left–right reversal which was commoner in dyslexics and in other linguistically retarded children, and not mere confusion of left and right. Belmont & Birch (1965) also found that dyslexic children of 9½–10½ years were inferior to normal readers in left–right discrimination and especially in complete reversal. They were also significantly inferior in formulating the left–right relations of external objects. Poor left–right discrimination in clinic cases of dyslexia has been reported by Rabinovitch *et al.* (1954), Kolson & Kaluger (1963), Gubbay *et al.* (1965) and Silver (1968).

Benton (1959) concluded that the real difficulty for the dyslexic was not a disturbance of the child's own body schema but the verbal formulation of the relation between himself and his spatial surroundings, including objects and other persons. Thus a conceptual disability was involved in the labelling of left and right; and hence a possible dependence on intelligence. Yet according to Belmont & Birch (1965) the deficiency was not associated with any significant inferiority in Verbal I.Q., though there was some inferiority in Performance I.Q. in which perception of spatial relations may be involved.

Another defect which has been associated with directional confusion is in finger localization, sometimes termed '*finger agnosia*', as shown in inability to judge which finger has been touched when one cannot see this. However, methods of testing finger localization have been variable, and in some cases it would seem to be the verbal labelling of the fingers which is affected rather than actual localization. Hermann (1959) required dyslexic children of 9–14 years to name the finger which had been touched, and found that 36 per cent were unable to do so, as compared with 16 per cent of normal readers aged 9–11 years and 3 per cent of those aged 12–15 years. Kinsbourne & Warrington (1963*a*) applied three tests not involving labelling to dyslexic children of 9–15 years of ability: (1) to state whether only one finger had been touched, or two simultaneously; (2) to say how many fingers there were between two which had been touched; (3) to match shapes by touch. Unfortunately the scores on these tasks were combined, although the third appears to involve factors other than finger localization. All the dyslexics with visuo-spatial defects performed the tasks poorly, and none of those who showed disordered language functions. In another study by Kinsbourne & Warrington (1963*b*), it was found that 43 per cent of a group of children aged 8–15 years referred to an English clinic for educational backwardness, and 24 per cent of a group of children aged 10–14 years attending the Word-Blind clinic in Copenhagen, failed on the tests. On the other hand, only a very small proportion of children attending school remedial reading classes failed. It would thus appear that deficiency in finger localization, which Kinsbourne & Warrington considered was associated with difficulty in the ordering of stimuli, is fairly frequent in dyslexic cases but not among backward readers in general.

The deficiency in finger localization may also be associated with late maturation. Thus Kinsbourne & Warrington (1963c) found that normal children under 6 years performed less well on their tests than did older children. Benton (1959) showed that ability to identify on a model a single finger touched increased from 68 per cent correct responses at 6 years to 93 per cent at 9 years. Ability to localize two fingers touched simultaneously increased from 37 per cent correct responses at 6 years to 63 per cent at 9 years. Shearer (1968) also found that finger localization improved between 8 and 11 years in both normal and severely retarded readers, but less in the latter than in the former. More of the latter showed gross disability.

Though 'finger agnosia' has been cited as a characteristic symptom in dyslexia by other writers, such as Clements & Peters (1962), Critchley (1970) regarded it as being of little importance, especially when finger localization was confused with finger naming. Again, Lyle (1969) found that finger localization as assessed by the first two tests of Kinsbourne & Warrington was unrelated to backwardness in reading in children of 7–12½ years. These findings are not surprising in view of the results obtained by Poeck & Orgass (1969). These investigators showed that in adult patients with cerebral injuries there was no significant correlation between verbal tests of finger naming, the two tests of Kinsbourne & Warrington of localization, and Benton's test of identifying on a model which finger had been touched; neither did the two types of non-verbal test correlate with each other. Performance on the verbal tests was highly correlated with the WAIS Verbal I.Q.; and performance on Benton's test with general mental deterioration. Thus Poeck & Orgass concluded that there was no genuine independent symptom of finger agnosia; though this could be true for adult brain-injured patients and not for dyslexic children. The symptom may have been emphasized because of its apparent significance in the so-called 'Gerstmann's syndrome' produced by injury to the left parietal cortex in adults. We shall discuss this in section (5).

No other symptom associated with dyslexia has attracted more attention than has defective *lateralization*; that is to say, the apparent failure to establish superior skill in one or other hand, or to show strong preference for using one hand rather than the other in performing skilled tasks. Normally of course this is the right hand; and the left hand of a left-handed person tends to be less skilled than the right hand of a right-handed person. Some people are said to show mixed handedness, in that they perform some tasks with the right hand and others with the left. 'Footedness' and 'eyedness' also tend to show lateral preference. The significance of lateralization is said to lie in its association with the established *dominance* of one cerebral hemisphere over the other; in the normally right-handed, of the left over the right hemisphere. This dominance was considered to be important particularly by Orton (1937), who hypothesized that 'engrams' or memory traces of letters and words were laid down in both hemispheres, those in the right being reversals of those in the left. If the dominance of the latter was incomplete, the reversed engrams of the former were incompletely suppressed and caused confusion and reversals in reading and writing.

There is no evidence to support the engram hypothesis. Nevertheless, other writers have considered lack of established cerebral dominance to be significant in dyslexia, for reasons which we shall discuss in section (5). Many investigations have been carried out on the incidence of left-handedness and mixed handedness in backward readers; and the earlier investigations were discussed at length by Vernon (1957). It was concluded that although some dyslexics exhibited left-handedness, or more commonly mixed handedness, this characteristic did not occur in all cases. In large-scale surveys little or no association might appear between laterality and backwardness in reading.

That there has been, and still is, disagreement as to the frequency and significance of imperfect lateralization is due, at least in part, to the variability in the methods employed in ascertaining handedness. Sometimes statements are obtained of preference for the right or left hand in performing various activities, for instance, in throwing a ball, hammering, cutting with a knife, combing the hair. But more commonly, especially with children, the actual performance of these activities is observed, and the preferences determined from observation. In other cases, the relative skill of the two hands is assessed by measuring the speed and accuracy with which they perform various tasks such as tapping, aiming, tasks of finger dexterity, etc. Or again the strength of grip may be measured. But the results obtained from these various measures are not always consistent, especially in children. In the first place, stated preference does not necessarily agree with measured relative skill or with actual preference. Again, neither preference nor skill are always consistent, but may vary according to the task performed. Thus it is desirable to assess the trend of handedness in a number of tasks. It may then be found that there is a considerable number of intermediate cases who are neither completely right-handed nor left-handed; this number tends to decrease with increasing age. Thus assessments of laterality based on one or two observations only have a low validity. Indeed, some investigators do not specify what tasks they have employed.

These variations were clearly demonstrated in a recent study by Annett (1970) of handedness in young adults. She required over 2000 University students and recruits to the Army to state the hand they preferred to use in performing twelve activities, and found that 72 per cent were right-handed in all activities, and 3 per cent left-handed. In the remaining 25 per cent with mixed handedness, 17 per cent performed more tasks with the right hand and 8 per cent more with the left. But there was a gradual scale of handedness in these cases between complete right- and complete left-handedness, with no point at which any cut could be made of the right- from the left-handed. In another group of adults and 12-year-old children, the speed of putting pegs into holes was measured. When the speed of movement of the right hand was subtracted from that of the left, a continuous scale was also obtained, which corresponded closely with the scale for hand preference. Thus preference and skill were closely associated in these cases. Annett concluded that lateral dominance is a phenomenon graded on a continuous scale from right to left, but with the preponderance of cases at the right-hand end. She also maintained that cases of mixed handedness were consistent in their performance of any one task, and that true ambidextrality – the performance of tasks with either hand at random – is very uncommon. This may indeed be so with adults and older children who have established strong habits of carrying out the tasks which are usually tested. But Annett did obtain answers of 'either hand' to some of her questions on preference, particularly the actions of unscrewing a jar and sweeping. In young children it might well be that a greater number of activities would be performed with either hand, since permanent habits of action would not have been fully established.

Annett also found that in those with mixed handedness, the degree of right- or left-handedness might depend on the particular tasks selected for report of preference. Thus the proportion of those using the left hand for cutting with scissors was much smaller than that of dealing cards with the left hand. By making a statistical analysis of her results, she established that certain activities were more highly correlated with each other as regards right- or left-handedness, than were others. She concluded that the actions most characteristic and representative of handedness were: writing, hammering, throwing a ball, using a racket, striking a match and using a toothbrush. The implication is that whether or not any particular individual is classified as left-handed or of mixed handedness may well depend on the particular tasks selected for report or testing.

Annett considered that since mixed handedness occurred in many of the University students she studied – indeed it was more frequent in them than in the Army recruits – it could not be associated with any immaturity in cognitive development. However, it should not be concluded that there is no such association in younger children; though it might be inconsistent rather than mixed handedness which is significant. There is considerable evidence for this in a study by Naidoo (1961), who administered ten tests of hand preference and skill to children of $4\frac{1}{2}$–6 years. Consistency of results was variable; but 33 per cent were fully right-handed and 4 per cent fully left-handed. In 13 per cent there was no strong lateral preference. The remaining 50 per cent were presumably inconsistent. Naidoo then selected 20 fully right-handed children, 20 fully left-handed and 20 with variable handedness, and administered further tests of motor skill, speech development, auditory and visual discrimination to these children. The right-handed performed the motor tasks more skilfully than did the other two groups with their preferred hand. The difference in skill between the two hands was least in the ambiguously handed. The more skilled hand was usually the preferred hand, but not always, especially in the ambiguously handed. The latter tended to be retarded in speech development and to perform visual matching tasks less well. They were not inferior in auditory discrimination, but could read fewer words than could the others. On the other hand, De Hirsch *et al.* (1966), who tested children at 6 years before they began learning to read, found that those who subsequently failed to learn showed no more ambilaterality than did those who subsequently succeeded.

Among unselected samples of school children it is usual to find little difference between reading achievement in the right-handed, the left-handed and those with mixed handedness. In some studies the tests have been inadequate. But Balow (1963), using fifteen tests of preference and relative skill designed by Harris (1957), found no significant difference between the reading test scores of right-handed, and combined left-handed and mixed-handed children of 6–7 years. Belmont & Birch (1965) also used ten of the Harris tests for hand preference, and found mixed laterality among 10-year-old boys, retarded by two or more years in reading, to be no more common than in normal readers. Again, Lyle (1969), using ten tests of hand preference, found no correlation between handedness and reading ability in children of 6–11 years, though some of the older children were severely retarded in reading.

With clinic cases of dyslexia, left or mixed handedness seems to occur more frequently. Thus Harris (1957) compared the hand preferences shown in ten tests and the relative skill in five tests of an unselected sample of 245 school children aged 7 and 9 years, and 316 children of 7–12 years who were attending clinics for severe reading disability. Among the unselected children, 18 per cent at 7 years and 8 per cent at 9 years showed mixed handedness. In the clinic children there was mixed handedness in 32 per cent at 7 years, in 25 per cent at 9 years and in 11 per cent at 12 years. Thus clearly more of the younger dyslexics possessed mixed laterality than of the normals. But though the mean difference disappeared at 10–11 years, it is possible that poor lateralization persisted in some severely dyslexic cases. Thus Ingram & Reid (1956), Zangwill (1960), Clements & Peters (1962), Kucera, Matejcek & Langmeier (1963) and Bender (1968) all reported weak lateralization as a characteristic feature of dyslexia. Hibbert (1961) noted it in 23 out of 27 cases of dyslexia. But Rabinovitch *et al.* (1954) stated that although it was common in dyslexics, it was by no means universal. And Silver (1968) and Doehring (1968) found it to be no more frequent in dyslexics than in normal readers. But the method of assessing laterality was seldom reported, and it is possible that disagreement in findings is due to unsatisfactory methods of assessment.

If indeed the failure to establish firmly the use of one hand rather than the other, and of superior skill in the preferred hand, is the consequence of lack of dominance by one cerebral hemisphere over the other, it might be expected that a similar failure in lateralization would appear in other bilateral functions, namely those of the feet and the eyes. It would appear that in most cases '*footed-*

ness', as assessed by preference in, for instance, kicking a ball, agrees with handedness. Clark (1957) found a fairly close correspondence between footedness and handedness, though not all the tests of the former gave consistent results.

The situation as regards '*eyedness*' is somewhat ambiguous (it was discussed in some detail in Vernon, 1957). Tests of eyedness are usually designed to show which eye is employed in sighting, when the observer has to choose between the two eyes. The relation of this choice to reading is obscure, though it is possible that in activities such as reading and scanning the field of view the dominant eye 'leads' the other. Zangwill (1960) reported a tendency in five of his twenty dyslexic cases to 'sinistrad scanning', presumably scanning from right to left rather than the more common left to right. It is not clear how this tendency was assessed.

All investigations have shown that left-eyedness is much more frequent than left-handedness; indeed it has commonly been found to occur in about 30 per cent of those tested (Harris, 1957; Clark, 1957). This suggests that eyedness is not associated with cerebral dominance in the same manner as is handedness; or it may be less affected by learning. Harris found that neither left-eyedness nor mixed or inconsistent eyedness were more common among his dyslexic cases than in normal readers, except perhaps at 7 years. Since more people are left-eyed than are left-handed, it is inevitable that a considerable number are '*cross-lateral*', that is to say, right-handed and left-eyed. At one time it was supposed, possibly on the basis of Orton's theory, that cross-laterality was even more likely to be associated with dyslexia than was weak handedness. Indeed, there appears to have been a slight excess of this in Harris's findings for both 7-year-old and 9-year-old dyslexics. Yet few of the more recent studies attribute great importance to it, since it must obviously occur in many cases with no reading disability.

The ambiguity of eyedness lies in the fact that eyedness in sighting is not related to the dominance of one visual field over the other, since both visual fields are represented in each cerebral hemisphere. However, McFie (1952) and other investigators attempted to show that there was a correspondence between handedness and the predominance of perception of apparent movement in one visual field over the other. In dyslexics, no clear dominance of visual field occurred, as it did in normal readers. However, the evidence was not very convincing (see Vernon, 1957).

It might be supposed that directional confusion, in so far as it indicates a confusion over the spatial relations of the body image, would be liable to occur particularly in cases of weak lateralization, because the child could not readily associate the right side of the field with his preferred hand. Benton (1959) found that children with confused left–right discrimination, that is to say, inconsistency of judgment, had a slight tendency towards weak lateralization. But those who completely reversed left and right, and were retarded in reading, showed normal lateralization. Harris (1956) considered that directional confusion could occur with almost any type of laterality, but that it was most frequent in cases of mixed handedness. Belmont & Birch (1965) found that lateralization was normally established some years before left–right discrimination became accurate. However, this does not prove that incompletely lateralized children were not slower to develop correct left–right discrimination. It is possible that the highly verbalized type of left–right discrimination is relatively independent of lateralization. But it would seem in general that the association between lateralization and left–right discrimination is doubtful.

There might also be some association between lateralization and finger localization. Reed (1967) tested finger localization in the two hands of children of $6\frac{1}{2}$ and $10\frac{1}{2}$ years, and compared the reading achievement of those who made more errors in localization with the right than with the left hand, and vice versa. There was no significant difference in the younger children; but among the older children, those who made more errors with the left hand were better readers than those who made more errors with the right. These results suggest that there may be some association between handedness and accurate finger localization; their import is not altogether clear.

It is possible that both weak lateralization and directional confusion are not only symptoms associated with the visual type of dyslexia, but also directly interfere with the child's capacity to write. Thus writing is easier when the right hand is used, and is relatively better than when neither hand is particularly skilled; and reading might be less proficient when writing was poor. It is also easier for the left-handed writer to write from right to left than from left to right; thus there might be a tendency to mirror reversal in the former, or even perhaps in the incompletely lateralized.

However, it would seem that a more important factor in dyslexia is the association between directional confusion and errors and reversals in sequential ordering, which we noted as characteristic features of reading difficulty. Indeed these may constitute two aspects of the same disability.

(4) LINGUISTIC DEFICIENCIES IN DYSLEXIA

We noted in Ch. IV that deficiencies in the development of speech and language were frequently associated with backwardness in reading. It is not surprising therefore to encounter many reports of dyslexic children in whom linguistic deficiencies are marked, and who may not possess the type of disability described in the previous section. We noted that Warrington (1967) found a considerable preponderance of children referred to clinics for reading difficulties whose Performance I.Q. markedly exceeded their Verbal I.Q. Moreover, in about half these cases there was history of slow speech development. This had also occurred in the five dyslexic cases selected by Kinsbourne & Warrington (1963 a) as having Performance I.Q.s exceeding their Verbal I.Q.s These cases showed additionally impairment in expressive language functions and on tests of naming and verbal learning.

Ingram & Reid (1956) carried out an investigation of seventy-eight dyslexics aged 6–15 years, all of normal intelligence, who had been referred to a clinic. Fifty-two of these cases were tested with the WISC, and were placed in one of three groups. In group (a), with 44 per cent of cases, Verbal I.Q. was superior to Performance I.Q. by an average of 21 points. In group (b), with 25 per cent of cases, Verbal I.Q. was inferior to Performance I.Q. by an average of 16 points. In the remainder, group (c), average Verbal and Performance I.Q.s were approximately the same. Reading retardation was greatest in group (b) and least in group (a). Many children in group (b), and also in group (c), suffered from what was termed 'developmental aphasia' or 'dysphasia' (Ingram, 1959a). Speech development had been retarded; and when the child did begin to speak, pronunciation had been so defective that speech was unintelligible, except to parents, up to 4–5 years in some cases. Other symptoms were similar in nature to those of the speech of younger children. The dysphasic children had difficulty in finding the right words to express themselves. They tended to omit words and syllables in words, and to say the latter in the wrong order, a possible sign of inadequate sequential processing (Ingram, 1959a). Comprehension was also poor; many common words were not understood, and often children could not obey commands until these were repeated. In reading, as we noted on p. 74, Ingram (1960) distinguished three types of disorder: primary difficulty in sounding printed letters, inability to construct words from letters correctly sounded, and difficulty in comprehension of meaning. The first type of disability was the most common.

It should be noted that group (a) resembled the cases described in the previous section. Speech development had been normal and there was no language disorder. But in reading, reversals were frequent, either of whole words or of syllables within words. In the WISC Performance tests, recall of shapes, analysis and synthesis of patterns and left–right orientation were all poor. The disability was most severe when lateralization was weakest. In the whole sample of seventy-eight cases there was a high proportion of incomplete lateralization; 71 per cent showed some degree of mixed handedness and 56 per cent of mixed footedness. There was no control group; but these figures are higher than those usually quoted for normal readers (see p. 142, Harris, 1957). Ingram & Reid concluded that in addition to those suffering from visuospatial disorders, there were numerous dyslexics with language deficiencies. In some cases these might be wholly responsible for the dyslexia, whereas in others they were accompanied by visuo-spatial disorders. The latter were the most severe cases, which might be irremediable (Ingram, 1960). In group (a) there were visuo-spatial disorders alone, with no language deficiencies. There were also cases with a minor degree of language deficiency, and with visuo-spatial disability predominant (Ingram, 1963a).

Other investigators have noted the frequency of language deficiencies among dyslexic children. Rabinovitch et al. (1954) found in some of his dyslexic cases language difficulties of the receptive, expressive and nominal types such as occur in adult aphasia. There were also numerous reversals of spoken words. But these authors noted, like Ingram, that in some cases it was the conceptual aspect of language which was particularly affected. Cohn (1961) showed that language ability and speech articulation were impaired in nearly all his forty-six dyslexic cases. In many there was also weakness in left–right discrimination, but not in lateralization. Benton (1959) also found a deficiency in the language functions of his backward readers with complete reversal of left–right discrimination, in whom there was no weakness in lateralization. In the twelve clinic cases of children aged 5–11 years with speech defects and language disorders described by Crookes & Greene (1963), reading quotients were much below I.Q.s. Left–right discrimination was poor and reversals of letters were frequent; but only four children showed inconsistency of handedness. On the other hand, the findings of Naidoo (1961) and of Kucera, Matejcek & Langmeier (1963) indicated an association between delayed speech development and imperfect lateralization. Naidoo noted the appearance of the first words to be particularly late in the least lateralized cases. It is not clear, however, if in such cases there was visuo-spatial as well as linguistic impairment. It was noted (p. 36) that Lyle (1969) carried out a factorial analysis of tests administered to backward readers which indicated the operation of two factors, one related to perceptuo-motor disorders, especially reversals, and the other to capacity for verbal learning. In a subsequent enquiry (Lyle, 1970) he obtained evidence from the mothers of these children as to difficulties which occurred during the children's early development. He found that early speech delays related to the perceptuo-motor deficiencies as well as to capacity for verbal learning. It might be, therefore, that there is a direct connection on some occasions of linguistic impairment with directional confusion and/or weak lateralization. We shall return to this matter in the next section.

Rawson (1968) carried out a study at an American independent primary school of fifty-six boys, aged 6–14 years, with varying degrees of reading achievement. These boys were of good intelligence, from middle and upper class homes with highly educated parents. Only one or two cases suffered from emotional disorder, and these were not dyslexics. But a considerable number exhibited a greater or less degree of language disability, the school being known to be successful in educating such children. The fifty-six boys were ranked in order of severity of symptoms and then classified into three groups: (1) twenty showing no signs of dyslexia whatever; (2) sixteen showing certain symptoms, such as slow speech development, late beginning of reading, difficulty in verbal formulation, but not considered to be dyslexic; and (3) eight classified as moderately dyslexic and twelve as severely dyslexic. The classification of dyslexia was based on failure to learn to read during the first year or two of teaching, and on case histories. These boys had shown symptoms of language disability during early childhood, with delayed speech development. Motor skill and control, auditory discrimination, lateralization and left–right discrimination were poor. When, with individual help, they began learning to read, reversals were frequent, and there were difficulties with phonics, including blending of phonemes, and with order of letters in words. Spelling was inferior to reading. But there appears to have been a continuous gradation from the non-dyslexic to the severely dyslexic, and it is not clear how Rawson arrived at the cut-off points of the three groups. Unfortunately there seems to have been no administration of standardized tests, other than the Stanford–Binet. Thus it is impossible to judge whether the criterion was number or severity of symptoms, or both. But it would seem that the diagnosis of dyslexia was not based on any all-or-none differentiation.

Other investigators have presented cases in which there were both linguistic and visuo-spatial defects. Thus for the children who subsequently failed in reading, De Hirsch, Jansky & Langford (1966) found visuo-spatial, auditory perceptual and oral language deficiencies in all cases; but there was no excess of ambilaterality. Doehring (1968) showed that older dyslexics, aged 10–14 years, were inferior to normal readers on most verbal tasks with both written and spoken language. The language deficit, which was particularly noticeable in certain complex performances, was accompanied by a visuo-spatial disability, though not in left–right orientation or in lateralization. The basic deficit in sequential processing affected both the visual and also the linguistic aspects of reading.

It might appear, therefore, that two distinct syndromes may be involved in dyslexia, one in which the perception of complex forms and their orientation is defective, the other in which there is linguistic impairment. A distinction of this kind was employed by Naidoo (1970) and Cotterell (1970). But several investigators have suggested that in only a comparatively small number of cases is only one of these syndromes operative. More commonly both are involved. In these, processes such as the association between sequences of printed and sounded letters are affected both visually and linguistically, and dyslexia tends to be severe. However, even when there seems to be a predominantly visual or verbal bias, it may be that the essential disability is in the process of conceptualization involved in the sequential processing of the visual and linguistic symbols employed in reading. This conceptual deficiency may be of more significance than are simple visual, auditory or linguistic defects. We noted in Ch. v that there was evidence of impairment in backward readers of other types of conceptual process.

(5) THE CAUSES OF DYSLEXIA

(A) *Neurological Impairment*

Many neurologists have been impressed by the similarity between the symptoms of developmental dyslexia and of *aphasia* produced in adults mainly by injury to the temporal lobe of the left cerebral hemisphere, though occasionally by right hemispherical lesions. The capacity to read and write may also be destroyed, in alexia and agraphia, or severely impaired, in *dyslexia* and *dysgraphia*. Some cases occur in which alexia or dyslexia are not accompanied by other types of language deficit, but these are not very common. Thus out of thirty-two aphasic patients studied by Rochford (cited by Williams, 1970), there were twenty-one with defects in reading and writing together with impairment of spoken language, seven with impaired speech alone and four with reading and writing defects alone. However, current investigations of aphasia suggest that these distinctions are seldom well defined, though errors and faults may be relatively greater in spoken language than in reading, or vice versa. In some dyslexic cases the main deficiency may be in the semantic aspects of reading, in others in word recognition; and verbal memory is generally poor. The exact nature of the failures and errors in reading seems to be extremely complex.

Dysphasia with reading and writing defects may be produced by brain damage to the dominant hemisphere in children also, and it is usually accompanied by articulatory disturbances. There may be recovery if injury occurs early in life.

There has been a tendency, therefore, in some quarters to attribute developmental dyslexia also to injury early in life to the left cerebral hemisphere, and especially to the temporal area. But some writers, notably Hermann (1959), have associated developmental dyslexia with another adult disorder, *Gerstmann's syndrome*, said to be produced by injury to a circumscribed area of the parietal lobe of the dominant hemisphere. The most notable feature of this disorder was claimed to be a disturbance in spatial orientation, in concepts of direction and in knowledge of the position of the body in space. Left–right discrimination was impaired, and there was finger agnosia. According to Hermann, this appeared mainly in inability to name the finger touched; but according to Williams (1970), finger location without naming might be more affected. Patients commonly exhibited agraphia and acalculalia (inability to do simple arithmetic). Reading was unaffected, but in oral spelling errors in the order of letters in words were unusually frequent (Kinsbourne & Warrington, 1964). Hermann considered that developmental dyslexia was not due to actual injury, but to a comparable innate dysfunction of the parietal lobe with regard to orientation and direction, which might be inherited. The reading disability of dyslexia, which did not occur in Gerstmann's syndrome, he attributed to confusion caused by inability to write and spell; the disordered writing and spelling of dyslexic children resembled those of adults with Gerstmann's syndrome.

However, Benton (1961) cast considerable doubt on the existence of Gerstmann's syndrome as an independent entity. He administered to a hundred patients, aged 6–64 years, his tests of left–right discrimination, finger identification on a model, constructional praxis (copying of stick and block designs) and visual memory for designs; and assessed performance in reading, writing and arithmetic. Performance of functions usually associated with Gerstmann's syndrome – that is to say, left–right discrimination, finger identification and writing – were no more closely correlated together than they were with constructional praxis, memory for designs and reading. This occurred even in patients with lesions of the left parietal area. Thus Benton concluded that patients exhibited a variety of symptoms; and that the particular group supposed to characterize Gerstmann's syndrome did not appear in isolation from other symptoms.

There is a considerable body of evidence to show that cases of alexia without language impairment may be associated with *visuospatial* disorders produced by lesions of the parietal area of the minor hemisphere. Patients with such injuries score better on the WAIS Verbal tests than on the Performance tests, whereas those with accompanying language disorders perform relatively better on the Performance tests. The former also do badly on Progressive Matrices. Warrington & James (1967) compared the performance of patients with right and left hemispherical lesions on the WAIS and on a variety of tests of recognition of pictures of objects, letters and meaningless patterns. Though patients with left hemispherical lesions made more errors than did those with right hemispherical lesions in naming, the reverse was true with errors of recognition, to which patients with right hemispherical lesions were particularly prone. Warrington & James concluded that the functioning of this area was essential for the efficient processing of information relating to the contours of shapes; and effective functioning was also necessary for adequate performance on tests such as Kohs Blocks. On the other hand, processes of 'apperception' of information and verbal association were affected by left hemispherical lesions. These differences between the functions of the two hemispheres was found by McFie (1961) not to appear with hemiplegia in infancy, but only if the children had reached the age at which differentiation of function had developed between the two hemispheres. Kinsbourne & Warrington (1962) had also found that patients with lesions of the right parietal area tended in their reading to substitute for the first parts of words, parts of other words, such as 'level' for 'novel' and 'eight' for 'tight'. Thus directional confusion was caused by reading the ends of the words only and guessing the beginnings. In some cases also patients tended to notice words at the end of the line before those at the beginning, another sign of directional confusion.

The association of reading difficulties with impairment of the left hemisphere was again suggested by the effects of section to the *corpus callosum*, the nerve tract joining the two hemispheres (Maspes, cited by Sperry, 1970). Letters, numbers and geometric figures were seen but not comprehended when they were projected to the non-dominant hemisphere of two patients with callosal section. Comparable effects have been obtained as the result of stimulating the left and right fields in normal individuals. Thus Kimura (1967) found that letters were perceived more accurately when presented in the right visual field than in the left. With meaningless patterns there was no significant difference between the two fields, except that estimation of number of forms was superior in the left. Wyke & Ettlinger (1961) showed that pictures of familiar objects were perceived more quickly in the right than in the left visual field, presumably because they were named; but there was no difference with unfamiliar shapes. Therefore it would seem that any verbal processing of material occurs in the left hemisphere, whereas the right hemisphere is responsible for shape perception. These results throw some doubt on any association between reading difficulties and injuries to the right hemisphere alone.

There have been numerous reports of *organic damage to the brain* in cases of dyslexia in children, as the result of some impairment during the antenatal period or at delivery, or of injury sustained during early childhood. Kawi & Passamanick (1959) stated that 16 per cent of 205 clinic cases of dyslexia had experienced some kind of abnormal effect during the antenatal period, as compared with only 1·5 per cent of normal controls. Lyle (1970) obtained evidence from mothers as to difficulties which had occurred during the antenatal or perinatal periods. He found that occurrence of perinatal brain injury was related to both perceptuomotor and verbal deficiencies in dyslexics. The former were also associated to some extent with antenatal difficulties, but less than was suggested by Kawi & Pasamanick. Kucera, Matejcek, & Langmeier (1963) stated that 46 per cent of a group of ninety-one dyslexic children aged 7–13 years showed brain disorders or lesions. In some of these cases there were deficiencies in visual and auditory perception, in speech development, in attention and concentration, and in motor control of hand movements. Impulsiveness and over-reaction also occurred. Shankweiler (1964) found evidence of brain damage in seven out of twelve dyslexic children aged $8\frac{1}{2}$–13 years. There was directional confusion and poor constructional ability, but no language impairment. Rabinovitch (1968) stated that actual or suggested brain damage occurred in 46 per cent of the sixty dyslexic children he studied.

Other investigators have been more cautious as to evidence for actual brain damage. Preston & Schneyer (1956) stated that three of their nine dyslexic cases showed actual damage, the remainder only the possibility of damage as indicated by abnormal antenatal and perinatal factors. Clements & Peters (1962) postulated only minimal brain damage. Lovell & Gorton (1968) administered a battery of tests to fifty school children aged 9–10 years, retarded by 1 s.d. on Schonell's Silent Reading Test B. They intercorrelated the test scores and submitted them to factorial analysis, extracting as their first factor what they termed 'neurological integrity impairment'. This correlated with audio-visual integration, directional confusion and spasmodic jerky movement. This factor did not appear in normal controls, but was found in 12 per cent of backward readers.

Evidence as to the existence of brain damage has often been based on *abnormalities in the EEG*. Statten (1953) found diffuse disturbances of the EEG, particularly slow rhythms in the occipital area, in a group of children with marked reading disability, and low scores on the WISC Object Assembly, Block Design and Coding sub-tests. The EEG disturbances were attributed to early *minimal brain damage*. Goldberg, Marshall & Sims (1960) observed EEG abnormalities in twenty-three out of twenty-five cases of dyslexia. The EEG showed disorganization, abundant slow activity and sharp waves in the parietal area. Cohn (1961) found EEG abnormalities in over 50 per cent of a group of forty-six dyslexic children aged 7–10 years, again with much slow wave activity particularly in the occipital area; these abnormalities had not disappeared two years later. Language ability was impaired in nearly all these cases, but there were also visual perceptual deficiencies and poor left–right discrimination. Mecke (1969) diagnosed minimal brain damage from EEG disorders in twelve dyslexic children, who also showed characteristic errors in the Bender test.

However, it is by no means certain that EEG abnormalities and excessive Bender test errors indicate brain damage, even of a minor kind. Benton & Bird (1963) pointed out that estimates as to the frequency of EEG abnormalities has varied from 28 per cent to 88 per cent of cases observed by different investigators. The variation may have been in part due to variation in the selection of cases, but also to the employment by different investigators of different criteria of EEG abnormality. Again, Preston (1969) considered that in the true dyslexic there is no history or evidence of brain injury, although fifteen out of the eighteen dyslexic cases on which he reported showed EEG abnormalities.

A symptom we have already noted which occurs in some dyslexics, and is frequently associated with brain damage, is *disordered motor control*, appearing in excessive restless jerky movement, fidgeting, clumsiness and uncontrolled impulsiveness. Cohn (1961) and Goldberg (1968) both found in their dyslexic cases poor muscular control and motor coordination, sometimes with excessive impulsivity. Gubbay *et al.* (1965) studied fourteen excessively clumsy and fidgety children, aged 9–17 years, in whom abnormal perinatal factors and mild EEG abnormalities suggested minimal brain damage, though there were no overt neurological symptoms. The WISC Verbal I.Q. was substantially above Performance I.Q. Ten cases showed poor left–right discrimination, and ten, finger agnosia. Only four were completely illiterate, but the majority were retarded in reading. Gubbay *et al.* regarded this disorder as being of the same nature as cerebral palsy, in which reading and writing disability commonly occur. The disorder is not associated with all cases of dyslexia. Brenner *et al.* (1967) found that a group of 8–9-year-old children with marked clumsiness and restlessness of movement and inferior performance on a variety of visuo-motor tests, including the Bender test, showed poor achievement in spelling, writing and arithmetic; but reading was fairly adequate. It was considered that these children, who had undergone numerous perinatal hazards, were suffering from a minor degree of cerebral dysfunction.

However, the whole concept of brain damage in its effects on children has been criticized by Herbert (1964). He cited Norris as finding that the Verbal *v.* Performance WISC I.Q. did not differentiate brain-damaged from non-brain-damaged children. As we noted, the Bender test has often been used to diagnose brain damage. Thus Quast (1961) found errors on the test to be considerable in number in children of 10–12 years suspected of brain damage, whereas in normal children such errors had usually disappeared by this age. But there has been disagreement between other investigators as to what are the characteristic features of performance by the brain injured. Silverman (cited by Herbert, 1964) found that dyslexic children produced significantly more distorted reproductions of the Bender test figures than did matched cases without reading disabilities, although the former possessed no known or suspected brain damage. However, Goldenberg (cited by Herbert, 1964) did find performance on both the Ellis Visual Designs test and the Marble Board test to be significantly impaired in brain-damaged children. But Pond (1961) considered that there were no unequivocal clinical signs or tests which could prove a relationship between brain damage and any particular type of disturbed behaviour. Even the classical syndrome of the hyperactive, distractable, impulsive and perceptually deficient brain-damaged child, which we have described, was of doubtful existence.

Herbert considered that difficulty in differentiating between brain-damaged and non-brain-damaged children was due partly to the effects of other factors such as age, intelligence, personality and other developmental characteristics. Effects on the brain were likely to be general and non-specific because in children the brain is less differentiated than it is in adults; thus these effects are less clearly localized. Nevertheless, he quoted some findings which suggested that there may be an association between a particular type of disorder and the locus of damage. Thus he cited Annett *et al.* as finding that in cases in which EEG foci of disturbance were contralateral to the preferred hand, performance was poor on language tests, especially of definition of words. With ipsilateral foci, there were deficits in tasks involving the reconstruction of material in new spatial relationships, such as the WISC Block Design, Picture Arrangement, Object Assembly and Coding subtests. McFie (1961) also found that impairment was greater on WISC Performance than on Verbal tests in children with right cerebral hemiplegia. However, these children were subnormal in all respects. Reed & Reitan (1969) studied thirty-five children with brain disorders in the right hemisphere and twenty-five with disorders of the left. These were infective disorders causing motor dysfunction which principally affected one hemisphere, though the other might also have been involved. There were no significant differences between the two groups in reading achievement, which was as expected for the somewhat subnormal mental age of the children; or between WISC Verbal and Performance I.Q.s.

It would be attractive to hypothesize that children exhibiting the predominantly dysphasic type of dyslexia were suffering from some kind of impairment of function in the temporal area of the left cerebral hemisphere; whereas those whose dyslexia was associated with visuo-spatial disorders were suffering from impairment of the right hemisphere, probably in the parietal area. However, the evidence from children was ambiguous; and even in adults the linguistic and visuo-spatial functions did not appear to be fully localized in the left and right hemispheres respectively. Moreover, it has been made clear that in many dyslexics both linguistic and visuo-spatial deficiencies occur. And perhaps the most important disorder is in the sequential ordering of both visual and verbal stimuli and their association together. This might suggest an impairment of functions of the parietal area analogous to Gerstmann's syndrome, except that the existence of this syndrome is doubtful. And verbal conceptual reasoning appears to be involved in the dyslexic's deficiencies in sequential ordering, not merely perception of order. Finally, it is doubtful if anything more than an analogy exists between the developmental dyslexic syndromes and those of adult disorders, which analogy may indeed be misleading (Critchley, 1970).

The concept of *minimal brain damage*, as distinct from damage accompanied by clear neurological signs of organic impairment, was severely criticized at a conference of neurologists, paediatricians, psychologists, etc. held in 1962 (MacKeith & Bax, 1963). In cases diagnosed as suffering from minimal brain damage, evidence of anatomical damage was absent, and there was often no evidence or history of any injuring process. There might be no signs of cortical dysfunction and abnormality in the brain. Ingram (1963 b) discriminated cases in which appeared definite clinical syndromes with consistent evidence of abnormality, such as minor cerebral palsy and hyper-kinetic (over-active) behaviour, from cases in which there was no such evidence of abnormality, as with dysphasia, dyslexia, dysgraphia and clumsiness. Francis-Williams

(1963) described three cases of children with an early history of brain damage. Two were dyslexic, one having a history of slow speech development but normal visuo-spatial perception, and the second with poor articulation and motor control and in addition visual disorders. The third case exhibited motor and visuo-spatial disorders, but could read well. All the cases suffered from secondary emotional difficulties; but in a fourth case there was emotional blockage only and no brain damage nor motor nor cognitive defects. It was suggested that the differentiating factor between the first three and the fourth case was minimal brain damage; and indeed the motor disabilities would appear to have been directly related to that. However the linguistic and visuo-spatial disorders may occur in cases in which no brain damage is apparent.

The conference finally decided that in future the term '*minimal cerebral dysfunction*' should be applied to all these cases. Yet no evidence seems to have been cited as to the nature of this dysfunction, other than in cases such as the three described by Francis-Williams. But minimal cerebral dysfunction is still diagnosed by certain clinicians, it would appear from the occurrence of EEG abnormalities and from so-called 'soft' signs which are the cognitive and motor defects we have described above. Thus in general the concept of minimal cerebral dysfunction would appear to have little descriptive or explanatory value as regards cases of dyslexia. However, it is sometimes employed as indicating a delay in maturation of certain cortical functions, as we shall consider in the next section.

We noted that several investigators observed the frequent appearance of incomplete lateralization in dyslexic cases with dysphasic disorders. It has sometimes been suggested that there is a direct neurological association between slow speech development and incomplete cerebral dominance; that is to say, in such cases the language functions are not completely lateralized. Thus it has been observed that language functions may be more completely lateralized in the right-handed than in the left-handed and ambidextrous. Whereas in the right-handed, lesions to the left cerebral hemisphere almost always produce aphasia, in the left-handed and ambidextrous aphasia may be caused by lesions to either hemisphere (Zangwill, 1963). It was also hypothesized by Travis (1931) that with incomplete cerebral dominance the mechanisms of speech were imperfectly controlled; hence, a greater incidence of stammering in the left-handed than in the right-handed. However, evidence for this association (discussed by Vernon, 1957) was not reliable. Indeed, as we have seen, there has been considerable disagreement as to the incidence of incomplete lateralization in dyslexics. The extreme emphasis on its importance given by Delacato (1966) would seem to be misplaced. It is possible however, that incomplete lateralization may be associated with general delay in cortical maturation.

New light on the neurological functions associated with lateral dominance in dyslexia was thrown by a recent study of Newton (1970). She compared the EEG recordings from the right and left temporal, parietal and occipital areas of the cortex in a group of dyslexic children, aged 8–13 years, within the normal range of intelligence but retarded in reading by an average of 4 years, with those of a group of matched controls who read normally. She found that the dyslexics showed more alpha and theta activity, demonstrating a low level of arousal, in the dominant hemisphere; or else little differentiation between the two hemispheres. The controls showed more such activity in the non-dominant hemisphere. Thus she concluded that lateral dominance in arousal was incomplete in the dyslexics. It appeared that in 40 per cent of these cases there was possible neurological impairment; in 35 per cent, genetic determination; and in 20 per cent, both factors.

(B) *Maturational Lag*

The theory which is perhaps most commonly held today with regard to dyslexia is that the majority of dyslexics are suffering from maturational lag, a failure in the normal maturation of certain functions of the cerebral cortex. The neurological patterns have shown slow differentiation and have remained immature. Thus clearly defined neurological patterns such as that of cerebral dominance have not been fully established, as perhaps in Newton's cases of deficient arousal in the major hemisphere in dyslexics. Thus lateralization is weak, as in younger children. We noted that Naidoo (1961) found that only 37 per cent of children aged $4\frac{1}{2}$–6 years were consistently and unequivocally right- or left-handed. Harris (1957) showed that lateralization was less complete in backward than in normal readers at 7 and 9 years, but was approximately the same by 11 years. However, it remained weak or inconsistent in some of Zangwill's older patients (Zangwill, 1960). We noted also that left–right discrimination improved with increase in age, and that significant differences between dyslexics and normal readers were in the more difficult left–right discriminations involving verbal functions. Cohen & Glass (1968) found that certain aspects of directional awareness were related to reading achievement in first grade but not in fourth grade children.

Again, reversals in reading and writing in dyslexics and some errors in the Gottschaldt and other perceptual tests resembled those occurring in younger normal readers. So also was 'primitivization' of reproductions in the Bender test. These tended to disappear in older dyslexics. Indeed Benton (1962) went so far as to state that deficiencies in visual perception were unimportant as correlates of dyslexia in older children of adequate intelligence. Again, Nielson & Ringe (1969) found that with children of 9–10 years there were no differences between those in remedial reading classes and normal readers on the Draw-a-Man and Frostig tests.

Deficiencies in dyslexics in auditory discrimination and in the matching of visual and auditory sequences resembled those occurring in younger normal children. And delayed development of speech and of the correct use of language characterized certain types of dyslexia. Thus it appeared that in some respects primitive perceptual and other cognitive processes which had disappeared in normal readers at a comparatively early age might persist till a later age in dyslexics, but might finally die out in them also.

On the other hand, it is not certain if all defects characteristic of dyslexia are similar in nature to those of younger normal children. The extremely bizarre writing and spelling (Fig. 8 on p. 129), the most distorted Bender test reproductions, and copies of objects such as those shown in Figs. 9 and 10 on pp. 132–3, would appear to have greater similarity to the productions of adult patients with parietal lobe injuries than to those of young children. Moreover, they would seem to occur in older dyslexics who might be expected to have grown out of such defects if they were caused by delayed maturation. De Hirsch, Jansky & Langford (1966) found that in dyslexic children of 11–15 years many of the symptoms of younger dyslexic children persisted: lack of differentiation and synthesis in Bender test reproductions, crude and primitive human figure drawings, diffuse auditory discrimination, linguistic deficiencies, uncontrolled hand movements and bad hand-writing. Again, the deficiencies in sequential ordering described by Doehring (1968) still existed in dyslexic children of 14 years. Thus there would appear to be some doubt whether symptoms can always be attributed to delayed maturation, or are the result of some permanent disability.

On the hypothesis of delayed maturation, it would be expected that children would also grow out of their dyslexia. Many do attain some ability in reading, though spelling continues to be impaired. Silver & Hagin (1964) found that twenty-four children followed up until 19 years of age still showed marked reading disability, together with difficulties in figure–ground discrimination and some degree of finger agnosia, although left–right discrimination had improved. About half the older cases of De Hirsch, Jansky & Langford (1966) had become fairly adequate readers through intelligent use of context, but most were poor at spelling. Rawson (1968) followed up her twenty dyslexic children and found that, after special individual teaching, their reading had greatly improved by the time they left the primary school. But 35 per cent were retarded by a half-year or more in reading, and 90 per cent were retarded in spelling. Though their subsequent careers were highly satisfactory, they were still not fluent in reading nor efficient in spelling. Thus it cannot be said that they entirely grew out of their dyslexia.

Bender (1968) considered that dyslexia was more likely to appear in cases of delayed maturation if the child was exposed to unfavourable environmental conditions, and also if the personality was immature. Zangwill (1960) suggested that cases of weak lateralization and imperfectly established cerebral dominance might be particularly vulnerable to emotional stress. Moreover, the development of spatial and directional orientation and of the ability to read and write were in these cases likely to have been disturbed by minimal brain injury at birth, and also by unfavourable environmental circumstances and especially by situations leading to emotional maladjustment in later childhood. The necessity of correcting a tendency to left-hand writing and to reversal might itself create stress. This hypothesis and that of Bender would suggest that any maturational lag in dyslexia may not be purely cognitive, but may be a more general personality characteristic.

This is also indicated in the findings of De Hirsch, Jansky & Langford (1966), which showed that the 6-year-old children they tested who subsequently failed to learn to read normally exhibited an accumulation of many of the characteristics of younger children, in general behaviour as well as in test performance. The tests which gave the best prediction of future reading achievement were those in which an improvement with increasing age was discernable in normal readers. Also several of the children who subsequently failed were physically immature. Some were hyper-active, impulsive and distractible; others were apathetic and incapable of co-ordinated movement. In general, behaviour and personality were infantile in nature. The children did not respond to testing in an organized and purposeful manner. They could not mobilize energy successfully in performing a task, nor carry out plans of action without immediate gratification, for instance by rewards of sweets. Some whined, cried and had to be comforted by the experimenter. A similar general immaturity occurred also in a group of prematurely-born children.

The failing children were compared with another group termed 'slow starters'. In the initial testing the latter performed adequately on the simpler tasks of figure–ground differentiation, organization of the visual field and auditory perception. Their drawings of human figures were also less primitive than those of the failing children, but their performance on the Bender test was poor. However, they did not exhibit the behavioural disorders found in the reading failures. They obtained zero scores on reading tests at the end of their first year of learning, but reached the expected level after two years. Spelling achievement was still inferior in half the group. Thus it is possible that these cases were suffering from a comparatively mild form of dyslexia, without general immaturity of personality.

The number of cases studied by De Hirsch, Jansky & Langford was small; there were only eight in the failing group and eight slow starters. Therefore there is some doubt as to the generality of these results. Dyslexic children studied by other investigators do not appear to have exhibited the same general personality characteristics. In many, the maturational lag, if it existed, seemed to be confined to certain rather specific cognitive processes. Indeed, Rawson's cases appear to have possessed superior personalities.

Birch (1962) considered that dyslexics have an inadequate capacity to integrate events in the visual and auditory modes, as in younger children. This did in fact appear in experimental observations described in Ch. IV (see p. 68). Backward readers were inferior to normal readers in readiness to respond to cross-modal stimulation; and also in matching auditory with visual rhythms. Birch found that the capacity to integrate visual and tactile–kinaesthetic stimulation was also poor in dyslexics; for instance, in matching shapes felt by touch against visually perceived shapes. Thus such children might have particular difficulty in applying their knowledge of printed word structure in writing; and writing would be inferior even to reading, which as we have noted frequently occurs in dyslexia.

It is possible therefore that a fundamental lag may affect the numerous processes of organization and integration which are essential in learning to read. In some cases this may be associated with general immaturity of personality, and the results of De Hirsch, Jansky & Langford suggest in these cases dyslexia may be severe. Alternatively, its effects may be aggravated by poor motivation or emotional stress. Such children are clearly not ready to begin formal instruction in reading when they first go to school. But if this were delayed until the processes essential for reading had developed to a more mature stage, they might have relatively little difficulty in learning.

However, there is also the possibility that there is some permanent dysfunction in the cerebral cortex which persists throughout life, even it its more harmful effects can be alleviated by suitable remedial teaching. There is no reliable evidence at present to determine whether this is so. Clearly it is inadvisable to disregard the condition in young children on the plea that they will grow out of it spontaneously. Remediation at the earliest possible opportunity is essential.

(c) *Hereditary Factors*

Finally, it has been suggested that there exists a *hereditary disposition* towards dyslexia, or perhaps towards the immaturity in neurological patterning on which dyslexia may depend. The most notable exponent of the inheritance of dyslexia was Hallgren (1950). He studied over 200 dyslexic children and their family histories, and claimed that in all but thirteen cases there was some evidence of reading disability in parents, siblings or other relatives. It appeared that the disability might be a Mendelian dominant, since in some cases it was reported as occurring in three successive generations. Few other investigators have claimed so high an incidence of inherited disability, though Hermann (1959) reported that 'information related to heredity' had been elicited in more than 90 per cent of his cases. In other studies, it has more commonly been stated that *some* cases exhibit a hereditary disposition. Thus Doehring (1968) found that 40 per cent of the parents of his dyslexic children had experienced reading problems, as against 10 per cent of normal controls. Newton (1970) found genetic factors in 55 per cent of her cases. But De Hirsch, Jansky & Langford (1966) obtained no significant correlations between reading achievement and any familial characteristics. It is often difficult of course to obtain reliable evidence as to the reading difficulties of parents and other relatives. But Drew (1956) examined in some detail two half-brothers and their father, all of whom suffered from dyslexia in some degree. He concluded that there was an inherited dominant trait appearing as a disturbance of Gestalt function which affected reading and spelling, and also performance of the WAIS Block Design and Digit-Symbol (Coding) sub-tests, and spatial orientation. He considered that the cause of this disorder might be delayed development of the parietal lobe.

Kolson & Kaluger (1963) hypothesized that the more severe cases of dyslexia, who made little or no progress under remedial treatment, suffered from primary dyslexia, for which there was an inherited disposition. This appeared also in difficulty in recognizing forms, in left–right discrimination and in finger agnosia. Secondary dyslexia was acquired through the operation of a number of factors, intellectual, sociological and emotional. McGlannan (cited by Harris, Otto & Barrett, 1969) studied three generations of each of sixty-five families in which children were severely dyslexic, and in which two or more members of the family had language disorders. He also found that left-handedness and ambidextrality were frequent in these cases. Rawson (1968) observed that for many of her dyslexic boys there was a family history of language disability and directional confusion. And Ingram (1959b) noted that in the dysphasic type of dyslexia family histories of speech disorder were frequent.

Ingram (1964) also reported a family history of weak lateralization in 40 per cent of his dyslexic cases. Indeed, it is sometimes claimed that the inherited disposition may appear in some cases only as left-handedness or mixed handedness. Zangwill (1960) quoted ten instances of this among twenty cases. Ettlinger & Jackson (1955) found that in five out of six dyslexic cases at least one member of the family was left-handed or ambidextrous, though in only one case was there a dyslexic member of the family. Doehring (1968) however found no difference in the distribution of handedness in the families of dyslexic and of normal readers. It should be noted that evidence as to laterality in the families of dyslexic children may be unreliable, since direct testing is usually impossible and reports of hand preference may be suspect. As

Annett (1970) showed, there is no discontinuity in the scale of handedness, and assessment may depend on the activities studied. She was inclined to favour a hereditary basis for handedness, based on several genetic factors rather than on a single one. But she did not investigate any relationship between inherited handedness and reading disability.

It has been argued, particularly by Hermann (1959), that the existence of a hereditary disposition to dyslexia is supported by evidence from its incidence in monozygotic and dizygotic *twins*. He cited Hallgren as finding that in three monozygotic pairs of twins, both twins were dyslexic; whereas in only one of three pairs of dizygotic twins were both dyslexic. Hermann also cited the work of Norrie on nine pairs of monozygotic twins who were both dyslexic; but in thirty pairs of dizygotic twins, both twins were dyslexic in only ten cases. Since the genetic disposition of monozygotic twins is identical, whereas that of dizygotic twins is more like that of other siblings, these findings seem to demonstrate the significance of inherited disposition.

Some authors, notably Critchley (1970) have advanced as evidence of a hereditary disposition the *sex difference* in incidence of dyslexia. It is a very general finding that this is higher in boys than in girls; and indeed in school samples the reading achievement of boys is usually inferior on the average to that of girls. This finding is not universal. But in clinic cases the ratio of boys to girls can be of the order of 4 or 5 to 1. Hence it has been suggested that the dyslexic disposition is a *sex-linked genetic characteristic*. But Hallgren (1950) found no evidence of sex-linked inheritance in his cases, and suggested that more boys than girls are referred to clinics for reading disability because school failure is more important in boys than in girls. De Hirsch, Jansky & Langford (1966) considered that the greater incidence in boys might be due to their greater physical immaturity and cited Tanner as finding that at 6 years boys lagged 12 months behind girls in skeletal age. It was observed in the study of De Hirsch, Jansky & Langford that some of the boys who became reading failures were physically immature. Recent work suggests the possibility also that lateralization of language functions in the dominant hemisphere occurs at an earlier age in girls than in boys. If further investigation proves that this is so, delay in learning to read may be associated with relative immaturity in boys of certain language functions.

It has indeed been suggested that boys are inferior to girls in linguistic development generally; though McCarthy (1953) threw some doubt on this. It could be associated with differences in interests. Thus boys as a rule are more interested in constructional and mechanical activities, and in consequence are often found to carry out Performance tests more efficiently than girls. They are relatively less interested and proficient in verbal activities. Girls appear to settle down more easily in school, to be less bored and to react less aggressively to unfavourable conditions than do boys (Kellmer Pringle, Butler & Davie, 1966). Hebron (1966) considered that the girl becomes accustomed during her upbringing to comply with her mother's wishes, in order to achieve security, and has learnt to meet criticism with increased effort. This behaviour is transferred to her interaction with her teachers. The boy on the other hand is more obstinate and aggressive, especially when he encounters difficulties. In a large survey of school behaviour, Highfield & Pinsent (1952) found that girls of 7–9 years showed more application to their work than did boys, more planning capacity and more purposeful persistence in difficulties. This difference disappeared by 10 years and was subsequently reversed. Such differences in attitude to school may well explain the better average reading achievement of girls than boys, but they would not seem to account for a higher incidence of dyslexia in the former, a difference which Ingram (1964) observed specifically in familial cases.

Thus it may be concluded that there is a hereditary disposition at least in some cases of dyslexia. But it would be unwise in the present state of evidence to decide that it is a dominant trait, or that it is sex-linked. It could be associated with more general developmental differences between the sexes.

(6) THE EFFECTS OF REMEDIAL TREATMENT
ON DYSLEXIA

We have already noted that the severe reading disability which normally occurs in dyslexia is often highly resistant to remedial teaching. Some cases may improve rapidly, but many show only very slow recovery, if any. Or some degree of reading ability may be achieved, but the children do not read fluently, and continue to spell badly. The variability of improvement appears particularly when there is *group remedial teaching*. Thus Collins (1961) found that a group of severely retarded readers given six months remedial teaching at a centre or in school showed considerably more improvement than did a control group who continued to receive ordinary school teaching. But when the children were tested again after $2\frac{1}{2}$ years, there was no significant difference between the groups. However, examination of the results of individual children showed that 38 per cent of all the children advanced about as much in reading age as in chronological age; 36 per cent gained more, and 26 per cent less. Six of the latter were still only semi-literate, with reading ages below 8 years. The percentages were not significantly different in the experimental and control groups. It seemed therefore that whereas some children improved considerably whatever teaching they received, there were others, probably dyslexic, who failed to profit even from remedial teaching.

A similar lack of over-all improvement was demonstrated by Cashdan & Pumfrey (1969), with 8-year-old boys retarded in reading by three years on the average. Though given remedial teaching for two terms in small groups of four, their average improvement was not significantly different from that of similar children who remained in their ordinary school classes. The same result was obtained when the children were retested about two years later. Cashdan & Pumfrey concluded that a longer period of remedial teaching is necessary to produce significant results.

A varied response to remedial teaching was obtained by other experimenters. Thus Hillman & Snowdon (1960) found that 9-year-old children, retarded in reading by two years on the average, who were sent to remedial classes for three terms, improved significantly more than did similar children who remained in their ordinary schools. But the improvement of the former varied from 8 months to 3 years of reading age. Lovell, Johnson & Platts (1962) compared the improvement shown by 10-year-old children with an average reading age of about 6 years, taught individually at a remedial reading centre, with that of similar children taught in small groups in their own schools by a visiting remedial teacher. At the end of this teaching the gain in reading age varied from 0–6·1 years in the first group and from 0–4·8 years in the second. At a later re-test, when the children had reached 12–13 years of age, 25 per cent of the first group and 37 per cent of the second still had reading ages of under 8½ years. Thus although the children who were taught individually showed rather more improvement than did those taught in groups, there were still many whose reading ability was poor.

It would appear that the degree of improvement resulting from remedial teaching depends partly on *age*. Thus Chansky (1963) found that with dyslexic children of 8–14 years, improvement from remedial teaching correlated negatively with age. Schiffman (cited by Goldberg, 1968) stated that 82 per cent of dyslexics diagnosed in the first two grades at school could learn to read normally as the result of remedial teaching, as against 46 per cent of those diagnosed in the third grade, 42 per cent in the fourth grade and 10–15 per cent in grades 5–7. This suggests that the children did not grow out of their reading disability without assistance, and that it became more deeply ingrained as time went on. However, it is probable that in the older children motivation was greatly impaired by persistent failure, frustration and discouragement. Thus Ablewhite (1967) considered that children who had failed to learn to read after three years in the primary school might develop definite personality problems. When very retarded readers entered the secondary school, they required special methods of arousing interest and changing attitudes to reading before remedial teaching could be effective.

Improvement also depends on the *efficacy and appropriateness* of remedial teaching. In the first place, it must be specialized in some manner. Friedmann (1958) found that 8-year-old children given three months' teaching in special remedial classes improved by over 3 months of reading age per month's teaching, whereas those left in ordinary schools progressed very little. We noted that Lovell *et al.* (1962) found greater improvement in children taught individually at a remedial centre than in those taught in small groups in their own schools. It is generally agreed that severely dyslexic children profit most from *individual teaching*; indeed, without it they may fail to learn. Thus Rawson's dyslexic boys were given individual teaching once it was found that they failed to learn from class teaching; and the majority acquired some capacity to read by the time they left school. It is probable that individual teaching improves motivation, as well as attacking directly the child's particular difficulties and correcting his errors before they are stamped in.

It might be supposed that if there are different types of dyslexia, visual and verbal, these would respond maximally to different kinds of *teaching method*. Indeed, it has been claimed that those whose defects are primarily visual are best taught by phonic methods, supplemented by recognition of whole forms and analysis of their details, perception of orientation and of sequences (Johnson & Myklebust, 1967). Those who suffer from auditory and linguistic deficiencies but are normal in visuo-spatial perception should be taught by whole word methods, with emphasis on auditory–visual correspondence and with additional training in auditory analysis and the perception of auditory sequences. The rationale of these methods appeared to be that initial learning to read should utilize those processes in which the child was adept; but supplementary training should also be given to overcome his weaknesses. This judgment was echoed by Naidoo (1970). But no evidence has been adduced as to the efficacy of these procedures.

Other writers have advocated some type of phonic method for all dyslexics. Bryant (1968) stated that the principal difficulties of dyslexics were in the extraction and recognition of details within wholes, either visual or auditory. Thus remedial teaching should begin by calling attention to these details, through writing and tracing and through practice in rapid discrimination of similar words. But also the capacity to associate sounds with printed letters was limited; thus associations should be taught a few at a time and blended into words, until they were learnt thoroughly. Though no data were given as to the effectiveness of this method, it resembles the Gillingham–Stillman method (see Orton, 1966) which Rawson (1968) found to be successful for children with linguistic difficulties. This began with the naming and sounding of a few letters, together with tracing and copying them. The consonants were presented as initial letters of words; but when a few vowels had been learnt, blending into familiar three-letter words was practiced. The sequence of letters and digraphs was from the easiest to the most difficult. Clearly the method depended on systematic building up from fundamental details. However, meaningful words and sentences were employed as soon as the child was able to use them. Again, it may be preferable for the child always to sound letters in word context, as in the method suggested by Miles (1970).

These methods emphasize the importance of writing, beginning with *tracing* from a model. This is the fundamental principle of Fernald's kinaesthetic method, which she claimed was successful with the most severely dyslexic children (Fernald, 1943). Indeed, it has been employed by many teachers with children who could learn in no other way. In this method, the child selected a few words which were written down for him in large letters. He then traced them over and over again with his forefinger while enunciating them, until eventually he could write them whenever he sounded them without looking at the original model. It was claimed that the method was particularly successful for children whose visual memory was poor. Talmadge, Davids & Laufer (1963) tested the effects of teaching reading by this method to dyslexic children suffering from cortical dysfunction caused by minimal brain damage and dyslexic children without brain damage. In a period of 3 months, the former improved by 1·04 years of reading age, the latter by 0·62 years. Similar children, with and without brain damage, taught by traditional methods, improved only by o·45 years. It was supposed by Fernald that the auditory patterns of the words became directly linked with the kinaesthetic patterns of movement of the hand in tracing. Thus the weak visual patterns were supplemented and reinforced. However, it may be that the effect is really to draw the child's attention to the structure of the letters and words, and the order of letters in words (Harris, 1956), hence reinforcing sequential processing. It would seem possible that the Gillingham–Stillman method, with its systematic sounding and tracing of letter–sound associations, would be more efficaceous. On the other hand, the Fernald method is claimed to appeal to the children's interests, through the use of words selected by the children themselves.

There are many other methods recommended for remedial reading teaching; Cotterell (1970) has discussed these procedures in some detail. Again, many of the methods proposed for teaching beginners are claimed to be appropriate for remedial teaching also. Thus Daniels & Diack (1956) found that their modified phonic method (see p. 48) was more successful in teaching word recognition to junior school non-readers, aged 8 years, than was a mixed phonic and whole word method. Unfortunately little validation has been attempted of the claims for other remedial teaching methods. It would appear that on the whole some type of phonic method is most effective. This indicates yet again that the dyslexic child's basic incapacity lies in associating the appropriate phoneme sequences to printed letter sequences, and synthesizing them correctly to form word sounds; that is to say, in grasping the correspondence between spatially extended letter sequences and temporally ordered phoneme sequences.

NOTE, 1973 In an investigation by S. Naidoo (*Specific Dyslexia*, Invalid Children's Aid Association, 1972), extensive testing and clinical interviewing were applied to boys of 8–13 years referred to a clinic for severe backwardness in reading and/or spelling. Some of these cases possessed a family history of reading and spelling difficulties and some appeared to suffer from neurological dysfunction; and among the former it was possible to distinguish those with auditory-linguistic deficiencies and those with poor visuo-spatial ability. Deficiencies in serial order processing were common throughout, A complex of contributory factors could be diagnosed in most cases, but clearly defined sub-groups could not be established by means of statistical cluster analysis.

CHAPTER VIII

CONCLUSIONS

It has appeared from the argument presented in the previous chapters that four principal types of psychological process are involved in reading; and that defective functioning of any of these may give rise to difficulty in learning to read.

(1) *Visual perception* of the printed material is basic and primary. This involves not merely the discrimination of simple shapes and patterns, but also the analysis of the complex forms of words into their constituent elements, the letters, and the recognition and identification of the essential shape and orientation of the latter. Hence good visual memory is necessary.

(2) *Auditory–linguistic perception* of and memory for speech sounds, not only of whole words and phrases, as in ordinary speech communication, but also in the analysis of these into their constituent phonemes, and the subsequent recognition of these. This is particularly difficult for young children, since they tend to apprehend words and even phrases as simultaneous unanalysable events. Some knowledge of the linguistic structure of continuous sentences is also involved.

(3) *Intellectual processes* which are various and ill-defined. It has been argued that conceptual reasoning is involved in understanding the symbolic nature of written language; in conceptualizing its essential visual and auditory components; and in associating these together. This necessitates the realization of the exact correspondence between spatially extended sequences of visual symbols and the temporally ordered sequences of phonemes.

(4) *Motivational processes*, adequate in strength and direction, also appeared to be essential. Children possessing the abilities necessary to perform the three types of cognitive process might fail to do so unless suitably motivated.

It seems likely that the abilities of children even within the range of normal reading achievement vary in degree, and hence the efficiency with which they perform these processes. We noted that variations in reading achievement were related to differences in general intelligence (g), verbal ability (v) and probably also in visuo-spatial ability. These abilities vary continuously in different children, from high to low. Thus the likelihood is that ability to perform the processes essential in reading varies similarly, along a continuous scale. It is also possible that the variations are, at least in part, innate in origin. We noted that general intelligence was in all probability subject to genetic variation, and it seems possible that auditory and linguistic abilities may show a similar innate variability. Certainly we know that children begin to speak at widely differing ages, though here environmental factors may be involved also. Again, sex differences in linguistic development might be in part genetic in origin. However, little appears to be known as to such innate variations; as also with variations in visuo-spatial ability.*

The effects of environmental influences are also frequently obscure. It appeared that linguistic ability, which was usually more deficient in backward readers than was visuo-spatial ability, was affected not only by gross deprivation of close contact with adults in infancy and early childhood, but also by lack of warm affectionate relationship with the mother or a mother substitute. Cultural deficiencies in the home, even if they did not impair development of the earliest language constructions, seemed to cause linguistic retardation at a later age. It has been suggested that gross deprivation of visual experience in infancy may affect the development of certain visual perceptual abilities. But such a deficiency may appear mainly in object recognition. There is no evidence, except in the tentative conclusions of P. E. Vernon

* A recent paper by Hartlage (1970) reported a study of the performance on a test of spatial ability of a hundred fathers, mothers, sons and daughters in twenty-five families. Significant correlations of 0·39 and 0·34 were obtained between the scores of mothers and sons, and fathers and daughters, respectively. Correlations between scores of fathers and sons and between mothers and daughters were not significant. Hartlage therefore concluded that there was evidence of sex-linked inheritance of spatial ability.

(1969), that minor degrees of environmenta restriction impair capacity for the visual analysis of form. However, a variety of factors was claimed by Vernon to affect the development of the intellectual capacities; and it would seem also that these might be influenced by the appropriateness of education. Nevertheless, it is difficult to trace any exact relationship between variation in the particular intellectual capacities involved in reading, and particular types of environmental influence.

As regards the motivational processes which are essential in stimulating the child to exercise his abilities: Again, we must suppose that there are certain innate differences in motivation in different children. Thus Escalona (1968) has demonstrated the effects on the behaviour of infants of apparently innate differences in responsiveness, excitability and energy in activity. It seems probable that these differences continue to operate in childhood; but undoubtedly they are modified to a very considerable extent by environmental influences, and particularly through the interaction of the child with his parents. These influences are so fundamental and far-reaching as to outweigh in importance those resulting from any other environmental circumstances. But we considered briefly the effects on motivation of school teaching and relationships with teachers.

Whatever the causes of variation, there appears to be sufficient evidence to show that the normal range of cognitive ability and of motivation in children may well be responsible for quite large differences in capacity to learn to read. It is then possible that unsatisfactory methods of teaching reading and lack of skill in teachers may affect particularly those children with lower degrees of cognitive ability and with poor motivation; while the more gifted, interested and responsive are able to learn in spite of inadequacy in teaching. Thus though some backwardness may be attributed solely to such inadequacy, or to the direct effects of, for instance, poverty and cultural deficiencies in the home, it is likely that in many if not the majority of cases the children are deficient in one or more of the basic cognitive abilities, or are failing to function effectively through impaired motivation. Were formal instruction postponed until the age of 6 years, or even later, both abilities and motivation might have developed and become more adequate. When teaching begins at too early an age, the child may be too immature to profit by it; and a succession of failures may produce such discouragement that it becomes increasingly difficult for him to learn.

We must then consider the questions: Is there, in addition to the normal variations in reading ability we have just discussed, an independent dyslexic syndrome or syndromes lying outside the normal range of variation? Are these innate disabilities, aggravated perhaps but not caused by environmental circumstances? And if so, is it possible to differentiate dyslexics from backward readers who should not be classified as dyslexic?

The evidence adduced in the preceding chapter would seem adequate to establish the existence of a basic disability in at least some backward readers. In these cases, the reading difficulty is not caused solely by poor intelligence, inadequate motivation or environmental circumstances such as uncultured homes or ineffective teaching, though all these factors may aggravate the effects of the basic disability. This disability appears principally in difficulty in grasping the sequential spatial relationships of printed letters and the temporal sequential relationships of phonemes in words; in associating these together; and in reintegrating them into meaningful wholes. It may be that in some cases there is greater weakness in analysing the essential formal and directional characteristics of printed words; in others it may lie in phonemic analysis, and the perception of temporal auditory patterns. But the deficiency is not purely perceptual; it affects the reasoning necessary to comprehend the exact correspondence and association between the spatially ordered visual sequences and the temporally ordered linguistic sequences. The elements of these sequences must be integrated together, and then coordinated into higher order sequences which have a regular and accepted grammatical structure and which also convey meaning. Normally the child has acquired the ability to inter-relate syntactic and semantic structure through the use of spoken language. But in reading he is required to reconstruct actively, first, word structures, then syntactic and semantic sequences in the form of phrases and sentences. This reconstruction is not a mere passive copy of his own speech constructions; the phrases and sentences he is required to read may differ considerably from these. Thus we noted in some dyslexics a deficiency in making spatial constructions, as with Kohs Blocks. Some cases might have difficulty not only in reconstructing words with correct sequential order of letters, but also in reconstructing sentences with correct sequential order of words. Thus in dyslexia there may be a single basic type of disability, in the reconstruction of particular kinds of sequential structure. It may arise mainly in conjunction with poor linguistic ability, especially in deficiencies in the analysis of linguistic structures; or mainly in conjunction with defective visual analysis of complex forms and their directional characteristics. These deficiencies may appear also in the performance of verbal and visuo-spatial tests, but most clearly when some process of ordered reconstruction is required.

As to the precise nature of the disability we know little, and much further experimental investigation is required to define this and to demonstrate exactly how it operates in creating reading difficulties. And as to the ultimate cause of the disability, the evidence is too weak and conflicting to do more than suggest certain highly speculative hypotheses. Actual injury in particular areas of the cerebral cortex seems to occur in only a small number of cases. In many there may be a retardation, termed maturational lag, in development of ability to perform certain of the cognitive processes essential for reading, especially in sequential processing. The lag may also appear in incomplete establishment of cerebral dominance; but there is no satisfactory evidence that this affects reading directly. In some cases delay in maturation may be associated with general immaturity of the personality or may be aggravated by emotional stress. Immature dyslexics may improve in reading as they grow older; and their difficulties might be obviated to some extent by a delay in the beginning of formal instruction. But in the most severe cases the disability would seem to be permanent, at least as regards spelling and the more advanced stages of reading.

The cortical basis of this disposition is unknown; but in an appreciable proportion of cases it appears to be not only innate but also inherited.

It is difficult in the present state of our knowledge to differentiate dyslexic from non-dyslexic backward readers. Indeed it may be impossible to do so with any precision. As we noted on p. 148, Rawson's cases exhibited a continuous scale of disability. However, one might classify as dyslexic only those suffering from a major defect in reading ability resulting from deficiencies in the capacity to associate visual and linguistic sequences. The deficiency would appear in excessive and persistent reversals in reading and writing, and in poor performance of tests of directionality, left–right discrimination, sequential ordering and reconstruction of complex forms. Failure on visuo-spatial tests of this nature would seem to be particularly characteristic of the constitutional disability of dyslexia, since it is not associated with environmental deficiencies. On the other hand, cases in which the disability is mainly linguistic in origin are more difficult to classify because of the impairment of linguistic development caused by adverse cultural factors. Indeed, some writers might prefer to term these cases dysphasic. Nevertheless, it would be important to differentiate cases of linguistic disability in which deficiencies in sequential processing were involved from any in which there were none.

It is possible that in many cases the constitutional disability may be so mild as to be easily overcome, given adequate intelligence and motivation, and favourable environmental circumstances. Where these circumstances are adverse, their improvement might relieve the child to such an extent that his motivation would be restored to normal and, given adequate teaching, he would overcome his constitutional disability and learn to read without great difficulty. It would seem important to differentiate those whose ability to learn to read is normal but inhibited by poor motivation or emotional disorder, from those suffering from a constitutional disability, however mild, such that one or more of the processes described above is not functioning effectively. The latter may have prolonged difficulty in learning even if environmental conditions are improved. It may also be much harder to increase effective motivation, since the child is likely to remain discouraged until he achieves some success in learning.

However, it is true that in many cases remedial teaching may enable children to acquire at least the basic stages of reading, though they may never become really fluent. Spelling appears to be less remediable. Although the effectiveness of remedial teaching depends on its skill and on the extent of the child's disability, good motivation is obviously important also, as was apparent in Rawson's cases. In some instances, as in the children described by De Hirsch, Jansky & Langford, there may be immaturity in the mobilization and direction of effort. Thus it is very important for the remedial teacher, not only to employ skilful methods of instruction, but also to apply the most appropriate means of stimulation and encouragement, of overcoming resistance or hopelessness, and of directing the child's efforts to the best advantage. Some of the most successful remedial teachers seem to possess a charismatic personality which enables them to convince the child that he can surmount his difficulties. Others may need training in the best methods of stimulation, as well as in teaching techniques.

It must be emphasized that individual teaching is always likely to be more effective than group teaching. In the first place, the teacher can establish a close relationship with the child, focus his attention and alleviate his discouragement and frustration by personal sympathy and encouragement. Secondly, she can ascertain the exact nature of his particular difficulties and adjust her teaching accordingly. Perhaps most important of all, she can immediately confirm or correct his responses, thus reinforcing the right responses and inhibiting the wrong ones, and ensuring that he does not remain in a state of doubt and confusion as to what he should have done.

Even if it is impossible to give individual remedial teaching to all backward readers, groups of children may be broken up and individual attention provided as frequently as possible. Without this, it seems likely that many severely backward readers will not improve.

CONCLUSIONS

Finally, it must be emphasized that severe backwardness should always be detected in the primary school, and remedial teaching provided immediately. As Ablewhite (1967) noted, it is difficult to overcome the resentment and despondency of dyslexic children in the secondary school, though he does suggest valuable procedures to attempting this. But at this stage the severely dyslexic may be difficult to help.

REFERENCES

ABLEWHITE, R. C. (1967). *The Slow Reader*. London: Heinemann.

ALTUS, G. T. (1956). A WISC profile for retarded readers. *J. Consult. Psychol.* **20**, 155.

AMES, L. B. & ILG, F. L. (1951). Developmental trends in writing behavior. *J. Genet. Psychol.* **79**, 29.

AMES, L. B., LEARNED, J., METRAUX, R. & WALKER, R. (1953). Development of perception in the young child as observed in responses to the Rorschach Test blots. *J. Genet. Psychol.* **82**, 183.

AMES, L. B. & WALKER, R. N. (1964). Prediction of later reading ability from kindergarten Rorschach and I.Q. scores. *J. Educ. Psychol.* **55**, 309.

ANDERSON, I. H., BYRON, O. & DIXON, W. R. (1956). The relationship between reading achievement and the method of teaching reading. *Univ. Mich. Sch. Educ. Bull.* **7**, 104.

ANDERSON, I. H., HUGHES, B. O. & DIXON, W. R. (1956). Age of learning to read and its relation to sex, intelligence and reading achievement in the sixth grade. *J. Educ. Res.* **49**, 447.

ANDERSON, I. H., HUGHES, B. O. & DIXON, W. R. (1957). The rate of reading development and its relation to age of learning to read, sex and intelligence. *J. Educ. Res.* **50**, 481.

ANISFELD, M. (1968). Language and cognition in the young child. In K. S. Goodman (ed.), *The Psycholinguistic Nature of the Reading Process*. Detroit: Wayne State Univ. Press.

ANNETT, M. (1970). A classification of hand preference by association analysis. *Brit. J. Psychol.* **61**, 303.

BABSKA, Z. (1965). The formation of the conception of identity of visual characteristics of objects seen successively. *Monog. Soc. Res. Child Devel.* **30**, No. 2.

BALOW, I. H. (1963). Lateral dominance characteristics and reading achievement in the first grade. *J. Psychol.* **55**, 323.

BARKER, P., FEE, R. & STURROCK, G. W. (1967). A note on retarded readers in Dundee. *J. Child Psychol. Psychiat.* **8**, 227.

BECK, F. (1968). Performance of retarded readers on parts of the Wechsler Intelligence Scale for Children. In H. M. Robinson & H. K. Smith (eds.), *Clinical Studies in Reading*, III, *Suppl. Educ. Monog.* No. 97.

BECK, R. & TALKINGTON, L. W. (1970). Frostig training with Head Start Children. *Percept. Motor Skills* **30**, 521.

BEERY, J. W. (1967). Matching of auditory and visual stimuli by average and retarded readers. *Child Devel.* **38**, 827.

BELMONT, L. & BIRCH, H. G. (1963). Lateral dominance and right–left awareness in normal children. *Child Devel.* **34**, 257.

BELMONT, L. & BIRCH, H. G. (1965). Lateral dominance, lateral awareness and reading disability. *Child Devel.* **36**, 57.

BELMONT, L. & BIRCH, H. G. (1966). The intellectual profile of retarded readers. *Percept. Motor Skills* **22**, 787.

BENDER, L. (1938). *The Visual Motor Gestalt Test and its Clinical Use.* New York: American Orthopsychiatric Association.

BENDER, L. (1968). Neuropsychiatric disturbances. In A. H. Keeney & V. T. Keeney (eds.), *Dyslexia.* St Louis: Mosby.

BENDER, L. (1970). Use of the Visual Motor Gestalt test in the diagnosis of learning disabilities. *J. Spec. Educ.* **4**, 29.

BENTON, A. L. (1959). *Right–Left Discrimination and Finger Agnosia.* New York: Hoeber & Harper.

BENTON, A. L. (1961). The fiction of the 'Gerstmann' syndrome. *J. Neurol. Neurosurg. Psychiat.* **24**, 176.

BENTON, A. L. (1962). Dyslexia in relation to form perception and directional sense. In J. Money (ed.), *Reading Disability.* Baltimore: Johns Hopkins Press.

BENTON, A. L. & BIRD, J. W. (1963). The EEG and reading disability. *Amer. J. Orthopsychiat.* **33**, 529.

BERKO, J. & BROWN, R. (1960). Psycholinguistic research methods. In P. H. Mussen, (ed.), *Handbook of Research Methods in Child Development.* New York: Wiley.

BERNSTEIN, B. (1958). Some sociological determinants of perception. *Brit. J. Sociol.* **9**, 159.

BIEMILLER, A. & LEVIN, H. (1968a). Pronounceability. In H. Levin, E. J. Gibson & J. J. Gibson (eds.), *The Analysis of Reading Skill.* U.S. Dep. Health, Educ. & Welfare.

BIEMILLER, A. & LEVIN, H. (1968b). Words with digraph spelling patterns. In H. Levin, E. J. Gibson & J. J. Gibson (eds.), *The Analysis of Reading Skill.* U.S. Dep. Health, Educ. & Welfare.

BING, E. (1963). Effect of childrearing practices on development of differential cognitive abilities. *Child Devel.* **34**, 631.

BIRCH, H. G. (1962). Dyslexia and the maturation of visual function. In J. Money (ed.), *Reading Disability.* Baltimore: Johns Hopkins Press.

BIRCH, H. G. & BELMONT, L. (1965). Auditory–visual integration, intelligence and reading ability. *Percept. Motor Skills* **20**, 295.

BLANK, M. (1968). Cognitive processes in auditory discrimination in normal and retarded readers. *Child Devel.* **39**, 1091.

BLANK, M. & BRIDGER, W. H. (1966). Deficiencies in verbal labelling in retarded readers. *Amer. J. Orthopsychiat.* **36**, 840.

BLANK, M., WEIDER, M. S. & BRIDGER, W. H. (1968). Verbal deficiencies in abstract thinking in early reading retardation. *Amer. J. Orthopsychiat.* **38**, 823.

BLIESMER, E. P. (1954). Reading abilities of bright and dull children of comparable mental ages. *J. Educ. Psychol.* **45**, 321.

BLOOMER, R. H. (1961). Concepts of meaning and the reading and spelling difficulty of words. *J. Educ. Res.* **54**, 178.

BLOOMFIELD, L. (1942). Linguistics and reading. *Elemen. Eng. Rev.* **19**, 125 & 183.

REFERENCES

BOND, G. L. & CLYMER, T. W. (1955). Interrelationships of the SRA Primary Mental Abilities, other mental characteristics and reading ability. *J. Educ. Res.* **49**, 131.

BOND, G. L. & TINKER, M. A. (1957). *Reading Difficulties: their Diagnosis and Correction.* New York: Appleton-Century-Crofts.

BONSALL, C. & DORNBUSH, R. L. (1969). Visual perception and reading ability. *J. Educ. Psychol.* **60**, 294

BORMUTH, J. (1968). New measures of grammatical complexity. In K. S. Goodman (ed.), *The Psycholinguistic Nature of the Reading Process.* Detroit: Wayne State Univ. Press.

BRADFORD, H. F. (1954). Oral–aural differentiation among basic speech sounds as a factor in spelling readiness. *Elemen. School J.* **54**, 354.

BRAINE, M. D. S. (1963). The ontogeny of English phrase structure: the first phase. *Language* **39**, 1.

BRAUN, J. S. (1963). Relation between concept formation ability and reading achievement at three developmental levels. *Child Devel.* **34**, 675.

BRENNAN, W. M., AMES, E. W. & MOORE, R. W. (1966). Age differences in infants' attention to patterns of different complexities. *Science* **151**, 354.

BRENNER, M. W. & GILLMAN, S. (1968). Verbal intelligence, visuomotor ability and school achievement. *Brit. J. Educ. Psychol.* **38**, 75.

BRENNER, M. W., GILLMAN, S., ZANGWILL, O. L. & FARRELL, M. (1967). Visuomotor disability in school children. *Brit. Med. J.* **4**, 259.

BROWN, R. (1957). Linguistic determinism and the part of speech. *J. Abn. Soc. Psychol.* **55**, 1.

BROWN, R. & BERKO, J. (1960). Word association and the acquisition of grammar. *Child Devel.* **31**, 1.

BRUCE, D. J. (1964). The analysis of word sounds by young children. *Brit. J. Educ. Psychol.* **34**, 158.

BRUININKS, R. H. (1969). Auditory and visual perceptual skills related to the reading performance of disadvantaged boys. *Percept. Motor Skills* **29**, 179.

BRUNER, J. S. (1966). On cognitive growth. In J. S. Bruner, R. R. Olver & P. M. Greenfield (eds.), *Studies in Cognitive Growth.* New York: Wiley.

BRYANT, N. D. (1968). Some principles of remedial instruction for dyslexia. In G. Natchez (ed.), *Children with Reading Problems.* New York: Basic Books.

BURT, C. (1921). *Mental and Scholastic Tests.* London: Staples.

BURT, C. (1937). *The Backward Child.* London: Univ. London Press.

CALDWELL, E. C. & HALL, V. C. (1970). Distinctive features versus prototype learning reexamined. *J. Exper. Psychol.* **83**, 7.

CARROLL, J. B. (1964). The analysis of reading instruction. In E. R. Hilgard (ed.), *Theories of Learning and Instruction.* 63rd Yearbook, Nat. Soc. for the Stud. of Educ. Part I.

CARTERETTE, E. C. & JONES, M. H. (1968). Phoneme and letter patterns in children's language. In K. S. Goodman (ed.), *The Psycholinguistic Nature of the Reading Process*. Detroit: Wayne State Univ. Press.

CASHDAN, A. (1970). Backward readers – research on auditory/visual integration. In *Reading Skills: Theory and Practice*. U.K. Reading Assoc.

CASHDAN, A. & PUMFREY, P. D. (1969). Some effects of remedial teaching of reading. *Educ. Res.* **11**, 138.

CHALL, J. S. (1967). *Learning to Read*. New York: McGraw-Hill.

CHALL, J. S., ROSWELL, G. F. & BLUMENTHAL, S. H. (1963). Auditory blending ability. *Reading Teacher*, **17**, 113.

CHANSKY, N. M. (1963). Age, I.Q. and improvement of reading. *J. Educ. Res.* **56**, 439.

CIPOLLA, C. M. (1969). *Literacy aud Development in the West*. Harmondsworth: Penguin Books.

CLARK, M. M. (1957). *Left-Handedness*. London: Univ. London Press.

CLARK, M. M. (1970). *Reading Difficulties in Schools*. Harmondsworth: Penguin Books.

CLARK, R. M. (1960). Maturation and speech development. In D. A. Barbara (ed.), *Psychological and Psychiatric Aspects of Speech and Hearing*. Springfield, Ill.: Thomas.

CLAY, M. M. (1969). Reading errors and self-correction behaviour. *Brit. J. Educ. Psychol.* **39**, 47.

CLEMENTS, S. D. & PETERS, J. E. (1962). Minimal brain dysfunction in the school age child. *Arch. Gen. Psychiat.* **6**, 185.

COHEN, A. & GLASS, G. G. (1968). Lateral dominance and reading ability. *Reading Teacher* **21**, 343.

COHN, R. (1961). Delayed acquisition of reading and writing abilities in children. *Arch. Neurol.* **4**, 153.

COLLINS, J. E. (1961). The effects of remedial education. *Educ. Monog.* Univ. Birmingham Inst. Educ. No. IV.

CONNERS, C. K., KRAMER, K. & GUERRA, F. (1969). Auditory synthesis and dichotic listening in children with learning disabilities. *J. Spec. Educ.* **3**, 163.

COTTERELL, G. C. (1970). Teaching procedures. In A. W. Franklin & S. Naidoo (eds.), *Assessment and Teaching of Dyslexic Children*. London: Invalid Children's Aid Assoc.

CRITCHLEY, M. (1964). *Developmental Dyslexia*. London: Heinemann.

CRITCHLEY, M. (1970). *The Dyslexic Child*. London: Heinemann.

CROOKES, T. G. & GREENE, M. C. L. (1963). Some characteristics of children with two types of speech disorder. *Brit. J. Educ. Psychol.* **33**, 31.

CROSBY, R. M. N. (1968). *Reading and the Dyslexic Child*. London: Souvenir Press.

CURR, W. & HALLWORTH, H. J. (1965). An empirical study of the concept of retardation. *Educ. Rev.* **18**, 5.

DANIELS, J. C. & DIACK, H. (1954). *Royal Road Readers*. London: Chatto & Windus.

DANIELS, J. C. & DIACK, H. (1956). *Progress in Reading.* Univ. Nottingham Inst. Educ.

DANIELS, J. C. & DIACK, H. (1960). *Progress in Reading in the Infant School.* Univ. Nottingham Inst. Educ.

DE HIRSCH, K. (1954). Gestalt psychology as applied to language disturbances. *J. Nerv. Ment. Dis.* **120**, 257.

DE HIRSCH, K., JANSKY, J. J. & LANGFORD, W. S. (1964). The oral language performance of premature children and controls. *J. Speech & Hearing Dis.* **29**, 60.

DE HIRSCH, K., JANSKY, J. J. & LANGFORD, W. S. (1966). *Predicting Reading Failure.* New York: Harper & Row.

DELACATO, C. H. (1966). *Neurological Organization and Reading.* Springfield, Ill.: Thomas.

DENMARK, F. L. & GUTTENTAG, M. (1969). Effect of integrated and nonintegrated programs on cognitive change in pre-school children. *Percept. Motor Skills* **29**, 375.

DEUTSCH, M. (1965). The role of social class in language development and cognition. *Amer. J. Orthopsychiat.* **35**, 78.

DIACK, H. (1960). *Reading and the Psychology of Perception.* Nottingham: Skinner.

DOEHRING, D. G. (1968). *Patterns of Impairment in Specific Reading Disability.* Bloomington: Indiana Univ. Press.

DOUGLAS, J. W. B. (1964). *The Home and the School.* London: MacGibbon & Kee.

DOUGLAS, J. W. B., ROSS, J. M. & SIMPSON, H. R. (1968). *All Our Future.* London: Davies.

DOWNING, J. (1969). The perception of linguistic structure in learning to read. *Brit. J. Educ. Psychol.* **39**, 267.

DREW, A. L. (1956). A neurological appraisal of familial congenital word-blindness. *Brain* **79**, 440.

DUNN-RANKIN, P. (1968). The similarity of lower-case letters of the English alphabet. *J. Verb. Learn. Verb. Behav.* **7**, 990.

DURKIN, D. (1966). *Children Who Read Early.* New York: Teachers' Coll., Columbia Univ.

EDELMAN, G. (1963). The use of cues in word recognition. In *A Basic Program in Reading.* Coop. Res. Proj. No. 639, U.S. Dep. Health, Educ. & Welfare.

EDWARDS, T. J. (1966). The Progressive Choice reading method. In J. Money & G. Schiffman, (eds.), *The Disabled Reader.* Baltimore: Johns Hopkins Press.

EISENBERG, L. (1966). The epidemiology of reading retardation and a program for preventive intervention. In J. Money & G. Schiffman, (eds.), *The Disabled Reader.* Baltimore: Johns Hopkins Press.

ELKIND, D., ANAGOSTOPOULOU, R. & MALONE, S. (1970). Determinants of part–whole perception. *Child Devel.* **41**, 391.

ELKIND, D. & DEBLINGER, J. A. (1969). Perceptual training and reading achievement in disadvantaged children. *Child Devel.* **40**, 11.

REFERENCES

ELKIND, D., HORN, J. & SCHNEIDER, G. (1965). Modified word recognition, reading achievement and perceptual de-centration. *J. Genet. Psychol.* **107**, 235.

ELKIND, D., KOEGLER, R. R. & GO, E. (1964). Studies in perceptual development, II. Part–whole perception. *Child Devel.* **35**, 81.

ELKIND, D. & WEISS, J. (1967). Studies in perceptual development, III. Perceptual exploration. *Child Devel.* **38**, 553.

ESCALONA, S. K. (1968). *The Roots of Individuality.* London: Tavistock.

ETTLINGER, G. & JACKSON, C. V. (1955). Organic factors in developmental dyslexia. *Proc. Roy. Soc. Med.* **48**, 998.

EWING, I. R. & EWING, A. W. G. (1954). *Speech and the Deaf Child.* Manchester Univ. Press.

FABIAN, A. A. (1955). Reading disability: an index of pathology. *Amer. J. Orthopsychiat.* **25**, 319.

FANTZ, R. L. (1958). Pattern vision in young infants. *Psychol. Rec.* **8**, 43.

FANTZ, R. L. (1964). Visual experience in infants: decreased attention to familiar patterns relative to novel ones. *Science* **146**, 668.

FELDMAN, S. C., SCHMIDT, D. E. & DEUTSCH, C. P. (1968). Effect of auditory training on reading skills. *Percept. Motor Skills* **26**, 467.

FELLOWS, B. J. (1968). *The Discrimination Process and Development.* Oxford: Pergamon.

FERNALD, G. M. (1943). *Remedial Techniques in Basic School Subjects.* New York: McGraw-Hill.

FLOWER, R. M. (1965). Auditory disorders and reading disorders. In R. M. Flower, H. F. Gofman & L. I. Lawson (eds.), *Reading Disorders.* Philadelphia: Davis.

FORD, M. (1967). Auditory–visual and tactual–visual integration in relation to reading ability. *Percept. Motor Skills* **24**, 831.

FRAISSE, P. & McMURRAY, G. (1960). Étude génétique du seuil visuel de perception pour quatre catégories de stimuli. *Anneé Psychol.* **60**, 1.

FRANCIS, H. (1969). Structure in the speech of a 2½-year-old child. *Brit. J. Educ. Psychol.* **39**, 291.

FRANCIS-WILLIAMS, J. (1963). Problems of development in children with 'minimal brain damage'. In R. MacKeith & M. Bax (eds.), *Minimal Cerebral Dysfunction.* London: Heinemann.

FRANKLIN, A. W. (ed.) (1962). *Word Blindness or Specific Developmental Dyslexia.* London: Pitman.

FRASER, C., BELLUGI, U. & BROWN, R. (1963). Control of grammar in imitation, comprehension and production. *J. Verb. Learn. Verb. Behav.* **2**, 121.

FRASER, E. (1959). *Home Environment and the School.* London: Univ. London Press.

FRIEDMANN, S. (1958). A report on progress in an L.E.A. remedial reading class. *Brit. J. Educ. Psychol.* **28**, 258.

FRIES, C. C. (1963). *Linguistics and Reading.* New York: Holt, Rinehart & Winston.

FRY, D. B. (1966). The development of the phonological system in the normal and the deaf child. In F. Smith & G. A. Miller (eds.), *The Genesis of Language*. Cambridge, Mass.: Mass. Inst. Tech. Press.

FURTH, H. G. (1964). Research with the deaf. *Psychol. Bull.* **62**, 145.

FURTH, H. G. (1969). *Piaget and Knowledge*. New Jersey: Prentice-Hall.

GAINES, R. (1969). The discriminability of form among young children. *J. Exper. Child Psychol.* **8**, 418.

GALIFRET-GRANJON, N. (1951). Le problème de l'organisation spatiale dans les dyslexics d'évolution. *Enfance* No. 4, 445.

GARDNER, D. E. M. (1942). *Testing Results in the Infant School*. London: Methuen.

GARDNER, D. E. M. (1950). *Long Term Results of Infant School Methods*. London: Methuen.

GATES, A. I. (1922). The psychology of reading and spelling. *Teachers' Coll. Contrib. Educ.* No. 129.

GATES, A. I. (1926). A study of the role of visual perception, intelligence and certain associative processes in reading and spelling. *J. Educ. Psychol.* **17**, 433.

GATES, A. I. (1968). The role of personality maladjustment in reading disability. In G. Natchez (ed.), *Children with Reading Problems*. New York: Basic Books.

GATTEGNO, C. (1962). *Words in Colour*. Reading: Educational Explorers.

GHENT, L. (1956). Perception of overlapping and embedded figures by children of different ages. *Amer. J. Psychol.* **69**, 575.

GIBSON, C. M. & RICHARDS, I. A. (1957). *First Steps in Reading English*. New York: Pocket Books.

GIBSON, E. J. (1965). Learning to read. *Science* **148**, 1066.

GIBSON, E. J. (1969). *Principles of Perceptual Learning and Development*. New York: Appleton-Century-Crofts.

GIBSON, E. J., GIBSON, J. J., PICK, A. D. & OSSER, H. (1962). A developmental study of the discrimination of letter-like forms. *J. Comp. Physiol. Psychol.* **55**, 897.

GIBSON, E. J., OSSER, H. & PICK, A. D. (1963). A study in the development of grapheme-phoneme correspondences. *J. Verb. Learn. Verb. Behav.* **2**, 142.

GIBSON, E. J., SCHAPIRO, F. & YONAS, A. (1968). Confusion matrices for graphic patterns obtained with a latency measure. In H. Levin, E. J. Gibson & J. J. Gibson (eds.), *The Analysis of Reading Skill*. U.S. Dep. Health, Educ. & Welfare.

GIBSON, E. J., SHURCLIFF, A. & YONAS, A. (1968). Utilization of spelling patterns by deaf and hearing subjects. In H. Levin, E.J. Gibson & J. J. Gibson (eds.), *The Analysis of Reading Skill*. U.S. Dep. Health, Educ. & Welfare.

GIBSON, J. J. & GIBSON, E. J. (1955). Perceptual learning: differentiation or enrichment? *Psychol. Rev.* **62**, 32.

GOINS, J. T. (1958). *Visual Perceptual Abilities and Early Reading Progress. Suppl. Educ. Monog.* No. 87.

GOLDBERG, H. K. (1968). Vision, perception and related factors in dyslexia. In A. H. Keeney & V. T. Keeney (eds.), *Dyslexia*. St Louis: Mosby.

GOLDBERG, H. K., MARSHALL, C. & SIMS, E. (1960). The role of brain damage in congenital dyslexia. *Amer. J. Ophthal.* **50**, 586.

GOODACRE, E. J. (1967). *Reading in Infant Classes*. National Foundation for Educational Research.

GOODACRE, E. J. (1968). *Teachers and their Pupils' Home Background*. National Foundation for Educational Research.

GOODACRE, E. J. (1970*a*). The concept of reading readiness. In M. Chazan (ed.), *Reading Readiness*. Univ. Coll. Swansea Faculty Educ.

GOODACRE, E. J. (1970*b*). Reading: what the teachers want. *Times Educ. Suppl.* 27 Nov., p. 4.

GORELICK, M. C. (1965). The effectiveness of visual form training in a prereading program. *J. Educ. Res.* **58**, 315.

GOTTSCHALDT, K. (1926). Über den Einfluss der Ehrfahrung auf die Wahrenhmung von Figuren. *Psychol. Forsch.* **8**, 261.

GOTTSCHALK, J., BRYDEN, M. P. & RABINOVITCH, M. S. (1964). Spatial organization of children's responses to a pictorial display. *Child Devel.* **35**, 811.

GRAHAM, E. E. (1952). Wechsler-Bellevue and WISC scattergrams of unsuccessful readers. *J. Consult. Psychol.* **16**, 268.

GRAHAM, F. K., BERMAN, P. W. & ERNHART, C. B. (1960). Development in preschool children of the ability to copy forms. *Child Devel.* **31**, 339.

GRAHAM, F. K. & KENDALL, B. (1946). Performance of brain-damaged cases on a Memory-for-Designs test. *J. Abn. Soc. Psychol.* **41**, 303.

GRUBER, E. (1962). Reading ability, binocular coordination and the ophthalmograph. *Arch. Ophthal.* **67**, 280.

GUBBAY, S. S., ELLIS, E., WALTON, J. N. & COURT, S. D. M. (1965). Clumsy children. *Brain* **88**, 295.

HALLGREN, B. (1950). Specific dyslexia. *Acta Psychiat. Neurol.* Suppl. No. 65.

HAMILTON, P. & OWRID, H. L. (1970). Reading and impaired hearing. *Reading* **4**, ii, 13.

HARLOW, H. F. (1949). The formation of learning sets. *Psychol. Rev.* **56**, 51.

HARRIS, A. J. (1956). *How to Increase Reading Ability*, 3rd ed. New York: Longmans Green.

HARRIS, A. J. (1957). Lateral dominance, directional confusion and reading disability. *J. Psychol.* **44**, 283.

HARRIS, A. J. (1961). *How to Increase Reading Ability*, 4th ed. New York: Longmans Green.

HARRIS, T. L., OTTO, W. & BARRETT, T. C. (1969). Summary and review of investigations relating to reading. *J. Educ. Res.* **62**, 291.

HARTLAGE, L. C. (1970). Sex-linked inheritance of spatial ability. *Percept. Motor Skills* **31**, 610.

HARVEY, O. J., PRATHER, M. S., WHITE, B. J., ALTER, R. D. & HOFF-

MEISTER, J. K. (1966). Teachers' belief systems and preschool atmospheres. *J. Educ. Psychol.* **57**, 373.

HEBRON, M. E. (1966). *Motivated Learning.* London: Methuen.

HENDRICKSON, L. N. & MUEHL, S. (1962). The effect of attention and motor response pretraining on learning to discriminate b and d in kindergarten children. *J. Educ. Psychol.* **53**, 236.

HENRY, S. (1947). Children's audiograms in relation to reading attainment. *J. Genet. Psychol.* **70**, 211 & **71**, 3, 49.

HERBERT, M. (1964). The concept and testing of brain damage in children. *J. Child Psychol. Psychiat.* **5**, 197.

HERMANN, K. (1959). *Reading Disability.* Copenhagen: Munksgaard.

HERSHENSON, M. (1967). Development of the perception of form. *Psychol. Bull.* **67**, 326.

HETZER, H. & TUDOR-HART, B. (1927). Die frühesten Reaktionene auf die menschliche Stimme. *Quel. u. Stud. z. Jugendk.* **5**, 103.

HIBBERT, F. G. (1961). Dyslexia. *J. Neurol. Neurosurg. Psychiat.* **24**, 93.

HIGHFIELD, M. E. & PINSENT, A. (1952). *A Survey of Rewards and Punishments in Schools.* National Foundation for Educational Research.

HILLMAN, H. H. & SNOWDON, R. L. (1960). Part-time classes for young backward readers. *Brit. J. Educ. Psychol.* **30**, 168.

HIMMELWEIT, H. T. (1963). Socio-economic background and personality. In E. P. Hollander & R. G. Hunt (eds.), *Current Perspectives in Social Psychology.* Oxford: Oxford Univ. Press.

HINE, W. D. (1970). The abilities of partially hearing children. *Brit. J. Educ. Psychol.* **40**, 171.

HINSHELWOOD, J. (1917). *Congenital Word Blindness.* London: Lewis.

HOGGART, R. (1957). *The Uses of Literacy.* London: Chatto & Windus.

HUELSMAN, C. B. (1970). The WISC subtest syndrome for disabled readers. *Percept. Motor Skills* **30**, 535.

HUTTENLOCHER, J. (1964). Children's language: word–phrase relationship. *Science* **143**, 264.

ILG, F. L. & AMES, L. B. (1950). Developmental trends in reading behavior. *J. Genet. Psychol.* **76**, 291.

INGRAM, T. T. S. (1959a). Specific developmental disorders of speech in childhood. *Brain* **82**, 450.

INGRAM, T. T. S. (1959b). A description and classification of the common disorders of speech in children. *Arch. Dis. Child.* **34**, 444.

INGRAM, T. T. S. (1960). Paediatric aspects of specific developmental dysphasia, dyslexia and dysgraphia. *Cerebral Palsy Bull.* **2**, 254.

INGRAM, T. T. S. (1963a). Delayed development of speech with special reference to dyslexia. *Proc. Roy. Soc. Med.* **56**, 199.

INGRAM, T. T. S. (1963b). Chronic brain syndromes in childhood other than cerebral palsy, epilepsy and mental defect. In R. MacKeith & M. Bax (eds.), *Minimal Cerebral Dysfunction.* London: Heinemann.

INGRAM, T. T. S. (1964). The dyslexic child. *The Practitioner* **192**, 503.

INGRAM, T. T. S. & REID, J. F. (1956). Developmental aphasia observed in a department of child psychiatry. *Arch. Dis. Child.* **31**, 161.

INHELDER, B. & PIAGET, J. (1964). *The Early Growth of Logic in the Child.* London: Routledge & Kegan Paul.

JEFFREY, W. E. (1958). Variables in early discriminatory learning, I. Motor responses in the training of left–right discrimination. *Child Devel.* **29**, 269.

JEFFREY, W. E. & SAMUELS, S. J. (1967). Effect of method of reading training on initial learning and transfer. *J. Verb. Learn. Verb. Behav.* **6**, 354.

JEFFRIES, C. (1967). *Illiteracy.* London: Pall Mall Press.

JENSEN, A. R. (1967). The culturally disadvantaged: psychological and educational aspects. *Educ. Res.* **10**, 4.

JOHNSON, D. J. & MYKLEBUST, B. R. (1967). *Learning Disabilities.* New York: Grune & Stratton.

JONES, J. K. (1967). *Colour Story Reading.* London: Nelson.

JONES, J. K. (1968). Comparing i.t.a. with Colour Story Reading. *Educ. Res.* **10**, 226.

JONES, J. K. (1970). Interim results in the Colour Story Reading experiment. In J. C. Daniels (ed.), *Reading: Problems and Perspectives.* U.K. Reading Assoc.

KAGAN, J. (1965). Reflection-impulsivity and reading ability in primary grade children. *Child Devel.* **36**, 609.

KAHN, D. & BIRCH, H. G. (1968). Development of auditory–visual integration and reading achievement. *Percept. Motor Skills* **27**, 459.

KATZ, P. A. & DEUTSCH, M. (1963). Relation of auditory–visual shifting to reading achievement. *Percept. Motor Skills* **17**, 327.

KAWI, A. A. & PASAMANICK, B. (1959). Prenatal and perinatal factors in the development of childhood reading disorders. *Monog. Soc. Res. Child Devel.* **24**, No. 4.

KEIR, G. (1970). The use of pictures as an aid to reading. *Reading* **4**, i, 6.

KELLMER PRINGLE, M. L. (1962). The long-term effects of remedial education. *Vita Humana* **5**, 10.

KELLMER PRINGLE, M. L. (ed.) (1965). *Deprivation and Education.* London: Longmans.

KELLMER PRINGLE, M. L., BUTLER, N. R. & DAVIE, R. (1966). *11,000 Seven-Year-Olds.* London: Longmans.

KELLMER PRINGLE, M. L. & NEALE, M. D. (1957). A note on the use of the Schonell and Gates Reading tests in the first year of the junior school. *Brit. J. Educ. Psychol.* **27**, 135.

KELLMER PRINGLE, M. L. & REEVES, J. K. (1968). The influence of two junior school regimes upon attainment in reading. *Human Devel.* **11**, 25.

KENDALL, B. S. (1948). A note on the relation of retardation in reading to performance on a Memory-for-Designs test. *J. Educ. Psychol.* **39**, 370.

KENT, N. & DAVIS, D. R. (1957). Discipline in the home and intellectual development. *Brit. J. Med. Psychol.* **30**, 27.

KEOGH, B. K. (1965). The Bender Gestalt as a predictive and diagnostic test of reading performance. *J. Consult. Psychol.* **29**, 83.

REFERENCES

KEOGH, B. K. (1968). The copying ability of young children. *Educ. Res.* **11**, 43.

KEOGH, B. K. & SMITH, C. E. (1967). Visuo-motor ability for school prediction. *Percept. Motor Skills* **25**, 101.

KERPELMAN, L. C. & POLLACK, R. H. (1964). Developmental changes in the location of form discrimination cues. *Percept. Motor Skills* **19**, 375.

KIMURA, D. (1967). Dual functional asymmetry of the brain in visual perception. *Neuropsychol.* **4**, 275.

KINSBOURNE, M. & WARRINGTON, E. K. (1962). A variety of reading disability with right hemisphere lesions. *J. Neurol. Neurosurg. Psychiat.* **25**, 339.

KINSBOURNE, M. & WARRINGTON, E. K. (1963a). Developmental factors in reading and writing backwardness. *Brit. J. Psychol.* **54**, 145.

KINSBOURNE, M. & WARRINGTON, E. K. (1963b). A survey of finger sense among retarded readers. In R. MacKeith & M. Bax (eds.), *Minimal Cerebral Dysfunction*. London: Heinemann.

KINSBOURNE, M. & WARRINGTON, E. K. (1963c). The development of finger differentiation. *Quart. J. Exper. Psychol.* **15**, 132.

KINSBOURNE, M. & WARRINGTON, E. K. (1964). Disorders of spelling. *J. Neurol. Neurosurg. Psychiat.* **27**, 224.

KLAPPER, Z. S. (1968). Psychoeducational aspects of reading disabilities. In G. Natchez (ed.), *Children with Reading Problems*. New York: Basic Books.

KNOBLOCK, P. (1965). A Rorschach investigation of the reading process. *J. Exper. Educ.* **33**, 277.

KOLERS, P. A. (1968). Reading temporally and spatially transformed text. In K. S. Goodman (ed.), *The Psycholinguistic Nature of the Reading Process*. Detroit: Wayne State Univ. Press.

KOLSON, C. J. & KALUGER, G. (1963). *Clinical Aspects of Remedial Reading*. Springfield, Ill.: Thomas.

KOPPITZ, E. M. (1958). The Bender Gestalt test and learning disturbances in young children. *J. Clin. Psychol.* **14**, 292.

KOPPITZ, E. M., MARDIS, V. & STEPHENS, T. (1961). A note on screening school beginners with the Bender Gestalt test. *J. Educ. Psychol.* **52**, 80.

KUCERA, O., MATEJCEK, Z. & LANGMEIER, J. (1963). Some observations on dyslexia in children in Czechoslovakia. *Amer. J. Orthopsychiat.* **33**, 448.

LACHMANN, F. M. (1960). Perceptual-motor development in children retarded in reading ability. *J. Consult. Psychol.* **24**, 427.

LEADER, A. B. (1968). Relationship of visual perception to word discrimination. In H. M. Robinson & H. K. Smith (eds.), *Clinical Studies in Reading, III. Suppl. Educ. Monog.* No. 97.

LEE, W. R. (1957). *Spelling Irregularity and Reading Difficulty in English*. National Foundation for Educational Research.

LEFEVRE, C. A. (1964). *Linguistics and the Teaching of Reading*. New York: McGraw-Hill.

LENNENBERG, E. H. (1962). Understanding language without ability to speak. *J. Abn. Soc. Psychol.* **65**, 419.

LENNENBERG, E. H. (1966). The natural history of language. In F. Smith & G. A. Miller (eds.), *The Genesis of Language*. Cambridge, Mass.: Mass. Inst. Tech. Press.

LEROY-BOUSSION, A. (1963). La fusion auditivo-phonétique d'un son consonne et d'un son voyelle en unité syllabique au debut de l'apprentissage de la lecture chez l'enfant. *Psychol. Franç.* **8**, 259.

LEVIN, H. & BIEMILLER, A. J. (1968a). Words vs. pseudo words. In H. Levin, E. J. Gibson & J. J. Gibson (eds.), *The Analysis of Reading Skill*. U.S. Dep. Health, Educ. & Welfare.

LEVIN, H. & BIEMILLER, A. J. (1968b). Contingent vs. non-contingent spelling patterns. In H. Levin, E. J. Gibson & J. J. Gibson (eds.), *The Analysis of Reading Skill*. U.S. Dep. Health, Educ. & Welfare.

LEVIN, H. & TURNER, E. A. (1968). Sentence structure and the eye–voice span. In H. Levin, E. J. Gibson & J. J. Gibson (eds.), *The Analysis of Reading Skill*. U.S. Dep. Health, Educ. & Welfare.

LEVIN, H. & WATSON, J. (1963). The learning of variable grapheme-to-phoneme correspondences. In *A Basic Research Program in Reading*. Coop. Res. Proj. No. 639. U.S. Dep. Health, Educ. & Welfare.

LEWIS, M. M. (1953). *The Importance of Illiteracy*. London: Harrap.

LEWIS, M. M. (1968). Language and mental development. In E. A. Lunzer & J. F. Morris. (eds), *Development in Human Learning*, II. London: Staples.

LIBERMAN, A. M., COOPER, F. S., SHANKWEILER, D. P. & STUDDERT-KENNEDY, M. (1967). Perception of the speech code. *Psychol. Rev.* **74**, 431.

LOVELL, K. (1963). Informal vs. formal education and reading attainments in the junior school. *Educ. Res.* **6**, 70.

LOVELL, K. & GORTON, A. (1968). A study of some differences between backward and normal readers of average intelligence. *Brit. J. Educ. Psychol.* **38**, 240.

LOVELL, K., JOHNSON, E. & PLATTS, D. (1962). A summary of a study of the reading ages of children who had been given remedial teaching. *Brit. J. Educ. Psychol.* **32**, 66.

LOVELL, K., SHAPTON, D. & WARREN, N. S. (1964). A study of some cognitive and other disabilities in backward readers of average intelligence as assessed by a non-verbal test. *Brit. J. Educ. Psychol.* **34**, 58.

LOVELL, K. & WOOLSEY, M. E. (1964). Reading disability, non-verbal reasoning and social class. *Educ. Res.* **6**, 226.

LURIA, A. R. (1961). *The Role of Speech in the Regulation of Normal and Abnormal Behaviour*. Oxford: Pergamon.

LYLE, J. G. (1968). Errors of retarded readers on block designs. *Percept. Motor Skills* **26**, 1222.

LYLE, J. G. (1969). Reading retardation and reversal tendency. *Child Devel.* **40**, 833.

REFERENCES

LYLE, J. G. (1970). Certain antenatal, perinatal and developmental variables and reading retardation in middle-class boys. *Child Devel.* **41**, 481.

LYLE, J. G. & GOYEN, J. (1968). Visual recognition, developmental lag and strephosymbolia in reading retardation. *J. Abn. Psychol.* **73**, 25.

LYLE, J. G. & GOYEN, J. (1969). Performance of retarded readers on the WISC and educational tests. *J. Abn. Psychol.* **74**, 105.

MACCOBY, E. E. & BEE, H. L. (1965). Some speculations concerning the lag between perceiving and performing. *Child Devel.* **36**, 367.

MACCOBY, E. E. & KONRAD, K. W. (1966). Age trends in selective listening. *J. Exper. Child Psychol.* **3**, 113.

MACCOBY, E. E. & KONRAD, K. W. (1967). The effect of preparatory set on selective listening. *Monog. Soc. Res. Child Devel.* **32**, No. 4.

MACFARLANE SMITH, I. (1964). *Spatial Ability.* London: Univ. London Press.

MACKAY, D., THOMPSON, B. & SCHAUB, P. (1970). *Break Through to Literacy.* London: Longmans.

MACKEITH, R. & BAX, M. (eds.). (1963). *Minimal Cerebral Dysfunction.* London: Heinemann.

MACKINNON, A. R. (1959). *How Do Children Learn to Read?* Toronto: Copp Clark.

MALMQUIST, E. (1958). *Factors Related to Reading Disabilities in the First Grade of the Elementary School.* Stockholm: Almqvist & Wiksell.

MANN, H. P. (1957). Some hypotheses on perceptual and learning processes with their applications to the process of reading. *J. Genet. Psychol.* **90**, 167.

MARCHBANKS, G. & LEVIN, H. (1965). Cues by which children recognize words. *J. Educ. Psychol.* **56**, 57.

MARTIN, C. (1955). Developmental inter-relationships among language variables in children of the first grade. *Elemen. School. J.* **32**, 167.

MASLOW, P., FROSTIG, M., LEFEVER, D. W. & WHITTLESEY, J. R. B. (1964). The Marianne Frostig Developmental Test of Visual Perception. *Percept. Motor Skills* **19**, 464.

MAXWELL, A. E. (1959). A factor analysis of the Wechsler Intelligence Scale for Children. *Brit. J. Educ. Psychol.* **29**, 237.

McCARTHY, D. (1953). Organismic interpretation of infant vocalizations. *Child Devel.* **23**, 273.

McCARTHY, D. (1960). Language development in children. In L. Carmichael (ed.), *Manual of Child Psychology*, 2nd ed. New York: Wiley.

McCARTHY, J. J. & KIRK, S. A. (1961). *Illinois Test of Psycholinguistic Abilities.* Urbana, Illinois: Inst. Res. Except. Children.

McCLEOD, J. (1965). A comparison of WISC sub-test scores of pre-adolescent successful and unsuccessful readers. *Austral. J. Psychol.* **17**, 220.

McFIE, J. (1952). Cerebral dominance in cases of reading disability. *J. Neurol. Neurosurg. Psychiat.* **15**, 194.

McFie, J. (1961). The effects of hemispherectomy on intellectual functioning in cases of infantile hemiplegia. *J. Neurol. Neurosurg. Psychiat.* **24**, 240.

McNeill, D. (1966). Developmental psycholinguistics. In F. Smith & G. A. Miller (eds.), *The Genesis of Language.* Cambridge Mass.: Mass. Inst. Tech. Press.

Mecke, V. (1969). Centration: a perceptual process diacritic of intellection and a differential diagnostic criterion. *Percept. Motor Skills* **29**, 827.

Menyuk, P. (1963*a*). A preliminary evaluation of grammatical capacity in children. *J. Verb. Learn. Verb. Behav.* **2**, 429.

Menyuk, P. (1963*b*). Syntactic structures in the language of children. *Child. Devel.* **34**, 407.

Miles, T. R. (1961). Two cases of developmental aphasia. *J. Child Psychol. Psychiat.* **2**, 47.

Miles, T. R. (1967). In defence of the concept of dyslexia. In J. Downing & A. L. Brown (eds.), *The Second International Reading Symposium.* London: Cassell.

Miles, T. R. (1970). *On Helping the Dyslexic Child.* London: Methuen.

Miller, G. A. (1956). The magical number seven plus or minus two. *Psychol. Rev.* **63**, 81.

Milner, E. (1951). A study of the relationship between reading readiness in grade one school children and patterns of parent–child interaction. *Child Devel.* **22**, 95.

Ministry of Education (1950). *Reading Ability.* Pamphlet No. 18. London: H.M.S.O.

Ministry of Education (1957). *Standards of Reading,* 1948–56. Pamphlet No. 32. London: H.M.S.O.

Mittler, P. & Ward, J. (1970). The use of the Illinois Test of Psycholinguistic Abilities on British four-year-old children. *Brit. J. Educ. Psychol.* **40**, 43.

Monroe, M. (1928). Methods for diagnosis and treatment of cases of reading disability. *Genet. Psychol. Monog.* **4**, Nos. 4 & 5.

Morgan, W. P. (1896). A case of congenital word-blindness. *Brit. Med. J.* **2**, 1378.

Morley, M. E. (1957). *The Development and Disorders of Speech in Childhood.* Edinburgh: Livingstone.

Morris, J. M. (1959). *Reading in the Primary School.* London: Newnes.

Morris, J. M. (1966). *Standards and Progress in Reading.* National Foundation for Educational Research.

Morrison, A. & McIntyre, D. (1969). *Teachers and Teaching.* Harmondsworth: Penguin Books.

Muehl, S. & Kremenak, S. (1966). Ability to match information within and between auditory and visual sense modalities and subsequent reading achievement. *J. Educ. Psychol.* **57**, 230.

Munsinger, H. & Gummerman, K. (1967). Identification of form in patterns of visual noise. *J. Exper. Psychol.* **75**, 81.

REFERENCES

MUSSEN, P. H. (1965). Individual differences in development. In R. M. Flower, H. F. Gofman & L. I. Lawson (eds.), *Reading Disorders*. Philadelphia: Davis.

MYKLEBUST, H. R. (1964). *The Psychology of Deafness*, 2nd ed. New York: Grune & Stratton.

NAIDOO, S. (1961). An investigation into some aspects of ambiguous handedness. *Unpublished M.A. Thesis*, Univ. of London.

NAIDOO, S. (1970). The assessment of dyslexic children. In A. W. Franklin & S. Naidoo (eds.), *Assessment and Teaching of Dyslexic Children*. London: Invalid Children's Aid Assoc.

NEISSER, U. (1963). The multiplicity of thought. *Brit. J. Psychol.* **54**, 1.

NEVILLE, D. (1961). A comparison of the WISC patterns of male retarded and non-retarded readers. *J. Educ. Res.* **54**, 195.

NEWSON, E. (1955). The development of line figure discrimination in pre-school children. *Unpublished Ph.D. Thesis*, Univ. of Nottingham.

NEWSON, J. & NEWSON, E. (1968). *Four Years Old in an Urban Community*. London: Allen & Unwin.

NEWTON, M. (1970). A neuro-psychological investigation into dyslexia. In A. W. Franklin & S. Naidoo (eds.), *Assessment and Teaching of Dyslexic Children*. London: Invalid Children's Aid Assoc.

NIELSON, H. H. & RINGE, K. (1969). Visuo-perceptive and visuo-motor performance of children with reading disabilities. *Scand. J. Psychol.* **10**, 225.

NODINE, C. F. & HARDT, J. V. (1970). Role of letter-position cues in learning to read words. *J. Educ. Psychol.* **61**, 10.

OLSON, A. V. (1966). Relation of achievement test scores and specific reading abilities to the Frostig Developmental Test of Visual Perception. *Percept. Motor Skills* **22**, 179.

ORTON, J. L. (1966). The Orton–Gillingham approach. In J. Money & G. Schiffman. (eds), *The Disabled Reader*. Baltimore: Johns Hopkins Press.

ORTON, S. T. (1937). *Reading, Writing and Speech Problems in Children*. London: Chapman & Hall.

OSSER, H., WANG, M. D. & ZAID, F. (1969). The young child's ability to imitate and comprehend speech. *Child Devel.* **40**, 1063.

PATERRA, M. L. (1963). A study of thirty-three WISC scattergrams of retarded readers. *Elemen. Eng.* **40**, 394.

PAYNE, C. S. (1930). The derivation of tentative norms for short exposures in reading. *Harvard Monog. Educ.* No. 10.

PETERS, M. L. (1967). *Spelling: Caught or Taught?* London: Routledge & Kegan Paul.

PHILLIPS, C. J. (1958). Retardation and the use of tests. *Educ. Rev.* **11**, 16.

PIAGET, J. (1955). *The Child's Construction of Reality*. London: Routledge & Kegan Paul.

PIAGET, J. (1961). *Les Mécanismes Perceptifs*. Paris: Presses Universitaires de France. Translated as *The Mechanisms of Perception*. London: Routledge & Kegan Paul, 1969.

PIAGET, J. & INHELDER, B. (1956). *The Child's Conception of Space.* London: Routledge & Kegan Paul.

PIAGET, J. & STETTLER-VON ALBERTINI, B. (1954). Observations sur la perception des bonnes formes chez l'enfant par actualization des lignes virtuelles. *Arch. de Psychol.* **34**, 203.

PIAGET, J. & VINH BANG (1961). Comparaison des mouvements oculaires et des centrations du regard chez l'enfant et chez l'adulte. *Arch. de Psychol.* **38**, 167.

PICK, A. D. (1965). Improvement of visual and tactual form discrimination. *J. Exper. Psychol.* **69**, 331.

PITMAN, J. & ST JOHN, J. (1969). *Alphabets and Reading.* London: Pitman.

PLOWDEN, LADY, (1967) *Children and their Primary Schools.* London: H.M.S.O.

POECK, K & ORGASS, B. (1969). An experimental investigation of finger agnosia. *Neurol.* **19**, 801.

POND, D. A. (1961). Psychiatric aspects of epileptic and brain-damaged children. *Brit. Med. J.* **2**, 1377, 1454.

PRESTON, R. C. (1969). An appraisal of medical research on dyslexia. In R. C. Staiger & O. Andresen. (eds.), *Reading: A Human Right and a Human Problem.* Newark, Delaware: International Reading Assoc.

PRESTON, R. C. & SCHNEYER, J. W. (1956). The neurological background of nine severely retarded readers. *J. Educ. Res.* **49**, 455.

QUAST, W. (1961). The Bender Gestalt: a clinical study of children's records. *J. Consult. Psychol.* **25**, 405.

RABINOVITCH, R. D. (1962). Dyslexia: psychiatric considerations. In J. Money (ed.), *Reading Disability.* Baltimore: Johns Hopkins Press.

RABINOVITCH, R. D. (1968). Reading problems in children: definitions and classification. In A. H. Keeney & V. T. Keeney (eds.), *Dyslexia.* St Louis: Mosby.

RABINOVITCH, R. D., DREW, A. L., DE JONG, R. N., INGRAM, W. & WITHEY, L. I. (1954). A research approach to reading retardation. *Res. Public. Assoc. for Res. in Nerv. and Ment. Dis.* **34**, 363.

RABINOVITCH, R. D. & INGRAM, W. (1968). Neuropsychiatric considerations in reading retardation. In G. Natchez (ed.), *Children with Reading Problems.* New York: Basic Books.

RAVENETTE, A. T. (1961). Vocabulary level and reading attainment. *Brit. J. Educ. Psychol.* **31**, 96.

RAVENETTE, A. T. (1968). *Dimensions of Reading Difficulties.* Oxford: Pergamon.

RAVENETTE, A. T. (1970). Reading difficulties – and what else? In *Reading Skills: Theory and Practice.* U.K. Reading Assoc.

RAWSON, M. B. (1968). *Developmental Language Disability.* Baltimore: Johns Hopkins Press.

REED, J. C. (1958). The relationship between the primary mental abilities and reading achievement at given developmental levels. *Amer. Psychol.* **13**, 324.

REFERENCES

REED, J. C. (1967). Lateralized finger agnosia and reading achievement at ages of 6 and 10. *Child Devel.* **38**, 213.

REED, J. C. & REITAN, R. M. (1969). Verbal and performance differences among brain-injured children with lateralized motor deficits. *Percept. Motor Skills* **29**, 747.

REID, J. F. (1966). Learning to think about reading. *Educ. Res.* **9**, 56.

REID, J. F. (1968). Reading. In H. J. Butcher & H. B. Pont (eds.), *Educational Research in Britain.* London: Univ. London Press.

ROBECK, M. C. (1964). Intellectual strengths and weaknesses shown by reading clinic subjects on the WISC. *J. Devel. Reading* **7**, 120.

ROBINSON, H. M. (1966). The role of auditory perception in reading. In J. Downing (ed.), *The First International Reading Symposium.* London: Cassell.

ROBINSON, J. S. & HIGGINS, K. E. (1967). The young child's ability to see a difference between mirror-image forms. *Percept. Motor Skills* **25**, 893.

ROSEN, C. L. (1966). An experimental study of visual perceptual training and reading achievement in first grade. *Percept. Motor Skills* **22**, 979.

RUDDELL, R. B. (1968). The relation of regularity of grapheme-phoneme correspondences and language structure to achievement on first-grade reading. In K. S. Goodman (ed.), *The Psycholinguistic Nature of the Reading Process.* Detroit: Wayne State Univ. Press.

RUDISHILL, M. (1956). Flashed digit and phrase recognition and rate of oral and concrete responses. *J. Psychol.* **42**, 317.

RUDNICK, M., STERRITT, G. M. & FLAX, M. (1967). Auditory and visual rhythm perception and reading ability. *Child Devel.* **38**, 581.

RYAN, T. J. & MUEHL, S. (1965). Perceptual recognition of words by grade school children. *Percept. Motor Skill* **20**, 1169.

SALAPATEK, P. & KESSEN, W. (1966). Visual scanning of triangles by the human newborn. *J. Exper. Child Psychol.* **3**, 155.

SAMPSON, O. C. (1962). Reading skill at eight years in relation to speech and other factors. *Brit. J. Educ. Psychol.* **32**, 12.

SAMPSON, O. C. (1966). Reading and adjustment. *Educ. Res.* **8**, 184.

SAMPSON, O. C. (1969). A study of incentives in remedial teaching. *Reading* **3**, i, 6.

SATTERLEY, D. (1968). Perceptual, representational and conceptual characteristics of primary school children. *Brit. J. Educ. Psychol.* **38**, 78.

SCARBOROUGH, O. R., HINDSMAN, E. & HARMAN, G. (1961). Anxiety level and performance in school subjects. *Psychol. Rep.* **9**, 425.

SCHWARTZ, S., DEUTSCH, G. P. & WEISSMAN, A. (1967). Language development in two groups of socially disadvantaged young children. *Psychol. Rep.* **21**, 169.

SEASHORE, H. G. (1951). Differences between Verbal and Performance I.Q.s in the Weschsler Intelligence Scale for Children. *J. Consult. Psychol.* **15**, 62.

SHANKWEILLER, D. (1964). A study of developmental dyslexia. *Neuropsychol.* **1**, 267.

SHEARER, E. (1968). Physical skills and reading backwardness. *Educ. Res.* **10**, 197.

SHERIDAN, M. D. (1948). *The Child's Hearing for Speech.* London: Methuen.

SIEGENTHALER, B. M. & BARR, C. A. (1967). Auditory figure–background perception in normal children. *Child Devel.* **38**, 1163.

SILVER, A. A. (1968). Diagnostic considerations in children with reading disability. In G. Natchez (ed.), *Children with Reading Problems.* New York: Basic Books.

SILVER, A. A. & HAGIN, R. A. (1964). Specific reading disability: follow-up studies. *Amer. J. Orthopsychiat.* **34**, 95.

SILVERMAN, J. S., FITE, M. & MOSHER, M. M. (1959). Clinical findings in reading disability children. *Amer. J. Orthopsychiat.* **29**, 298.

SLOBIN, D. I. (1966). Grammatical transformation and sentence comprehension in childhood and adulthood. *J. Verb. Learn. Verb. Behav.* **5**, 219.

SMITH, C. E. & KEOGH, B. K. (1962). The group Bender–Gestalt as a reading readiness screening instrument. *Percept. Motor Skills* **15**, 639.

SMITH, H. P. & DECHANT, E. V. (1961). *Psychology in Teaching Reading.* New York: Prentice-Hall.

SMITH, N. B. (1928). Matching ability as a factor in first grade reading. *J. Educ. Psychol.* **19**, 560.

SNYDER, R. T. & KALIL, J. (1968). Item analysis, inter-examiner reliability and scoring problems for Koppitz scoring on the Bender Gestalt for six-year-olds. *Percept. Motor Skills* **27**, 1351.

SOUTHGATE, V. (1970). The importance of structure in beginning reading. In *Reading Skills: Theory and Practice.* U.K. Reading Assoc.

SOUTHGATE, V. & ROBERTS, G. R. (1970). *Reading – Which Approach?* London: Univ. London Press.

SPACHE, G. D. (1957). Personality patterns of retarded readers. *J. Educ. Res.* **50**, 461.

SPACHE, G. D. (1968). Contributions of allied fields to the teaching of reading. In H. M. Robinson (ed.), *Innovation and Change in Reading Instruction.* 67th Yearbook, Nat. Soc. for the Study of Educ., Part II.

SPERRY, B., STAVER, N., REINER, B. S. & ULRICH, D. (1958). Renunciation and denial in learning difficulties. *Amer. J. Orthopsychiat.* **28**, 98.

SPERRY, R. W. (1970). Physiological plasticity. In P. C. Dodwell (ed.), *Perceptual Learning and Adaptation.* Harmondsworth: Penguin Books.

STATTEN, T. (1953). Behavior patterns, reading disabilities and EEG findings. *Amer. J. Psychiat.* **110**, 205.

STAUFFER, R. G. (1968). Individualized and group type directed reading instruction. In G. Natchez (ed.), *Children with Reading Problems.* New York: Basic Books.

STERRITT, G. M. & RUDNICK, M. (1966). Auditory and visual rhythm perception in relation to reading ability in fourth grade boys. *Percept. Motor Skills* **22**, 859.

STEWART, R. S. (1950). Personality maladjustment and reading achievement. *Amer. J. Orthopsychiat.* **20**, 410.

STOTT, D. H. (1964). *Roads to Literacy.* Glasgow: Holmes.

STRAUSS, A. A. & LEHTINEN, L. E. (1947). *Psychopathology and Education of the Brain-Injured Child.* New York: Grune & Stratton.

TALMADGE, M., DAVIDS, A. & LAUFER, M. W. (1963). A study of experimental methods for teaching emotionally disturbed, brain damaged, retarded readers. *J. Educ. Res.* **56**, 311.

TAYLOR, J. A. & WALES, R. J. (1970). A developmental study of form discrimination in pre-school children. *Quart. J. Exper. Psychol.* **22**, 720.

TEMPLIN, M. C. (1957). *Certain Language Skills in Children.* Univ. Minnesota Press.

TEMPLIN, M. C. (1966). The study of articulation and language development during the early school years. In F. Smith & G. A. Miller (eds.), *The Genesis of Language.* Cambridge, Mass.: Mass. Inst. Tech. Press.

THOMAS, H. (1968). Children's tachistoscopic recognition of words and pseudo-words varying in pronounceability and consonant–vowel sequence. *J. Exper. Psychol.* **77**, 511.

THOMPSON, B. B. (1963). A longitudinal study of auditory discrimination. *J. Educ. Res.* **56**, 376.

THWEATT, R. C. (1963). Prediction of school learning disabilities through the use of the Bender Gestalt test. *J. Clin. Psychol.* **19**, 216.

TIKOFSKY, R. S. & McINISH, J. R. (1968). Consonant discrimination by 7-year-olds. *Psychonom. Sci.* **10**, 61.

TJOSSEM, T. D., HANSEN, T. J. & RIPLEY, H. S. (1962). An investigation of reading difficulty in children. *Amer. J. Psychiat.* **118**, 1104.

TRAVIS, L. E. (1931). *Speech Pathology.* New York: Appleton.

TRAXLER, A. E. (1960). Sequential studies of pupil achievement. In H. M. Robinson (ed.), *Sequential Development of Reading Abilities. Suppl. Educ. Monog.,* No. 90.

TRIESCHMANN, R. B. (1968). Undifferentiated handedness and perceptual development in children with reading problems. *Percept. Motor Skills* **27**, 1123.

UPSON, P. G. (1968). The psychodynamics of reading disability. *Brit. J. Project. Psychol.* **13**, 15.

VERNON, M. D. (1949). The relation of cognition and phantasy in children. *Brit. J. Psychol.* **30**, 273.

VERNON, M. D. (1957). *Backwardness in Reading.* London: Cambridge Univ. Press.

VERNON, M. D. (1969). *Human Motivation.* London: Cambridge Univ. Press.

VERNON, M. D. (1970). *Perception Through Experience.* London: Methuen.

VERNON, P. E. (1950). *The Structure of Human Abilities.* London: Methuen.

VERNON, P. E. (1958). The relation of intelligence to educational backwardness. *Educ. Rev.* **11**, 7.

REFERENCES

VERNON, P. E. (1960). *Intelligence and Attainment Tests.* London: Univ. London Press.

VERNON, P. E. (1965). Environmental handicaps and intellectual development. *Brit. J. Educ. Psychol.* **35**, 9, 117.

VERNON, P. E. (1969). *Intelligence and the Cultural Environment.* London: Methuen.

VORHAUS, P. G. (1968). Rorschach configurations associated with reading disability. In G. Natchez (ed.), *Children with Reading Problems.* New York: Basic Books.

WALLACH, M. A. (1963). Perceptual recognition of approximations to English in relation to spelling achievement. *J. Educ. Psychol.* **54**, 57.

WALTERS, R. H. & DOAN, H. (1962). Perceptual and cognitive functioning of retarded readers. *J. Consult. Psychol.* **26**, 355.

WARBURTON, F. W. & SOUTHGATE, V. (1969). i.t.a.: *An Independent Evaluation.* London: Murray and Chambers.

WARRINGTON, E. K. (1967). The incidence of verbal disability associated with reading retardation. *Neuropsychol.* **5**, 175.

WARRINGTON, E. K. & JAMES, M. (1967). Disorders of visual perception in patients with localized cerebral lesions. *Neuropsychol.* **5**, 253.

WATTS, A. F. (1944). *The Language and Mental Development of Children.* London: Harrap.

WEBER, R.-M. (1968). First graders' use of grammatical context in reading. In H. Levin, E. J. Gibson & J. J. Gibson (eds.), *The Analysis of Reading Skill.* U.S. Dep. Health, Educ. & Welfare.

WECHSLER, D. (1939). *The Measurement of Adult Intelligence.* Baltimore: Williams & Wilkins.

WECHSLER, D. & HAGIN, R. A. (1964). The problem of axial rotation in reading disability. *Percept. Motor Skills* **19**, 319.

WEDELL, K. & HORNE, I. E. (1969). Some aspects of perceptual–motor disability in 5½-year-old children. *Brit. J. Educ. Psychol.* **39**, 174.

WERNER, E. E., SIMONIAN, K. & SMITH, R. S. (1967). Reading achievement, language functioning and perceptual–motor development of 10- and 11-year-olds. *Percept. Motor Skills* **25**, 409.

WERTHEIMER, M. (1923). Untersuchungen zur Lehre von der Gestalt. *Psychol. Forsch* **4**, 301.

WHIPPLE, C. I. & KODMAN, F. (1969). A study of discrimination and perceptual learning with retarded readers. *J. Educ. Psychol.* **60**, 1.

WHIPPLE, G. (1961). The culturally and socially deprived reader. In H. M. Robinson (ed.), *Controversial Issues in Reading and Promising Solutions. Suppl. Educ. Monog.*, No. 91

WILEY, W. E. (1928). Difficult words and the beginner. *J. Educ. Res.* **17**, 278.

WILLIAMS, J. P., BLUMBERG, E. L. & WILLIAMS, D. V. (1970). Cues used in visual word recognition. *J. Educ. Psychol.* **61**, 310.

WILLIAMS, M. (1970). *Brain Damage and the Mind.* Harmondsworth: Penguin Books.

REFERENCES

WILSON, F. T. & FLEMMING, C. W. (1938). Correlations of reading progress with other abilities and traits in grade I. *J. Genet. Psychol.* **53**, 33.

WISEMAN, S. (1964). *Education and Environment.* Manchester Univ. Press.

WITKIN, H. A. (1950). Individual differences in ease of perception of embedded figures. *J. Person.* **19**, 1.

WOHLWILL, J. F. & WIENER, M. (1964). Discrimination of form orientation in young children. *Child Devel.* **35**, 1113.

WYKE, M. & ETTLINGER, G. (1961). Efficiency of recognition in left and right visual fields. *Neurol.* **5**, 659.

ZANGWILL, O. L. (1960). *Cerebral Dominance and its Relation to Psychological Function.* Edinburgh: Oliver & Boyd.

ZANGWILL, O. L. (1963). The cerebral localization of psychological function. *Advance. Sci.* **20**, 335.

ZAPOROZHETS, A. V. (1965). The development of perception in the preschool child. *Monog. Soc. Res. Child Devel.* **30**, No. 2.

ZIMMERMAN, I. L. & ALLEBRAND, G. N. (1965). Personality characteristics and attitudes towards achievement of good and poor readers. *J. Educ. Res.* **59**, 28.

INDEX OF AUTHORS

Ablewhite, R. C. 116, 169, 180
Ahlstrom, K. G. 57
Allebrand, G. N. 106
Altus, G. T. 90
Ames, E. W. 11
Ames, L. B. 12, 26, 30
Anagnostopoulou, R. 16
Anderson, I. H. 61, 85, 110
Anisfeld, M. 78
Annett, M. 139, 140, 141, 156, 166

Babska, Z. 12
Balow, I. H. 141
Barker, P. 2
Barr, C. A. 45
Barrett, T. C. 165
Bax, M. 157
Beck, F. 90
Beck, R. 21
Bee, H. L. 12
Beery, J. W. 68
Bellugi, U. 42
Belmont, L. 57, 67, 89, 135, 136, 141, 144
Bender, L. 15, 16, 32, 128, 142, 161, 162
Benton, A. L. 134, 135, 136, 137, 144, 147, 151, 154, 160
Berko, J. 41, 42
Berman, P. W. 13
Bernstein, B. 99
Biemiller, A. 28, 53, 54, 56
Bijou, S. W. 22
Bing, E. 108
Birch, H. G. 20, 37, 57, 67, 89, 135, 136, 141, 144, 163
Bird, J. W. 154
Blank, M. 66, 68
Bliesmer, E. P. 85
Bloomer, R. H. 28, 29
Bloomfield, L. 55
Blumberg, E. L. 25
Blumenthal, S. H. 66
Boguslavskaya, Z. M. 13
Bond, G. L. 89, 118
Bonsall, C. 28
Bormuth, J. 60
Bower, T. G. R. 11

Bradford, H. F. 51
Braine, M. D. S. 40
Braun, J. S. 81
Brennan, W. M. 11
Brenner, M. W. 92, 155
Bridger, W. H. 68
Brown, R. 41, 42
Bruce, D. J. 51
Bruinincks, R. H. 66
Bruner, J. S. 12, 19, 20
Bryant, N. D. 170
Bryden, M. P. 20
Burt, C. 97, 128
Butler, N. R. 2, 105, 167
Byron, O. 110

Caldwell, E. C. 26
Cane, B. S. 6
Carroll, J. B. 58
Carterette, E. C. 44
Cashdan, A. 69, 168
Chall, J. S. 24, 48, 57, 59, 66
Chansky, N. M. 169
Chazan, M. 115
Chomsky, N. 43
Cipolla, M. 1
Clark, M. M. 2, 66, 68, 74, 89, 91, 129, 131, 143
Clark, R. M. 70
Clay, M. M. 62
Clements, S. D. 131, 137, 142, 153
Clymer, T. W. 89
Cohen, A. 160
Cohn, R. 72, 147, 154, 155
Collins, J. E. 109, 168
Conners, C. K. 52
Cooper, F. S. 39
Cotterell, G. C. 149, 172
Crane, J. A. 118
Critchley, M. 125, 128, 132, 137, 157, 166
Crookes, T. G. 72, 147
Crosby, R. M. N. 31, 128, 131, 132
Curr, W. 86

Daniels, J. C. 48, 57, 172
Davids, A. 171

14-2

Davie, R. 2, 105, 167
Davis, D. R. 107
Deblinger, J. A. 76
Dechant, E. V. 61, 81
De Hirsch, K. 32, 35, 66, 72, 73, 131, 134, 141, 149, 161, 163, 164, 166, 179
Delacato, C. H. 159
Denmark, F. L. 75
Deutsch, C. P. 75, 100
Deutsch, M. 68, 100
Diack, H. 4, 24, 48, 57, 172
Dixon, W. R. 85, 110
Doan, H. 33
Doehring, D. G. 36, 54, 69, 74, 142, 149, 161, 164, 165
Dornbush, R. L. 28
Douglas, J. W. B. 84, 95, 105, 106, 107, 115, 117
Downing, J. 49
Drew, A. L. 164
Dunn-Rankin, P. 27
Durkin, D. 101, 112
Durrell, D. 24

Edelman, G. 25
Edwards, T. J. 48
Eisenberg, L. 95, 96
Elkind, D. 16, 19, 76
Ernhart, C. B. 13
Escalona, S. K. 175
Ettlinger, G. 152, 165
Ewing, A. W. G. 64
Ewing, I. R. 64

Fabian, A. A. 118
Fantz, R. L. 11, 12
Fearn, D. 69
Fee, R. 2
Feldman, S. C. 75
Fellows, B. J. 22
Fernald, G. M. 171
Fite, M. W. 116, 117, 118
Flax, M. 20
Flemming, C. W. 24
Flower, R. M. 66
Ford, M. 68
Fraisse, P. 28
Francis, H. 44
Francis-Williams, J. 157, 158
Franklin, A. W. 126
Fraser, C. 42

Fraser, E. 100, 104
Friedmann, S. 170
Fries, C. C. 55
Fry, D. B. 40
Furth, H. G. 87

Gaines, R. 89
Galifret-Granjon, N. 31, 131
Gardner, D. E. M. 110
Gates, A. I. 30, 116, 118
Gattegno, C. 50, 110
Ghent, L. 15, 16, 88
Gibson, C. M. 55
Gibson, E. J. 10, 13, 14, 18, 19, 20, 23, 25, 26, 33, 39, 52, 54
Gibson, J. J. 33
Gillman, S. 92
Glass, G. G. 160
Go, E. 16
Goins, J. T. 22, 31, 81
Goldberg, H. K. 154, 155, 169
Goldenberg, S. 156
Goodacre, E. J. 3, 24, 47, 96, 97, 104, 112
Gorelick, M. C. 21
Gorton, A. 153
Gottschaldt, K. 15
Gottschalk, J. 20
Goyen, J. 35, 90, 91
Graham, E. E. 89, 90
Graham, F. K. 13, 34
Greene, M. C. L. 72, 147
Gruber, E. 37
Gubbay, S. S. 136, 155
Guerra, F. 52
Gummerman, K. 17
Guttentag, M. 75

Hagin, R. A. 35, 161
Hall, V. C. 26
Hallgren, B. 164, 166
Hallworth, H. J. 86
Hamilton, P. 65
Hansen, T. J. 131
Hardt, J. V. 28
Harlow, H. F. 85
Harman, G. 117
Harris, A. J. 119, 141, 142, 143, 144, 146, 160, 172
Harris, T. L. 165
Hartlage, L. C. 174
Harvey, O. J. 115

Hebron, M. E. 167
Heil, L. M. 115
Hendrickson, L. N. 22
Henry, S. 64
Herbert, M. 155, 156
Hermann, K. 125, 128, 129, 134, 135, 136, 150, 151, 166
Hershenson, M. 11
Hetzer, H. 38
Hibbert, F. G. 142
Higgins, K. E. 18
Highfield, M. E. 108, 167
Hillman, H. H. 168
Himmelweit, H. T. 107
Hindsman, E. 117
Hine, W. D. 64
Hinshelwood, J. 125
Hoggart, R. 1
Horn, J. 19
Horne, I. E. 32
Huelsman, C. B. 89, 90, 91
Hughes, B. O. 85
Huttenlocher, J. 41

Ilg, F. L. 26
Ingram, T. T. S. 57, 71, 74, 87, 92, 93, 97, 118, 130, 142, 157, 165, 167
Ingram, W. 74, 116, 145, 146, 147
Inhelder, B. 13, 20, 78

Jackson, C. V. 165
James, M. 151, 152
Jansky, J. T. 32, 72, 73, 134, 149, 161, 162, 163, 164, 166, 179
Jeffrey, W. E. 22, 52
Jeffries, C. 1
Jensen, A. R. 100, 103, 112
Johnson, D. J. 66, 170
Johnson, E. 169
Jones, J. K. 50
Jones, M. H. 44

Kagan, J. 82
Kahn, D. 20
Kalil, J. 15
Kaluger, G. 136, 165
Kass, C. E. 74
Katz, P. A. 68
Kawi, A. A. 153
Keir, G. 24
Kellmer Pringle, M. L. 2, 47, 84, 95, 105, 111, 120, 122, 167

Kendall, B. 34, 35
Kent, N. 107
Keogh, B. K. 15, 18, 32
Kerpelman, L. C. 19
Kessen, W. 19
Kimura, D. 152
Kinsbourne, M. 92, 130, 132, 136, 137, 145, 151, 152
Kirk, S. A. 73
Klapper, Z. S. 79
Knoblock, P. 31
Kodman, F. 33, 34
Koegler, R. R. 16
Kolers, P. A. 6
Kolson, C. J. 136, 165
Konrad, K. W. 45, 46
Koppitz, E. M. 31, 32, 92
Kramer, K. 52
Kremenak, S. 67
Kucera, O. 77, 142, 147, 153

Lachmann, F. M. 31, 131
Langford, W. S. 32, 72, 73, 134, 149, 161, 162, 163, 164, 166, 179
Langmeier, J. 77, 142, 147, 153
Laufer, M. W. 171
Leader, A. B. 33
Lee, W. R. 56
Lefevre, C. A. 38
Lehtinen, L. E. 131
Lennenberg, E. H. 43, 46, 71
Leroy-Boussion, A. 52
Levin, H. 25, 28, 53, 54, 56, 62, 80
Lewis, M. M. 2, 87
Liberman, A. M. 38, 39
Lovell, K. 82, 91, 111, 153, 169, 170
Luria, A. R. 12
Lyle, J. G. 35, 36, 90, 91, 137, 142, 147, 153

Maccoby, E. E. 12, 45, 46
Macfarlane Smith, I. 88
Mackay, D. 43, 61
MacKeith, R. 157
Mackinnon, A. R. 55
Mackworth, N. H. 19, 20
Malmquist, E. 83, 85, 101, 116
Malone, S. 16
Mann, H. P. 119
Marchbanks, G. 25
Mardis, V. 32
Marshall, L. 154

Martin, C. 72
Maslow, P. 35
Maspes, P. E. 152
Matejcek, Z. 77, 142, 147, 153
Maxwell, A. E. 90
McCarthy, D. 60, 167
McCarthy, J. J. 73
McCleod, J. 89, 90
McFie, J. 143, 152, 156
McGlannan, F. K. 165
McInish, J. R. 40
McIntyre, D. 111, 115
McMurray, G. 28
McNeill, D. 41
Mecke, V. 154
Menyuk, P. 43, 44
Miles, T. R. 128, 129, 133, 171
Miller, G. A. 53
Milner, E. 104, 107
Mittler, P. 73, 87
Monroe, M. 35
Moore, R. W. 11
Morgan, W. P. 125
Morley, M. E. 71
Morris, J. M. 2, 6, 7, 84, 98, 101, 110,
    113, 114, 123, 124, 126
Morrison, A. 111, 115
Mosher, M. M. 116, 117, 118
Muehl, S. 22, 28, 29, 67
Munsinger, H. 17
Mussen, P. H. 117
Myklebust, H. R. 63, 64, 66, 170

Naidoo, S. 74, 141, 147, 149, 160,
    170
Neale, M. D. 84
Neisser, U. 26
Neville, D. 89
Newson, E. 22, 100, 101
Newson, J. 100, 101
Newton, M. 127, 159, 164
Nielson, H. H. 160
Nodine, C. F. 28
Norrie, E. 166

Olson, A. V. 35
Orgass, B. 137, 138
Orton, J. L. 171
Orton, S. T. 125, 138, 143
Osser, H. 42, 52
Otto, W. 165
Owrid, H. L. 65

Pasamanick, B. 153
Paterra, M. L. 89
Payne, C. S. 28
Peters, J. E. 131, 137, 142, 153
Peters, M. L. 49, 57
Phillips, C. J. 84
Piaget, J. 10, 13, 17, 18, 19, 20, 38, 78,
    82, 83, 86, 87
Pick, A. D. 26, 52
Pinsent, A. 108, 167
Pitman, J. 9, 49, 58
Platts, D. 169
Plowden, Lady, 47, 126
Poeck, K. 137, 138
Pollack, R. H. 19
Pond, D. A. 156
Poole, I. 40
Preston, R. C. 153, 154
Pumfrey, P. D. 168

Quast, W. 155

Rabinovitch, M. S. 20
Rabinovitch, R. D. 74, 77, 82, 116,
    127, 136, 142, 153
Ravenette, A. T. 72, 74, 84, 92, 119
Rawson, M. B. 129, 130, 148, 161,
    163, 170, 171, 178, 179
Reed, J. C. 87, 144, 156
Reeves, J. K. 111
Reid, J. F. 2, 77, 92, 93, 97, 118, 130,
    142, 145, 146
Reitan, R. M. 156
Richards, I. A. 55
Ringe, K. 160
Ripley, H. S. 131
Robeck, M. C. 90
Roberts, G. R. 9, 56
Robinson, H. M. 40
Robinson, J. S. 18
Rochford, G. 150
Rosen, C. L. 21
Rosenstein, J. 54
Ross, J. M. 106, 107
Roswell, G. F. 66
Ruddell, R. B. 59, 60
Rudishill, M. 29
Rudnick, M. 20, 67
Ryan, T. J. 28, 29

Salapatek, P. 19
Sampson, O. C. 72, 114, 115

Samuels, S. J. 52
Satterley, D. 17
Scarborough, O. R. 117
Schapiro, F. 26
Schaub, P. 43, 61
Schiffman, G. 169
Schmidt, D. E. 75
Schneider, G. 19
Schneyer, J. W. 153
Schwartz, S. 100
Seashore, H. G. 93
Shankweiler, D. 133, 153
Shapton, D. 82
Shearer, E. 135, 137
Sheridan, M. D. 45, 65, 70
Shurcliff, A. 52, 54
Siegenthaler, B. M. 45
Silver, A. A. 66, 73, 131, 136, 142
Silverman, J. S. 116, 117, 118, 155
Simonian, K. 102
Simpson, H. R. 106, 107
Sims, E. 154
Slobin, D. I. 43
Smith, C. E. 32
Smith, H. P. 61, 81
Smith, N. B. 27
Smith, R. S. 102
Snowdon, R. L. 168
Snyder, R. T. 15
Sokhina 21
Southgate, V. 9, 50, 56, 110
Spache, G. D. 62, 74, 117
Sperry, B. 119
Sperry, R. W. 152
Statten, T. 154
Stauffer, R. G. 112
Stephens, T. 32
Sterritt, G. M. 20, 67
Stettler-von Albertini, B. 17
Stewart, R. S. 117, 119
St John, J. 58
Stott, D. H. 114
Strauss, A. A. 131
Sturrock, G. W. 2

Talkington, L. W. 21
Talmadge, M. 171
Taylor, J. A. 14
Templin, M. C. 59, 71
Thomas, H. 54
Thompson, B. 43, 61
Thompson, B. B. 44

Thurstone, L. L. 87
Thweatt, R. C. 32
Tikofsky, R. S. 40
Tinker, M. A. 118
Tjossem, T. D. 131
Travis, L. E. 159
Traxler, A. E. 7
Trieschmann, R. B. 14
Tudor-Hart, B. 38
Turner, E. A. 62

Upson, P. G. 120

Vernon, M. D. 11, 15, 20, 37, 66, 67, 106, 138, 143, 144, 159
Vernon, P. E. 83, 84, 86, 87, 88, 89, 101, 102, 104, 109, 120, 174, 175
Vinh Bang 19
Vorhaus, P. G. 119

Wales, R. J. 14
Walker, R. N. 30
Wallach, M. A. 29
Walters, R. H. 33
Wang, M. D. 42
Warburton, F. W. 9, 50
Ward, J. 73, 87
Warren, N. S. 82
Warrington, E. K. 92, 93, 130, 132, 136, 137, 145, 151, 152
Washburne, C. 115
Watson, J. 80
Watts, A. F. 46
Weaver, W. W. 62
Weber, R.-M. 60, 62, 63
Wechsler, D. 35, 90
Wedell, K. 32
Weider, M. S. 68
Weiss, J. 19
Weissman, A. 100
Wepman, J. M. 40, 66
Werner, E. E. 102, 103
Wertheimer, M. 15
Whipple, C. I. 33, 34
Whipple, G. 99
Wiener, M. 17, 18
Wiley, W. E. 27, 28
Williams, D. V. 25
Williams, J. P. 25
Williams, M. 150
Wilson, F. T. 24
Wiseman, S. 97

INDEX OF AUTHORS

Witkin, H. A. 88
Wohlwill, J. F. 17, 18
Woolsey, M. E. 98
Wyke, M. 152

Yonas, A. 26, 52, 54

Zaid, F. 42
Zangwill, O. L. 131, 132, 133, 142, 143, 159, 160, 162, 165
Zaporozhets, A. V. 13, 21
Zimmerman, I. L. 106

INDEX OF SUBJECTS

ability
  perceptual 88–9, 174
  practical 88–9, 109
  spatial 88–9, 174
  verbal 86–7, 94, 101, 108–9, 174
achievement quotient 86
aggression 117–19, 122, 167
anxiety 107, 116, 117–19, 130
attention
  centration in 19, 20
  direction of 19, 23
articulation 39
  defects in 70–2, 146–7, 158
auditory
  development in children 38–47
  discrimination 39–40, 44–5, 148–9, 160
Colour Story Reading 50
conceptual
  ability 94
  deficiencies 147, 149, 176
  reasoning 21, 77–83, 87, 94
congenital word blindness 125
dependence 119, 122
deprivation 100, 101–3
dyslexia, in adults 150, 151–3
  visuo-spatial disorders in 151–3
dyslexia, specific developmental 125–72
  causes of 149–67
  characteristics of 128–30
  delayed maturation in 37, 137, 141, 159–64, 177
  directional confusion in 134–6, 144–5, 148, 153, 160, 162, 165
  disordered motor control in 155, 158, 161, 162
  EEG abnormalities in 154–5, 156
  existence of 125–7, 176
  frequency of 127
  finger localization in 136–8, 144, 161, 165
  hereditary factors in 164–7
  left–right discrimination in 134–6, 147, 148, 154, 155, 160, 161, 165
  linguistic deficiencies in 145–9, 153, 154, 157, 158, 160, 161, 165, 176–8

neurological impairment in 153–9, 162, 171, 177
  sex differences in 166–7
  in twins 166
  visual deficiencies in 130–45, 146–7, 149, 153, 154, 155, 156, 157, 158, 160, 161, 176–8
dysphasia, in adults 150
dysphasia, developmental 146, 157, 158, 178
emotional disturbance, maladjustment 108, 115–22
  in dyslexics 129–30, 158
familiarity
  of letter groups 54–6
  with printed words 28–9
  with spoken words 46
  with syntactic structure 29
form, forms
  analysis of 30–1, 33, 36, 37, 94
  complex 15–17, 22, 33, 131–4
  details of 12, 15, 23
  identification of 22
  integration of 15, 16, 17, 23, 32–3, 36
  memory for 13, 14, 18, 34–5, 36, 88
  perception of 10–23, 88–9, 131–4, 149
  reproduction of 12–13, 15, 23, 31–3, 131–4
Gerstmann's syndrome 138, 150–1, 157
hearing loss 63–5
Initial Teaching Alphabet 49–50, 110
intelligence 83–94, 97–8, 101–2, 174
  in dyslexics 129
invariants 10, 11, 39, 52
inversion
  of forms 17–18
  of letters 27
lateralization 138–45
  in dyslexics 142–5, 146, 147, 148, 149, 158–9, 160, 165–6
letters
  chunks, clusters of 52–6
  identification of 24, 79
  memory for 24, 25, 26

letters (*cont.*)
  perception of 23–7
  pronounceability of 52–4
  shape and sound association of
    47–50, 52, 74, 77, 80–1, 82, 171
linguistic
  ability 73, 75–6, 81, 87–8, 99–100,
    174
  development in children 38–47,
    59–60, 71–4, 167
  grammatical constructions 42–4,
    62–3
  imitation 40
  impairment 70–5, 94, 99–100, 103
  inflexions 42–3
  patterns 41, 45
  semantic structure 62–3
  training 75–6
  transformations 43–4
listening, selective 45–6
methods of investigation of reading
  7, 8
motivation 103–15, 173, 175, 178–9
  achievement 106–7
order
  of forms 20, 35, 131
  of letters 27–8, 131, 145
  of phonemes 57
  of syllables 57
orientation
  of forms 13, 15, 17, 22, 31, 33, 35,
    149
  of letters 36, 128, 130
parental
  deprivation 120–2
  education 101
  encouragement 104–7
  relationship to children 105–9,
    113, 118–19, 120–2
patterns, visual
  identification of 11
  perception of 11–12
perceptual activity 19
pictures
  perception of 20, 24
  reproduction of 12
phonemes
  acoustics of 38–9
  blending of 51–2, 66–7
  discrimination of 39–40, 47–52,
    65–6, 70, 79–80
  hearing of 38, 45, 64

phonemic pattern or structure
  analysis of 45, 50–2, 55–6, 59
  hearing of 38–9, 45, 47
  reconstruction of 51–2, 57
reading readiness 22, 28, 111–12
reversals
  of forms 13, 14, 18, 35–6
  of letters 27
  in words 27, 128, 145, 146, 147,
    148, 160
rotation
  of forms 13, 14, 15, 18, 31
  of letters 26
sentences
  complexity of 59–60
  context in 50, 57, 61–2
  hearing of 42, 44–6
  length of 59–60
  reading of 58–63
  speaking of 40–4, 59, 72, 74
sequences, sequential patterns
  association of 67–70, 75, 82, 94,
    149, 160, 163, 176–7, 178
  of forms 20, 23, 35–6, 37, 70
  of ideas 69
  memory for 67
  of phonemes 57, 83
  of printed letters 28–9, 83
  of sounds 57, 67–70
  verbal labelling of 68
  of words 146, 149, 157, 161, 177
socio-economic status 95–103
spelling
  in dyslexics 128–9, 148, 161, 163,
    177
  irregularity of 56, 58
  rules of 58
strephosymbolia 126
surveys of reading 6, 7
symbolization 77
teachers' skill 113–15
teachers' encouragement 114–15
teaching methods
  discovery 109–10, 111
  efficacy 3–4, 8–9
  formal and informal 109–11
  Gillingham–Stillman 171, 172
  language experience 60–1
  linguistic 55, 59, 80
  phonic 47–8, 59, 170
  remedial 168–72, 179–80
  sentence 58–9

teaching methods (*cont.*)
  tracing 171
  whole word 4, 24–5, 48, 170
test
  Bender 15, 16, 18, 31–3, 86, 88, 92,
    103, 131, 132, 154, 155, 156, 160,
    161, 163
  Crichton Vocabulary 73, 84
  Draw-a-Man 88, 133, 160
  Frostig 21, 35, 160
  Gottschaldt figures 15, 17, 19, 21,
    25, 50, 86, 88, 109, 160
  Horst Reversals 36
  Illinois, of Psycholinguistic Abilities
    73–4, 87, 100
  Kohs Blocks 88, 89, 109, 131, 177
  Memory-for-Designs 34, 36
  N.F.E.R. Picture Vocabulary 73, 84
  Neale 111
  non-verbal intelligence 84, 98
  Peabody Picture Vocabulary 22
  reading 6, 7, 8
  Rorschach 30
  Schonell Graded Word Reading 84,
    93
  Southgate 95
  Terman–Merrill 134
  Thurstone's Primary Mental Abili-
    ties 89, 102–3, 108
  verbal intelligence 83–4, 98
  Vernon Graded Word Reading 111
  Watts English language 72, 82
  WISC 64, 89–93, 108, 132, 145,
    146, 154, 155, 156, 157
  Wepman, of Auditory Discrimina-
    tion 66
training, teacher 2, 3
  in perception 21–2, 23
vision, disorders of 37
Words in Colour 50, 110
words
  analysis of 25, 47, 48–50
  hearing of 39–47, 64, 66
  memory for 47, 73
  reconstruction of 51–2, 74
  visual perception of 28–30